The Bully Society

DATE D

Apr 17 20'
2.9.2⁻

INTERSECTIONS

Transdisciplinary Perspectives on Genders and Sexualities
General Editors: Michael Kimmel and Suzanna Walters

Sperm Counts:
Overcome by Man's Most Precious Fluid
Lisa Jean Moore

The Sexuality of Migration:
Border Crossings and Mexican Immigrant Men
Lionel Cantú, Jr.
Edited by Nancy A. Naples and Salvador Vidal-Ortiz

Moral Panics, Sex Panics:
Fear and the Fight over Sexual Rights
Edited by Gilbert Herdt

Out in the Country:
Youth, Media, and Queer Visibility in Rural America
Mary L. Gray

Sapphistries:
A Global History of Love between Women
Leila J. Rupp

Strip Club:
Gender, Power, and Sex Work
Kim Price-Glynn

Sex for Life: From Virginity to Viagra:
How Sexuality Changes Throughout Our Lives
Edited by Laura M. Carpenter and John DeLamater

The Bully Society:
School Shootings and the Crisis of Bullying in America's Schools
Jessie Klein

The Bully Society

*School Shootings and the Crisis
of Bullying in America's Schools*

Jessie Klein

NEW YORK UNIVERSITY PRESS
New York and London

NEW YORK UNIVERSITY PRESS
New York and London
www.nyupress.org

References to Internet websites (URLs) were accurate at the time of writing.
Neither the author nor New York University Press is responsible for URLs that
may have expired or changed since the manuscript was prepared.

Library of Congress Cataloging-in-Publication Data

Klein, Jessie.
The bully society : school shootings and
the crisis of bullying in America's schools / Jessie Klein.
p. cm.
Includes bibliographical references and index.
ISBN 978–1–4798–6094–4 (pb : alk. paper)
ISBN 978–0–8147–4888–6 (cl : alk. paper)
ISBN 978–0–8147–7149–5 (ebook)
ISBN 978–0–8147–6371–1 (ebook)
1. Bullying—United States. 2. Bullying in schools—United States.
3. School shootings—United States. 4. School discipline—United States. I. Title.
BF637.B85K584   2011
302.34'30973—dc23   2011039377

New York University Press books are printed on acid-free paper,
and their binding materials are chosen for strength and durability.
We strive to use environmentally responsible suppliers and materials
to the greatest extent possible in publishing our books.

Manufactured in the United States of America

To Lev, Susan, Justin, and Daisy,

and in loving memory to Louis and Milty,

and to all children (and adults): may you thrive

in compassionate communities.

A note on the data for this book

To see comprehensive data on school shootings in the United States, visit Jessie Klein's website at www.jessieklein.com.

Contents

Acknowledgments

I was inspired by so many people as I was researching and writing this book. Here, I've tried to thank those most directly involved. I can only hope that if I have understated or neglected to mention anyone's contribution, they will know in their hearts how much I appreciated their support.

I am grateful to several friends who read complete drafts or selected chapters of *The Bully Society* and provided excellent comments, questions, suggestions, and other feedback: Shari Cohen, Beth Fertig, Jean Halley, Anne Kornhauser, Nadine Lemmon, Helaine Olen, Michael Putnam, Laurence Sachs, Deborah Siegel, Maia Szalavitz, and especially David Lipsky, who contributed epic personal help and sharp, critical feedback along the journey, and Michele Wucker, my shining star, who read through the manuscript more than a few times, always providing superb aid.

Nothing I can say is worthy of Jean Casella's editorial and emotional support, her incredible heart, talent, devotion, and hard work. Jean read every page of *The Bully Society* of almost every draft, cared authentically about the issues it raised, and gave brilliant and meticulous feedback at every turn. Looking forward to Jean's insightful responses, I never felt alone in the many hours I spent writing and rewriting.

The suggestions of my New York University Press editor, Ilene Kalish, improved the book significantly, and editorial assistant Aiden Amos was particularly effective in moving the book along its best possible path. Elisabeth Magnus did a fantastic copyediting job; and Despina Gimbel managed the project with a touching combination of kindness and expertise; Martin Tulic contributed a comprehensive index.

My research assistant, Gaia Fried, was extraordinarily helpful, especially on issues relating to race. Talitha Douglas worked tirelessly and with extreme care to help transform the reference style in the book, just in time, and Jamilah Maiga helped finish that job. My students at Adelphi University and at CUNY/Lehman College contributed thoughtful comments and questions, as did all the people I interviewed for this book—students, parents, teachers, administrators, and colleagues. I hope, as they do, that their participation will contribute to eradicating school bullying in the future.

I am grateful as well to all the people from Humanities Preparatory Academy and the two Camp Thoreaus—exceptional examples of the compassionate communities that ground this book and illustrate the tremendous potential inherent in helping people thrive and care about one another.

Very special thanks to my mentors, whom I love deeply: Stanley Aronowitz, Lynn Chancer, and Michael Kimmel, who read and enthusiastically supported early drafts of *The Bully Society*—providing invaluable feedback. Stanley's friendship, writings, wisdom, and intellectual passion are a constant source of inspiration. He introduced me to many of the most scintillating books, theories, and people that have helped shape my thinking, and he continues to do so. Lynn's scholarship has had a significant impact on my perspective and this book; her generous collaboration launched my career, and her belief in this book helped make it happen. She is a cherished friend and an extraordinary support, and I am eternally grateful to her. I felt so honored when Michael, my hero, read my first publication and made the effort to find me. Since then, as a loving friend and phenomenal colleague, he has done everything possible to make sure my intellectual contributions, including this book, are further published and widely read. I adore him.

My dear friend David Callahan encouraged me when I was discouraged and motivated me further when I was already exhilarated. David is a friend in the most beautiful sense of the word. I thank him for carefully reading every page and for providing such profound and acutely targeted feedback. Dave has encouraged me to publish a book since we met in college—and has never failed in his confidence that I would accomplish this and many other great things. A friend that sees and fosters your strengths and potential when they are less visible to yourself is a rare gem, and I am grateful every day for the love and support Dave has shown me over almost thirty years. Thanks also to David's mother, Sydney Callahan, without whom I might never have discovered my love and passion for sociology.

I am grateful to the many friends, students, and relatives who shared important ideas, information, and help, especially Vincent Brevetti, Monique Daniel, Stephen Lewandowski, Maxine Grant Steele, Katherine Stevens, and Adrian Stone.

Brett Kuehner came to the book's technological rescue on many occasions—at a moment's notice and with good humor—and is a cherished and talented friend.

My childhood friend Ricky Snyder emerged as a powerfully uplifting force whose support and warmth was palpable. Ricky also reviewed, checked, crunched, and double-crunched many of the statistics reported in the book, a mammoth contribution.

My colleagues provided warm support and intellectual stimulation, especially Lina Beydoun, Melanie Bush, Dean Sam Grogg, Provost Gayle Insler, Jacqueline Johnson, Stephanie Lake, Deborah Little, Sal Primeggia, Sally Ridgeway, and Dean Steve Rubin.

Others provided personal support: Anna Panurach, who blesses our lives in being so loving, highly competent, calm, and generous—she is cherished; and Claudia Heilbrunn, whose unparalleled talent, wisdom, love, and brilliance helped me develop into a happy, high-functioning, and energized writer, teacher, and mother. Claudia teaches empathy as a principle for creating, maintaining, and growing healthy relationships with self and others; her work is a beautiful model for creating compassionate communities, and her thoughts on sections of this book were critical contributions.

My mother encouraged me to get my PhD and was excited about my every achievement on the road to publishing this book. I could not have written such a book without the enduring love and learning I received from her, not to mention the ethical and intellectually thought-provoking upbringing she gave me. I know that my father would be so proud of me too. I can see the tears rolling down his face as he holds the book in his hands. This book is a tribute to his powerful integrity and compassion and the many beautiful lessons he taught me. I know too that his brother, my uncle, would be thrilled to see *The Bully Society* in print. His memory emboldens me. I also thank my brother and sister-in-law for their very welcome and consistent enthusiasm.

I thank my husband, whom I love so much, for being proud of me, supporting me emotionally and otherwise, doing everything he could to give me the time I needed to finish *The Bully Society*, and laboring over the book's sentences and words with his own professional editing expertise. His love, sharp critical thinking, worldly stories, and compassionate and principled heart bless and light my life. And I thank our children, whose beautiful spirits make each moment magical. I continuously learn from their love and creativity and their voracious curiosity and passion; they inspire me daily.

I wrote this book to address school conditions which have caused monstrous pain. To that end, I thank everyone who is working hard to create safer and more compassionate learning environments.

Introduction

The Gender Police

In October 1997, I heard on the radio that Luke Woodham, a sixteen-year-old, had killed two classmates and wounded seven others in a school shooting in Pearl, Mississippi. In a note, Luke declared: "I am not insane. I am angry. I killed because people like me are mistreated every day."[1] He explained that he was tired of being called a "faggot"; he was additionally enraged that his girlfriend—whom he killed in the shooting—had broken up with him.

At the start of the Woodham case, I began examining school shootings. Two months after the massacre in Mississippi came a shooting in Kentucky, then one in Arkansas that same month, and then another in Arkansas three months later in March 1998. There was a shooting in Pennsylvania that April, in Tennessee that May, and then in Oregon that same month, where two students were killed and twenty-two wounded. A year and a half later, on April 20, 1999, as I was driving home from my job as a school social worker, I heard about the Columbine shooting on the radio. I pulled the car over and sat paralyzed as I heard the latest terror unfold.

I continued to study these cases and began to look at shootings prior to Woodham, while also watching one after another take place. This book covers shootings over three decades: 1979 to 2009. I am still struck by the similarities among them. In almost every one, perpetrators targeted other boys who had called them names associated with homosexuality, girls who had rejected them, or both. Even in cases when the shooters lashed out against their schools for perceived injustices related to discipline or academic assessments, gender pressures often played a role: the shooters talked about these actions as challenges to their masculinity.

1

It became clear, as I uncovered the roots of these shootings, that children and teens continue to feel forced to conform to a narrow set of gender expectations in order to be accepted. Things have clearly grown worse, however, since my own childhood, when the dozen or so school shootings that occurred in the seventies barely registered in the national consciousness. It is more common today for those victimized in school to pick up guns and turn them on fellow students.

Some difficult economic and social circumstances have developed over these three decades, and since the turn of the century new challenges have surely made life even harder for children and adults alike. These forces add pressure to school environments, which are often the only social spaces children have. In many of the towns and cities where school shootings took place, everyone attended the same school. For those who were tormented during the school day, extracurricular activities were just extensions of the same environment. Many of these children seemed to have no way out. They felt beleaguered by other youth in their school, as well as by some school faculty who spoke derisively to them or who even joined in the bullying.

Ideally students shouldn't need to find alternative spaces to feel safe and accepted. Schools are responsible for helping students become self-reflective, self-actualized, compassionate, and civic-minded people. Instead, teachers often become resented authority figures, while students become passive and docile, or rebellious and then accused of "acting out." The obsession with gender, status, obedience, and competition that occupies our students undermines their relationships with themselves and with others, as well as their ability to learn and thrive. In many of our schools, precious opportunities for creating community and developing critical thinking are lost; instead, perhaps more than ever before, cutthroat competition, cruelty, isolation, and anxiety prevail.

Over the last thirty years, school shootings have gone from a rare occurrence to a frequent tragedy. From 1969 to 1978, there were 16 school shootings in the United States. (Interestingly, 3 of them were committed by state police against student protesters.) From 1979 to 1988, there were 29 school shootings, almost double those in the previous decade. Between 1989 and 1998, school shootings just about doubled again, to 52; and from 1999 to 2008 they increased again, as 63 new shootings took place. Shootings continue to increase in number; there were 22 in 2009 alone. By my count, there have been 166 shootings in schools in the last three decades (182 in the last forty years). Yet even as they become more common—with more than 500 students and 150 parents, school faculty, and other adults killed or wounded—these cases are persistently viewed as "aberrations." Each new incident provokes surprise and shock.

Many of these mass shootings or rampages took place in predominantly white, middle-class or upper-class suburbs or small towns and have been treated by other scholars and critics as an isolated and unique phenomenon, sharing nothing with gang-related or single-targeted shootings or other forms of school violence. In my research, however, while there are some disparities, I found more similarities among these various forms of violence. Experts also tend to fix blame on factors external to schools: severe mental illness, access to guns, or media violence, especially video games. While these issues surely play a role in the high incidence of such events, we need to ask a more fundamental question: What occurs in schools themselves—the sites, after all, of the shootings—that causes so many students to become unhappy, anxious, depressed, and motivated by rage?

This book proposes that there are inextricable connections between school shooting outbursts, the "everyday" violence of bullying, and the destructive gender pressures and social demands created by the larger culture and endured by virtually all children in our schools. Although the forms of school violence may differ, the same patterns emerge. Boys (and, increasingly, girls) lash out to prove that they can fulfill their narrow gender prescriptions. Nearly all the school shooters were violently reacting to oppressive social hierarchies in their schools.

As I will show, the conditions that have helped spark school shootings are not aberrations; they are the norm. The hurtful and violent bullying with which teens contend has become commonplace and has reached disturbing levels. Our ubiquitous zero-tolerance policies help schools suspend or expel students who commit violence, but they do not prevent the specter of violence from returning again and again. They certainly do nothing to halt the quieter violence—the violence students do to themselves, the depression and suicide, for instance, fostered by the same conditions. To stop school shootings as well as the more common culture of despair in our schools, we will need to transform our schools' cultures.

In addition to examining a wide range of studies, I conducted more than sixty interviews with children and adults in the United States between March 2006 and March 2008. Since I had worked in schools for over twenty years, I had access to people in school communities that I might not otherwise have had. I found quickly that most people had a story about either being bullied or witnessing bullying incidents. I share their stories in *The Bully Society* to bring to life the common situations our children experience and to show the similarities between the school shooters' complaints and those of average American children and adults from our schools.

My interviews included working-class, wealthy, and middle-class families from rural, inner-city, and suburban communities. Most of the people I interviewed were white, but I also interviewed people with African American, Latino, and other ethnic backgrounds. I conducted slightly more interviews with white middle-class students from suburbs, since most of the school shootings took place within this demographic. I also interviewed more people from the Northeast. Fewer school shootings took place in this region, yet the same bully cultures that led to so many shootings in midwestern and southern states persist there. Students ranged in age from approximately eleven to twenty-six. I also interviewed some teachers and related professionals in their thirties and forties who reflected on the bully cultures in their schools when they had been younger. They came from places including the inner cities of Manhattan and the Bronx, rural Maine, Connecticut, North Carolina, Texas, and New York State, especially Long Island and Westchester.

I have changed the names of my respondents, and I mention their demographics in general terms to protect their privacy. I refer to my student and parent interviewees by a first name only and my school faculty respondents by only a last name. Actual first and last names are used only for those individuals whose stories have been reported in the media and for individuals who wanted to be named directly. I have allowed people to speak for themselves, both in public testimonies and in interviews I conducted myself. Sometimes people used less respectful language in their anecdotes; but I am hopeful that both young people and their elders will speak more civilly when the concerns of so many students, school faculty, and parents are more effectively addressed.

As you will see, the stories and concerns shared here illuminate three key traits of everyday school culture discussed in *The Bully Society*.

The first is *gender policing*, or pressure to conform to gender expectations. Students (and adults) engage in constant surveillance of themselves and others to enforce boy and girl codes. Most people in a given school community tend to become members of the "gender police," correcting their own and one another's behaviors, attitudes, and dress according to their perceived expectations for proper gender performance.

The second is a set of *masculinity imperatives.* Hypermasculinity is the dominant gender norm imposed by the gender police. Boys—but also girls—obtain status by displaying aggression and a willingness to demonstrate power at another's expense.

The third is *normalized bullying.* Bullying is the tool by which the most aggressive members of the gender police use coercive and often violent power to acquire and maintain high social status. By participating in gender policing, and targeting students they perceive to be failing in the task of meeting masculinity norms, students elevate their social status.

The rigid status hierarchies found in today's schools have not developed in a vacuum. They come from a larger, more encompassing set of values, generated by what I call a *bully economy.* Economic and cultural trends associated with extreme capitalism, including severe income disparities and related values pervasive in popular media, have helped institutionalize masculinity prescriptions (i.e., aggression and dominance) and intensified gender policing in multiple forms.

Children today learn that status is everything, as described in chapter 1, "Social Status Wars." Race and class are our most typical indicators of power, and conformity to gender expectations is paramount. This chapter explains how students become gender police recruits—and how their policing fuels battles over status and power in schools.

Chapter 2, "Masculinity and White Supremacy," examines theories of masculinity and their relevance both to school shootings and to the everyday violence that has become accepted in our schools. Boys are expected to be powerful and dominant and then are often attacked and ridiculed if they appear gay, poor, or nonwhite or have any number of other perceived differences. A recipe for violence ensues when boys are pressured to be hypermasculine and then are marginalized through classism, racism, heterosexism, or other forms of prejudice.

"Violence against Girls," chapter 3, addresses how boys learn from an early age that they assert manhood not only by being popular with girls but also by wielding power over them—physically, emotionally, and sexually. This chapter examines school shootings where the perpetrators specifically targeted girls who rejected them and where they lashed out indiscriminately as a result of perceived damage to their manhood after being "dumped." These shootings reveal other problems in schools too, including a high level of sexual harassment and dating violence.

Chapter 4, "Gay Bashing," examines the fate that awaits many boys who are perceived as failing to meet accepted parameters of masculinity and whose peers label them "gay." These boys, judged as wanting by students as well as adults—the school's gender police—are taunted and abused. Many of the school shooters were heterosexually identified victims of relentless gay bashing; many cited revenge against such masculinity challenges as a motivation for their shooting. Boys are expected to demonstrate what I have called a *flamboyant heterosexuality*—flaunting and bragging about sexual exploits with girls—with aggression and disdain. A successful image imbued in sexist and heterosexist expectations can vault a boy to the top of his school's status hierarchy. Conversely, failure to conform to this image (by being respectful to girls, for instance) can quickly render boys vulnerable to harassment and assault.

As discussed in chapter 5, "Girl Bashing," girls are themselves driven to conform to superficial and destructive gendered standards. Female teens and tweens navigate a minefield: they are judged by conventional standards regarding their body type and their ability to attract boys, but they are also increasingly pressured to be "tough" in today's hypercompetitive and pervasively masculine society. These pressures encourage girls to use violence as a means of proving themselves and help explain the dramatic increases in violence committed by girls as outlined by recent research.

Much of the violence girls (and boys) wield is through text messages and in cyberspace, as addressed in chapter 6. Slut bashing and gay bashing are common and persistent in these venues. Each technological innovation (texting, instant messaging, e-mail) makes this type of insidious bullying more painful and intimate. It was bad enough when students were harassed on Facebook pages, but now they are tormented by text messages sometimes nonstop; or they may be victims of "sexting," in which sexual photos of them are widely distributed to embarrass and humiliate them and ruin their reputations.

Chapters 7 and 8, "Adult Bullies" and "The Bully Economy," trace the competitive pressures that pervade our schools to our economy and politics. While schools serve as pressure cookers where ruthless competition and other hypermasculinity imperatives are expressed in extreme form, adults inadvertently or explicitly play out the same social status conflicts relating to wealth, race, looks, and sexuality, as well as grown-up versions of gay and girl bashing, dating violence, and harassment. The same ruthless social hierarchies and hurtful cliques can be found among adults: many parents and teachers bully one another, and bully children and students too.

An increasingly unfettered capitalist economy has both fed and been fed by these values. Adults continue to work long hours and weeks to be able to purchase the clothes and lifestyles that help them achieve status among each other. Often the business tactics necessary to achieve such wealth require the same objectification found in our schools—that is, a casual disregard for the feelings and lives of others.

Chapters 9 and 10 discuss whether particular educational policies and typical school cultures are likely to encourage or mitigate bullying and violence. Chapter 9, "America Is from Mars, Europe Is from Venus," compares the more "masculine," punitive, individually focused policies prevalent in the United States with the more "feminine" relationship- and community-oriented policies that are common in European and Nordic countries. Many U.S. anti-bullying programs focus on helping students to stand up for themselves and talk back to potential bullies. Research has shown, though, that developing bonds among school faculty and students and helping students and faculty support one another in such situations are more effective. Chapter 10, "Creating Kinder Schools and Cyberspaces," highlights some excellent and successful programs in the United States and across the world, with a particular focus on programs that help develop a collective courage.

The Bully Society concludes by pointing toward the necessity for change: dismantling our schools' bully society, which is driven by our contemporary bully economy. The following pages present insights necessary for understanding and undertaking this challenging and essential task; together, as the conclusion shows, we can transform our schools into more humane and compassionate communities.

Working on this book led me to reflect on my own early experiences in schools and what might have been different then, when school shootings were comparatively rare. When I felt excluded at school, I didn't fantasize about an attack on my tormentors. I wanted to tell everyone why I thought they had certain values wrong. I wanted to improve my environment, not destroy it. Gender, though, was also at the core of my own difficult experiences in school.

My troubles began on the cusp of adolescence, when I became a "girl" instead of a kid in my local public elementary school. In fifth grade, pressure to demonstrate typical gendered behaviors began to permeate our school days. Competition and backbiting replaced what I had previously experienced as a positive and enjoyable school environment. Until then, I had been perceived as popular and had been voted president of my class every year. Now suddenly I was the class pariah. A girl in the class had started making comments about me—saying I had too many boyfriends and telling different boys who she believed liked me that I liked a different one better. Like many girls across the country, I had my first experience with what I refer to in this book as slut bashing—in which girls or boys question the sexual legitimacy of a target and then lash out at her with vicious names conveying that she is worthless.

These unpleasant experiences continued in sixth grade, and the negative social culture changed only slightly when I went to a private middle school. I quickly discovered that I didn't have the right clothes, the right look, the right gestures, or the right things to say. I was dismayed by the flood of new rules and expectations and realized that I needed to change everything about myself if I wanted to be accepted in this new environment. The gender prescriptions in private school were not only strict but expensive. In public school I needed Keds and then Pro-Ked sneakers; now I needed pricey designer jeans (Sassoon or Jordache), and I was expected to go on shopping "dates" with certain girls to be included in after-school social events and activities. It was a lot of work to become a "popular girl" in this school, and everyone seemed to be striving to achieve this goal. But even when I wore the right clothes, talked to the right girls, and hung out with the right crowd, I felt somehow disconnected. I felt alone as I struggled to be accepted by a group of people who were themselves working hard to be included. The popular codes inflicted expectations on everyone, effectively building impenetrable obstacles to authentic self-expression and connection. Instead, people talked about each other in ways I thought were mean as they jockeyed for status among the "in" groups.

While my childhood challenges were mild in comparison with what millions of American children endure today in their schools, I was often miserable, and I longed for some alternative safe space. I found some reprieve at the time in a community-oriented summer camp. For many of us there, camp became a preserve, a salvation from the rougher social environments we experienced during the rest of the year at school. This community, and others where I've worked as a professional since then, showed me that compassion and connection with others are vital for learning and thriving. Such support should be available to all youth. People shouldn't have to wait until they get through their school years before it presumably gets better; growing up shouldn't have to be quite so hard.

I've worked for decades to change schools and the larger social environment that tends to breed violence and other bullying behavior. For eleven years I worked in secondary schools; I served as a conflict resolution coordinator, a teacher, a substance abuse prevention counselor, and a school social worker and guidance administrator, often dealing directly with bullies and their targets. I listened to students in different kinds of educational environments—from the elite and exclusive to those from inner cities—as they complained about feeling frightened and confused, detached and lonely. More recently, I have worked in public and private universities as a sociology, social work, and criminal justice professor. My research has focused primarily on the links between school violence and gender. Through it all, I have studied what would help students—male and female—to feel supported, recognized, and empowered by other students, as well as by teachers and parents.

In 2000, as a school social worker, I helped 100 percent of my students at an at-risk New York City public school gain entrance to four-year colleges—35 percent of them with full scholarships to excellent private universities. Many of these students emerged from violent gang and drug cultures in their neighborhoods, homelessness, sexual abuse, extreme depression and anxiety, truancy, and other conditions that might have been predicted to doom their futures. These students were instead inspired by the community-oriented focus of their public school and the work they themselves contributed to making the school more compassionate and supportive. The community support they received at school helped them become potential future leaders, instead of remaining in conditions of poverty and violence.

As I discuss in the book's later sections, I've seen students leave gangs and become part of mediation teams, working heroically to recruit record numbers of new students to their school's conflict resolution program. Some of my students initiated and wrote the first sexual harassment policy in their school, then worked tirelessly to get it the respect and support it needed to be instituted schoolwide.

Students collaborated to create different kinds of helpful programs and then thrived in the smaller communities we created. The warmth generated by these affirming and safe environments had positive effects on the students' lives—attendance, grades, behavior, graduation rates, and entry to college. They also enhanced the larger school environment. Many of my students had been brutally gay-bashed and slut-bashed in previous schools—whereas we worked together to support these students and addressed such concerns effectively in communitywide meetings. Methods for creating compassionate communities in schools are literally infinite.

I became a school counselor because I wanted to help those who struggled in school. I believed then and believe now that it is possible to create more supportive and empowering school environments. Right now the gender police dominate our schools: students and adults often monitor themselves and one another for perceived infractions against respective gender codes, in gangs as well as in more common social cliques. To create safe schools, we need to examine the forces that turn them into gender police training grounds inciting so many forms of violence.

This book aims to help concerned families, schools, and communities understand the dangers of oppressive gender expectations—and offers alternatives. I hope it helps fuel the quest for the kind of community-oriented and caring schools children need to thrive.

1

Social Status Wars

The twenty-three-year-old Virginia Tech gunman Cho Seung-Hui had been relentlessly teased and bullied throughout middle school and high school. He was angry at what he perceived as an unjust school hierarchy that privileged the wealthy. Before he killed thirty-two people and then himself in a 2007 rampage, Cho raged against the rich, declaring his shooting a response to the "brats" and "snobs" at his school who were not satisfied with their "gold necklaces" and "Mercedes." The South Korean-born Cho, whose parents ran a dry-cleaning business, seemed to believe he had been bullied because of his lower economic status and his race. His peers said they couldn't understand his accent and way of speaking and told him to "go back to China" one of the rare times he mustered up the courage to speak in class.[1]

When Eric Harris and Dylan Klebold sauntered into the Columbine High School library, they were similarly angry at those with higher status in their school. Armed with a rifle, a shotgun, handguns, knives, and bombs, the first thing they shouted was "All jocks stand up. We're going to kill everyone one of you."[2]

These were vicious and devastating attacks that grabbed headlines all over the world. The media presented a parade of analysts and experts trying to figure out why two middle-class boys or a quiet college student had become mass murderers. Few of them looked at the high school culture that places a diminished value on students who are perceived as not measuring up. In today's high schools, race and class, the historical purveyors of American status, are still important factors, but gender is also crucial. Students are measured against reductive and stereotypical standards for what it means to be the "right" kind of girl or boy. Children may be perceived as not good-looking or affluent enough; boys are judged for being not sufficiently masculine or athletic; and girls are scrutinized for the extent to which they are pretty and popular with boys. Children found lacking are pushed to the bottom of their school's social hierarchy, where life can feel unbearable.

The French sociologist Pierre Bourdieu explains in his groundbreaking works the dynamics of power in social relationships. Social inequality becomes reified among adults through the acquisition of different forms of capital.[3] Young people also find that to win power and influence in a given community they have to have a certain kind of body (body capital), be friends with certain people (social capital), participate in particular activities that are valued in a given school (cultural capital), be up on the latest gossip (information capital), and of course have a certain amount of money (economic capital) and the material possessions that money can buy (symbolic capital).

Children who come up short in one or more of these categories are often deprived of basic opportunities to fulfill their potential. A bully culture instead circumscribes their lives. Students who don't achieve the prescribed status markers can be shunned, taunted, assaulted, and otherwise forced to pursue their education in a hostile environment. Children who do score high on these measures are not necessarily much better off, since these goals encourage an obsession with external approval that rarely leaves room for young people—or adults—to express their authentic selves.

The status systems in schools reflect familiar forms of institutionalized discrimination in which some members of society continue to be treated as second-class citizens. Many of the stories I heard from people around the country centered on bullying behavior that took place on their school bus and brought to mind the history of racial segregation on public vehicles. Older students or students perceived as more popular tend to claim a certain part of the bus—front or back—and other students are often forced to sit in the remaining spaces, if they are allowed to sit at all.

Rebecca, from an upper-class northeastern suburb, talked about how she had joined the bullies after years of being harassed about her weight. "What is she wearing?" "What was she thinking?" she and her friends would whisper loudly about the other girls. "If someone was wearing something really off the wall, we would laugh about it." Rebecca had a keen sense of who was higher or lower on the hierarchy. "I had graduated to the back of the bus," where the older kids would sit, Rebecca recalled, "and all the way in the front of the bus, this girl called me a 'fat bitch.' She said it in front of everyone. So I grabbed her by her hair and smacked her in the face and said, 'Don't you ever call me that again.'" What seemed to concern Rebecca most was that the girl was younger than she was: "It might have been different if she was older. I couldn't get over that this little girl who annoys the whole bus was going to say this to me." She reasoned to herself that "if I didn't do it, someone else would." If you're a "freshman in high school, you're the little guy. Unless you have a big brother on campus, you don't run your mouth. It's a known thing; when you're the youngest grade in a school, it is known that you have to keep a low profile until you gain experience at that school."

Shantique, from an impoverished southern rural area, also remembers the bus as the scene where the most ferocious jockeying for status took place, and the worst bullying. "I was always the last person to get on my bus so I would have to negotiate to get a seat. No one wanted to move over. It was high school kids who drove the bus and no one would let me sit down. One little guy sometimes let me sit down, and then they would pick on him." The powerful girls sat at the back, she said, and controlled the whole bus. They were particularly horrible to one girl because her family had even less money than those of the other girls on the bus. "They picked on her mercilessly, extorted money from her whatever she had, and they made fun of her and called her names. She would cry hysterically and cut school as a result." Finally the girl told her parents what was going on because she was missing so much school. "They got her on another bus," Shantique said, "but then the [powerful] girls would go after her in school."

The rigidity of the school status system often remains hidden from adults. Students who are tormented and ostracized at school come home sullen, depressed, angry, or otherwise distressed, but many say they don't want to talk about their treatment because it is humiliating, and they don't even want their parents to know that others don't seem to like them. Abused young people bring home a host of upsetting feelings and problems that can overwhelm family members—who, even if they are informed about the situation, may also feel helpless and at a loss about what they can do to make it stop. Sadly, some adults who are informed dismiss or minimize the problem.

Eric Harris and Dylan Klebold and their bullies were in fact living in a typical American high school culture where, in a microcosm of an authoritarian state, kids were made to conform to constrained parameters of acceptable behavior that were often vicious and hostile. If you didn't accept the school leaders and the imposed culture, you were against them and would be severely punished for it, said Columbine classmate Brooks Brown in his book *No Easy Answers: The Truth behind Death at Colum-*

bine. Brooks, who considered himself Dylan's good friend, sometimes hung out with the social group the bullies at Columbine referred to as the Trench Coat Mafia.[4]

Eric and Dylan were seen as weak, nerdy, and weird; in short, they were way outside the narrow ideal of what people in their school and their community believed a boy should be, and therefore they were treated as less than human, Brooks explained. Eric had two strikes against him. He had a slight deformity that left his chest a bit sunken. When he undressed in gym class, the bullies were ready to mock him. "Mocking a guy for a physical problem he can't control is one of the most humiliating ways to bring him down," wrote Brooks. Eric was also the shortest in the group. "The rest of us, as we got older, became well over six feet in height; Eric never did," Brooks continued. "He was small, he was a 'computer geek,' and he wasn't even from Colorado to begin with. He was as prime a target as the bullies at Columbine could have asked for."[5]

Brooks Brown describes some of what the bullies' targets endured: "At lunchtime, the jocks would kick our chairs, or push us down onto the table from behind. They would knock our food trays onto the floor, trip us, or throw food as we were walking by. When we sat down, they would pelt us with candy from another table. In the hallways, they would push kids into lockers and call them names while their friends stood by and laughed."[6] Brooks recalled another incident "when a bunch of football players drove by, yelled something and threw a glass bottle that shattered near Dylan's feet. I was pissed, but Eric and Dylan didn't even flinch. 'Don't worry about it, man,' Dylan said. 'It happens all the time.'"[7] Someone reported to school authorities that the two boys had drugs "as a way to harass them." They were removed from class and searched, and their cars and lockers were searched as well. "No drugs were turned up," Brooks writes, "but the two of them had been humiliated nonetheless."[8]

In his 2005 book on rage in contemporary America, *Going Postal,* Mark Ames writes that Eric and Dylan "were so marked for abuse that even talking to them was dangerous. One female student recounted how, when she was a Columbine freshman, some 'jocks' spotted her talking to Dylan Klebold in the school hallway between classes. After she walked away from him, one of them slammed her against the lockers and called her a 'fag lover.' None of the students came to help her—and when asked later why she didn't report the incident to the administration, she replied, 'It wouldn't do any good because they wouldn't do anything about it.'"[9]

Even after the shooting, many students seemed to see nothing wrong with bullying students like Eric and Dylan. Elliot Aronson writes in *Nobody Left to Hate,* "Most members of the 'in group' considered taunting 'outsiders' a reasonable thing to do."[10] Aronson quotes one member of the Columbine football team, who said, "Columbine is a good, clean place except for those rejects. Most kids didn't want them there. Sure we teased them. But what do you expect with kids who come to school with weird hairdos and horns on their hats? It's not just the jocks; the whole school's disgusted with them. . . . If you want to get rid of someone, usually you tease 'em. So the whole school would call them homos."[11] Kevin Koeniger, at the time seventeen years old and a junior on Columbine's Rebels Football Team, told a reporter, "If they were different, why wouldn't we look at them as weird?" Another student from the soccer team, Ben Oakley, agreed. "They're freaks."[12]

In this case, the "freaks" struck back. With guns in their hands they were, for a moment, at the top of the pecking order, and they doled out humiliation, abuse, and death not only to the students who bullied them but to everyone in their path. The teacher who was hiding in the library during the massacre recalled hearing the shooters say, "Kill all the jocks." But she also heard them say, "What do we have here, a nigger?" just before they shot Isaiah Shoels, an African American and a star football player. They said to someone else: "Whatta we got here, a fat boy?" And they taunted a student with glasses. While they had compiled a "hit list" in advance, their real hope, Harris wrote in his diary, was that they could use explosives to simply blow up the whole school, reducing the site of their torment to rubble.[13]

In *Comprehending Columbine*, Ralph W. Larkin writes, "They apparently wanted to target the entire peer structure, in which they were at the very bottom. Although they were harassed by a small minority of the student population, they blamed everyone in the school for their own degraded social status,"[14] perhaps because no one helped them and because many seemed to have watched their humiliation with either indifference or some degree of pleasure.

Eric and Dylan internalized the status hierarchies in their school. They despised the "bullies" who tormented them, but they didn't seek to defend other targets of bullying. Instead they became the biggest bullies, in an apparent effort to momentarily be at the top of the school hierarchy themselves—torturing those they had learned to believe were categorically inferior.

Why Did They Shoot?

As the Columbine shooting took its place among an escalating number of school shootings in the 1990s, most observers asked: "What was different about those boys, what was it that made them reject common social and moral standards?" Such questions belie the fact that in some sense Eric and Dylan were affirming, rather than rejecting, some of the prevailing social and moral standards at their schools. These expectations push boys to achieve certain kinds of status at all costs—and in particular link the achievement of this status to a narrow definition of masculinity that values power and dominance above all else. A close look at three decades of school shootings shows how tightly school social expectations and the school shooters' responses are intertwined.

If they want to be popular, male students in American high schools are often expected to conform to hypermasculine values. Boys are pressured to be successful at sports, highly competitive, dominant with girls, emotionally detached, able to hold their own in a fight, disdainful of homosexuality, and derisive toward academics. More often than not, they are expected also to be affluent, with a nice car, expensive clothes, and money to throw around—more evidence of their power and success. The recognition that boys gain if they exhibit these qualities allows them to climb up their school hierarchy and maintain a high social status.

Living as they do within such a strict and punitive social hierarchy, boys are told in one way or another to prove their manhood and, in some cases, to prove that they exist at all. Many boys feel they must go to great lengths to differentiate themselves from those perceived as gay, feminine, poor, intellectual, or weak. They'll harass, bully, demean, humiliate, and generally try to crush the social value of anyone who doesn't fit in, all in an effort to secure their own social standing. By calling another student "gay," a boy demonstrates to others that he is successfully heterosexual, while a boy who "beats up" another student proves how powerful he is compared with the injured party. Such bullying techniques are pervasive across American schools as children work desperately to prevent their own social demise and to raise their otherwise fragile status; without this violence, boys, in particular, fear that they might not get recognized at all, or worse, could become the targets of the abuse themselves and lose any opportunity for social connection. In various ways, boys of all races and economic groups, across the country, feel compelled to demonstrate an aggressive masculinity. What's more, "dominance bonding" tends to be socialized through school athletics as well as other school institutionalized activities.[15]

Of the 166 school shooting perpetrators whose identities are known, 147 were male. Most of those who committed the massacres, as revealed in the examination of their cases, struggled for recognition and status among their peers. The majority of them languished at the bottom of the social hierarchy. They tended not to be athletic, and they were often described in the media as skinny, scrawny, short, lanky, or pudgy. They were teased for looking feminine or gay. They tended to be academically oriented. They were generally unsuccessful with girls. Many of them were also significantly less wealthy than the popular teens at their schools. As a result of these perceived failures, they were mercilessly teased and abused.

Without even a shred of the status necessary for surviving socially in their schools, these boys repeatedly chose to prove their masculinity through overwhelming violence. Many of them targeted more popular kids who had harassed them and girls who had rejected them. They believed their violent response, a powerful demonstration of masculine prowess, would win them the recognition they desperately craved. Whether they were dead or alive, free or behind bars, one after another, the perpetrators spoke about their yearning for notoriety. They could no longer imagine achieving recognition in their present reality, so they dreamed of receiving it in some form of afterlife obtained through violence and infamy. Most people work hard to get recognized and seen— a basic human need. Without more constructive vehicles in schools and elsewhere in the community, these youth turned to any means necessary.

Some of the shooters who survived—who didn't kill themselves or get killed in the mayhem—expressed these feelings explicitly. Fifteen-year-old Michael Carneal told psychiatrists he was proud of himself after he shot and killed three girls, including two who had rejected him, in West Paducah, Kentucky, in 1997.[16] Michael told the psychiatrists that he wasn't sure why he had started shooting that day. "I didn't expect to kill anyone. I was just going to shoot. I thought maybe they would be scared and then no one would mess with Michael."[17] "Murder is gutsy and daring," bragged Luke Woodham after his 1977 shooting in Mississippi.[18]

In fact many of them did become nationally or internationally known figures after their shootings rather than merely abused and tormented "social rejects." Sadly, it did seem to take the shootings to "broadcast" to the society at large the message that millions of students were suffering terribly at school every day. Suddenly, the school pecking order—and the dreadful plight of those at its bottom end—were exposed to public view. People began to notice that the periodic outbursts of violence seemed to be taking place not just at "disadvantaged" inner-city high schools but at "good" schools in suburban and small town America. Tamar Lewin, writing in the *New York Times*, observed, "Compared with big-city schools, these schools look homogeneous: the majority of the students are white, middle class, dressed in the same handful of brand names. But the reality is far more complex." Lewin quoted Carol Miller Lieber, a former principal and director of high school programs at Educators for Social Responsibility, who spoke of the "winner culture" at many of the schools where mass shootings took place—an environment dominated by jocks, student government, and other "in" groups. "But the winners are a smaller group than we'd like to think, and high school life is very different for those who experience it as the losers. They become part of the invisible middle and suffer in silence, alienated and without any real connection to any adult."[19]

Writing in the *New York Times Magazine* four months after the Columbine shooting, Adrian LeBlanc outlined the hierarchy in a suburban American high school in 1999, complete with the names of each of the stratified groups:

> The popular kids tend to be wealthier and the boys among them tend to be jocks. The Gap Girls, Tommy Girls, and Polo Girls compose the pool of desirable girlfriends, many of whom are athletes as well. Below the popular kids, in a shifting order of relative unimportance, are the druggies (stoners, deadheads, burnouts, hippies or neo-hippies), trendies or Valley Girls, preppies, skateboarders and skateboarder chicks, nerds and techies, wiggers, rednecks, and Goths, better known as freaks. There are troublemakers, losers and floaters—kids who move from group to group. Real losers are invisible.[20]

It was from the ranks of these "invisible losers" that many of the school shooters came. While only a fraction of bullied students respond with lethal force, thousands more suffer relentless hostility and humiliation at the hands of their peers. Both statistics and anecdotes show that bullying is an intrinsic part of the cutthroat status wars that have become commonplace at school. As one boy who felt compelled to become a school bully put it: if another boy challenged him at school, "they were trying to get my status. But they got their ass kicked instead."[21] What are they fighting over? What's at stake in these status wars, and how do students gauge who is winning and who is losing?

The Power of Wealth

Among adults, members of all social classes tend to socialize with others like themselves. They quickly learn to recognize one another: even minor differences in clothing, gestures, and speech can signal economic wealth and social prestige, creating cliques that are impenetrable to those outside. Similarly, school cliques tend to be exclusive and powerful.

Among kids today, designer clothes, the latest hairstyles, expensive cars, and the ability to participate in status-building activities—from shopping to luxurious vacations to high-class partying—send powerful signals to other students. In the PBS documentary *People Like Us: Social Class in America*, students at Anderson High School in Austin, Texas, spoke about the influence of family wealth on the school's social hierarchy. "Everybody's really close-minded about who they will and will not associate with," said one girl, "and if you're not wearing these clothes, and driving these cars, and if you don't have Mommy and Daddy's credit card and your own little Structure card, then you can't hang out with us, you know?"[22]

Wendy, now nineteen, experienced the brutality of the status wars when her family moved to an affluent northeastern suburb from an inner city. Wendy's mother is from the Dominican Republic and her father is from Egypt; she spent her early years in public school in a racially mixed, urban working-class neighborhood. "It was so diverse. I didn't know I was different," she said. "I never felt out of the loop. Everyone was accepting. I miss it." In her new school in the suburbs, "I was miserable. . . . Everyone wanted to know what street you live on, because that's who you were . . . It was all materialistic, where you lived and what you owned." Wendy continued: "They would question my clothing. I used to wear cartoon character T-shirts and overalls, but most people it seemed would shop at the boutiques . . . and buy Juicy Couture and Tiffany jewelry." Wendy tried her best to get in line. In elementary school, she said: "I was dying to get a charm bracelet that everyone had. I begged and pleaded. And my parents got me a fake one, but I didn't know. The second I came into school, this girl ran over to me and picked up the bracelet and said: 'Oh, it's fake,' and she dropped it. I felt betrayed by my parents." While Wendy felt she desperately needed the expensive bracelet, she says she now understands why her parents didn't want to buy it for her. "Why spend $150 on a brace-let for a young girl? They thought little kids wouldn't know. But they are trained. My bracelet said 'Tiffany and Co.,' but it wasn't the same writing. They knew."

Status is perceived as something passed down from upper- and mid-dle-class parents to their children. In adult society, those from a higher socioeconomic background are often affiliated with prestigious organi-zations, companies, and social groups. The ability to participate in this culture of prestige enables individuals to maintain their high status, per-petuating a closed society.[23] This system is also mirrored in high school cliques, which block lower-income students from mixing with more afflu-ent groups.

Lenny, who grew up in a working-class northeastern urban commu-nity, was just as aware of the class distinctions in his school as any youth from a wealthy suburb. He explained, "If you wear something preppie like a college shirt, you get called 'preppie'; if you wear baggy clothes with your hat backwards you get called 'thug,' or 'hoodlum'; you need to wear brand names or they call you 'poor,' or 'broke,' or 'welfare child.' You've got to wear some brand—Polo, Hilfiger, Jenco, Lacoste—it doesn't mat-ter which; you got to wear something that makes you not look like you're broke."

Mr. Lang, a high school teacher in a predominantly working-class northeastern rural area, said the same thing. "Kids who are poor get bul-lied. . . . If they want to belong in a certain social group, they know they have to buy the right uniform." Students work hard to try to prove they have money in a culture that values economic capital so highly.

"You have to succumb to the pressure of wearing what everyone else is wearing," Lenny continued. "Black kids wear oversized shirts and baggy pants to prove they're tough. If they wear the button-down shirt like the white preppies they can't hang out with the other black kids. That's the way life is, decide who you are and you follow."

One African American university student in one of the classes I taught said that the pressure he experienced as a high school student was unre-lenting. "You had to wear clothes that were two sizes too big on you or you get called gay. I was a medium and I had to get all extra large clothes, 'cause if it wasn't baggy, you were done for. You want to fit in and you don't want to look stupid," he explained.

In a lower-middle-class northeastern urban school, Jessina saw serious violence over the consumer items students felt pressured to purchase. An acquaintance of hers, Adrian, accidentally spilled some juice on another guy's expensive Michael Jordan sneakers in the locker room. In no time, the boy who owned the sneakers, Daniel, pounced on Adrian with the aid of four of his friends and beat him so badly that when the ambulance arrived Adrian was shaking and convulsing. Adrian spent two weeks in the hospital with a concussion and serious cuts and bruises, and his parents were too frightened to allow him to return to the school.

The sneakers were not just expensive; they were considered a status symbol and a ticket to popularity, explained Jessina. "People get very upset if someone steps on these sneakers or dirties them in any way." No one had had a problem with Adrian before the sneaker incident—but given how integral these sneakers were to being accepted in school, the juice accident was perceived as a major threat to Daniel's status and prestige. The incident Jessina described was part of a disturbing trend referred to as "sneaker murders," where students mugged other youth for their high-status shoes.[24]

Jessina said there were many items like the sneakers that kids in her school believed they needed in order to be accepted. "You needed name-brand clothes, name-brand sneakers, the newest electronics, and the right book bag." Jansport book bags were big at her school. But you needed more than one. "Every book bag came with a little string to open the zipper and the more of these you collected the more cool you were." If you had those strings, people knew you had so many Jansport book bags, and you had to guard all these items—bags, phones, strings—because people would steal them in an instant. The clothes at her school were Phat Farm for boys and Baby Phat for girls, as well as Roca Wear—clothes by big-name entertainers in urban music. When Jessina went to a university with a significant upper-class student body, she found there were new purchases she needed. Instead of Baby Phat, the students wore Juicy Couture and Louis Vuitton. There's a tacit contest between who has nicer things, who has the newest and most expensive bags, Jessina explained. "Everybody has Uggs [boots], so you feel you have to get a pair. You feel pressure because everyone else has them. If you don't have a Coach bag you can't compete with the other girls. I had to get a Coach bag to fit in or be on an equal level with them is the thinking. Obviously they are expensive and if you can afford them that says something about you."

Jessina reflected that in both her lower-middle-class urban high school and her upper-class suburban university you had to spend money on certain brands to be accepted. The items valued by the lower economic groups did not necessarily cost less; they were just different kinds of brands that referenced different identities. Jessina described how important expensive North Face down jackets became in her high school. "Every single person in that school had a jacket, and if you didn't you weren't cool. They were three hundred dollars per coat, and the particularly popular coats, the Snorkel, had fur on the hat and they were even more money. Then North Face started putting out even more expensive coats, from six hundred to eight hundred dollars. If you could only afford one you'd get the black one, but you were more popular if you could get more of the coats, and eventually people collected the gray and red and other colors too. People would get beat up all the time because someone wanted that coat or the Jansport bag." Kids would work extra jobs, beg their parents for holiday presents, or steal them, said Jessina. These items were tickets to getting accepted and having a circle of friends of some kind, and kids would do whatever it took to acquire them.

Rebecca, who is now a teacher herself, recalls the same conditions in her white, upper-class southern suburban schools: "You don't fit into this mold, you don't share the same things at least somewhat, you're an outcast, and that's it for you." Each clique associated itself with a different brand name, but you were completely ostracized if you didn't wear any brand at all. "I couldn't keep up with the way some of the girls dressed," Rebecca confided, but "if you're not wearing the right clothes, you won't be accepted. If I didn't dress the right way I would be an outcast." But these girls were wearing Louis Vuitton and Prada. "I couldn't afford that, but I found ways to look good. Kids who couldn't go shopping were in trouble. The parking lot was like a car show; these were sixteen-year-olds with Hummers, Audis, and Land Rovers." It was a lot of pressure, but Rebecca worked hard to maintain appearances in her wealthy school. "They didn't know I was middle class," Rebecca said with some relief.

Rebecca finds the same pressure among the kindergarten students with whom she now works. "They were forming a popular table and wouldn't let one girl sit there because of her clothes and this other girl because of her hair. Some of these five-year-olds are wearing designer clothes, and the girl who didn't wasn't allowed at the popular table." These kids are African American and Latino from a lower-income community—yet the pressures they experience are like the ones Rebecca once endured in her wealthy mostly white suburb. The only difference is in the particular brands.

The status wars that can begin as early as preschool also continue through higher education. Raquel shared her experiences in a northeastern university dominated by upper-class students. "More people are judgmental towards one another here," she said. "Parents have money, expensive bags, and go tanning. If you don't have Coach bags and you don't have Tiffany jewelry, people won't talk to you unless you're forced to in groups in some classes. People who have Tiffany and Coach are friends with each other. If you ask them a question they brush you off; they have an attitude about themselves." "Is it real?" is a common question. Young women get points for donning designer clothing, but the knockoffs just breed scorn.

In one of the gender studies classes I taught, female students talked about the tremendous pressure they had felt to keep up with the latest status symbols in high school. One young woman said, "First you had to get the 'I Love New York' shirts, and then a moment later—you weren't cool if you had one." "Yes, I remember that," murmured another student, resentfully. "I hated them."

Some of the male students in the class insisted that boys were less concerned than girls about fashion and other status symbols—until someone brought up cars. "In my school you had to have a BMW, a Hummer, Mustang or a Range Rover," said one young man. "The guys who had shitty cars had a hard time." Another student added, "You were really in trouble if you took a cab."

Even the religious schools and other private and public schools that require uniforms, in part to help kids opt out of the status wars, end up failing to achieve this goal. My students who attended suburban religious schools said that pressure to have the right look still operates despite the uniform dress code: "In my school girls had to wear their skirts short. Then the administration said we had to wear pants, so the girls wore skin-tight pants. Any girl who didn't do it was looked upon differently," said one. One single mom from a more urban community told me that the uniforms at her daughter's Catholic school were made by the same "must-have" designers that were part of the problem in the first place. Then her daughter besieged her with demands for the shoes and phones that "all the other girls had." A boy explained how important it was to sport a Rolex watch in his Catholic school. In the context of this kind of status competition, uniforms fail to fix the problem as students find other ways to flaunt brand-name objects.

In most schools, both boys and girls feel pressured to have the newest and hippest electronic communications devices and related status technology too. "You had to have the latest cell phone," one of my students recalled. "I got it too, but then something else came out, and you had to keep up." "I thought my social problems would be over when I finally got a cell phone," one young woman commented, "but then they made fun of me because mine didn't have the antennae that came out . . . I was crying. I pulled out my phone so proudly, and I thought, 'Finally I'm going to be cool like everyone else,' and then the antennae didn't pull up, and I still wasn't good enough."

According to a September 2008 survey, four out of five American teens have cell phones, and "teens feel that cell phones have become a vital part of their identities. They also believe that they can gauge a peer's popularity or status by the phone he or she uses."[25] "It's not even about what you look like," said one of my students. "I mean, the cell phones aren't even about your hair or your body—it's just something to buy."

As the discussion continued, my class erupted in indignation over the material items they had felt forced to buy in high school—and in many cases in their college years as well. "Everyone had to go to work to have the money needed to buy brands," said one. "You needed to show you had money and could buy whatever was 'in.'" The big corporations that create these "status" products—from Abercrombie and Fitch, Louis Vuitton, and Baby Phat to Verizon, Apple, and Nokia, along with a host of others—make millions off of children's fragile self-esteem and vulnerable social ties.

Girls and boys alike are often too willing to do whatever it takes to conform to the requirements for popularity in their schools—in large part because the alternatives are so intolerable. They spend money that they and their parents don't have and trade in authentic selves and meaningful connections with others for superficial status markers and membership in the right cliques. The corporations that profit from the consumer culture encourage them to believe that success is impossible without the correct purchases, and the adult society they see around them only reinforces this message. It is hardly surprising, then, that young people fall in line.

This extreme competition in high schools regarding wealth and appearance of wealth fosters bullying, but school administrators often look away when white wealthy students are the ones causing trouble. Affluent teens boost the image of the school and of the community. In addition, adults approach students' behavior with their own prejudices. Many are reluctant to believe that well-dressed, well-spoken youth from financially well-off families could be involved in thuggish acts; in racially mixed schools, white kids are likely to benefit—and minority students suffer—from the preconceived biases of adults.

In schools where many of the shootings took place, the perpetrators were less wealthy—sometimes marginally, sometimes markedly—than the students referred to as jocks and preps who were often their tormentors. Both Evan Ramsey, who shot a classmate who had bullied him and then shot his principal in Bethel, Alaska, in 1997, and Luke Woodham, the Pearl, Mississippi school shooter, were poor by the standards of their schools—and their economic disadvantages became more fodder for ridicule.

Many of the other shooters came from financially stable, suburban homes, but this does not discount class issues. Eric Harris's father entered the oil industry during the late 1970s boom and was apparently a casualty of the subsequent bust. Part of Eric's motivation may have come from his family's loss of strength and power.[26] Certainly, class was a factor in the pecking order at Columbine. "Jocks have more money," said Meg Harris, a sixteen-year-old sophomore at the time of the shootings. "One jock has a Hummer. He totaled one Hummer and his Dad bought him another."[27]

From the outside, these towns may have looked uniform in their racial and class makeup. This only means that less obvious distinctions were employed to determine social status. These less visible differences, expressed in particular gestures, habits, tastes, and access to exclusive social institutions in a given community—Bourdieu's symbolic, cultural, and social capital—can represent extreme variations in status and power. In addition, these small differences are even less likely to be tolerated than they might be in more diverse settings.

Economic capital can be used in a sense to purchase other forms of capital too. For instance, some parents pay for their children to attend expensive sports camps where youth are trained to excel in the competitive sports designed to win them further status.

The Jock Cult

Success for today's adolescents is narrowly defined—not just by peers but by parents, school faculty, and athletic coaches and in images across the media. For boys in American high schools, athletics, in particular, is often the golden road to status. In schools across the country, the best athlete is, by and large, also the most popular boy, and among the different sports, football reigns supreme. The deeper meanings that coaches and often fathers (and mothers) attach to these kinds of sports tend to revolve around themes of masculine power: distinctions between boys and men, physical size and strength, and emotional self-control.

Even the most seemingly masculine athletes bear the social burden of constantly proving their manhood through aggression to maintain their high status. The boys most successful at staying on top are actually a small minority—and they can never relax their vigilance. Through the shoving, pushing, and roughhousing that takes place in school hallways, in locker rooms, and on playing fields, the boys perceived as most popular continue to assert power among each other, as well as over the weaker kids whom they try to keep in their place. Likewise, persecuting boys who don't live up to these masculinity values by calling them names like "fag," "sissy," and "homo" produces status for the popular boys by creating distance from femininity and homosexuality and distance from other groups identified as pariahs in the school.

Students, faculty, and administrators alike are notorious for looking past the negatives of the hypermasculinity celebrated in schools, seeing only the glow of masculine power in athletic success. Parents and other adults outside school are likewise often willing to look the other way if the local "jocks" behave badly. The whole town enjoys a higher status when the high school boys win games, and the larger society frequently condones unethical and even illegal actions by professional athletes, provided they keep winning. All this reinforces the school sports stars' sense that they can and should do just about anything they like—including abusing others—with impunity.

Columbine student Brooks Brown writes in his 2002 book about the mentality that "equates sports with status: 'I am a football player, and therefore I'm better than you. I am a basketball player, and therefore I deserve to make out with all the cheerleaders. Pathetic geeks like you are not on my level.'" He continues, "I don't mean to imply that all the jocks in the world are jerks. . . . The thing is, Columbine's culture worshipped the athlete, and that unconditional adulation had a pretty bad effect on many of the jocks at our school."[28]

In an article on "Columbine's cult of the athlete," Lorraine Adams and Dale Russakoff of the *Washington Post* describe the extent of the special treatment given to student athletes:

The state wrestling champ was regularly permitted to park his $100,000 Hummer all day in a 15-minute space. A football player was allowed to tease a girl about her breasts in class without fear of retribution by his teacher, also the boy's coach. The sports trophies were showcased in the front hall—the artwork, down a back corridor.

Columbine High School is a culture where initiation rituals meant upper class wrestlers twisted the nipples of freshman wrestlers until they turned purple and tennis players sent hard volleys to younger teammates' backsides. Sports pages in the yearbook were in color, a national debating team and other clubs in black and white. The homecoming king was a football player on probation for burglary.[29]

Tommy told me that his friends who weren't athletes struggled in his northeastern public middle school in a wealthy suburb; they were bullied by the athletes, ignored by the faculty, and quickly sent to the principal for the slightest infraction. The "jocks" would "open up a kid's book bag while he was walking down the hall, and all his books would fall out; and then people would just trample right over you. They put tacks and glue on people's seats without them knowing. If you put your bag down to go to the bathroom, they would put it in the garbage can." Athletes, on seeing a nonathlete with a hot lunch, would "shake him up and laugh as his food slid all over him." They put water or baby oil on the floor so that other students would slip.

Tommy himself became an outcast in fourth grade because he wasn't interested in one of the sports mandatory for social acceptance—football, travel soccer, lacrosse. It just was "not my thing," he explained. Instantly, he was teased by students who had been his best friends just the year before. "You're not a man," they chided him. "You're a baby if you can't do this." When he did play, he heard threats: "If you don't score a goal, I'm going to kill you," one student said to him. The student punched him in the face, but when he went to the principal's office, nothing happened. "The kid was a soccer player, one of the best in the county. They didn't want his record tarnished," Tommy said. "Athletes who could barely write their name got easy As and Bs in my school. Teachers pushed sports and substituted that for academics. They didn't have to work for what they got. Others busted tails to get a C."

The school shooters, by and large, failed to live up to the standards of the jock cult. Instead of playing football like the popular students in the school, Michael Carneal, the Kentucky shooter, played in the band that performed at football games, a role that the "jocks" apparently viewed as demeaning and for which they tormented him. Michael made it clear that he wanted to kill the "popular, preppie students" whom he blamed for his mistreatment.[30]

Andrew Golden was the eleven-year-old who joined thirteen-year-old Mitchell Johnson in firing into a crowd at their Jonesboro, Arkansas, school in 1998; they killed a pregnant teacher and four girls. Andrew wanted to play football and basketball. But he was "too slight" for one and "too short" for the other. Shooting was what he did best, his grandfather told reporters.[31]

Kipland Kinkel's family also put a high value on athletic prowess. His father, a tennis coach, spoke of his son's lack of athletic skill with disappointment and noted that his son "wanted to be big."[32] Kip killed his parents before killing two classmates and wounding twenty-five others in Springfield, Oregon, in 1998. The two boys he killed were considered jocks in his school and had tormented him for being "small."[33]

In one school massacre after another, the shooters cited harassment by "jocks," sometimes also referred to as "preps," as a motivating factor in their crimes. They sought revenge against those athletes who had pushed them to the lowest rungs of the school's social order—not just isolating them from potential friendships but branding them as losers.

A closer look at the jock cult in schools, however, reveals that being the jock invites painful pressures too. For these boys the message is also clear: "underachieving" means they are associated with women (sissies) or homosexuals (gay), and their social acceptance plummets with these labels. The school hierarchy punishes everyone. The demonization of whatever is considered "feminine" forces these boys to sacrifice depth and intimacy in their relationships with themselves and other people; they spend their lives instead, working to prove that they are adequately aggressive and invincible. At the same time, parents, coaches, and others often push them beyond their physical capacities; masculine power becomes increasingly difficult for jocks to achieve or maintain as the stakes get higher and expectations for athletic performance more fierce.

In an article titled "By the Numbers: Bigger and Better?" sportswriter Allen Barra notes that professional athletes are bigger than in times past. The average weight for a football offensive lineman is now three hundred pounds—more than fifty pounds heavier than the average during the era of Vince Lombardi. Athletes are at the same time pressured to be quicker and more agile and to have more endurance. It is not just because they are using more steroids, Barra writes. Professional athletes now train year-round; gone are the days when baseball players used "spring training" to get into shape.[34] These new standards of athletic achievement are even reflected in children's toys. In the 1960s, the biceps of a G.I. Joe were the equivalent of twelve-inch biceps in a full-sized human. In 1999, the doll's biceps were the equivalent of twenty-seven inches, as much an anatomical impossibility as Barbie's proportions.[35]

Boys report pressure to look "bigger and stronger" than was necessary in past generations, which has led some to develop eating disorders, previously rare among boys. This type of eating disorder has become common enough to sport a new name: "bigorexia."[36] There is also evidence of increases in steroid use among high school athletes as they work tirelessly to meet virtually impossible physical expectations.[37]

Boys police one another's efforts to demonstrate the invincible masculinity expected of them. In one elite all-boys urban school, the boys gave each other "birthday punches"—an institutionalized form of bullying. "They punch hard," explained a teacher there—and "as many times as years for your birthday. Kids have gotten badly bruised." The message is that boys need to prove yet again that they "can take it," even when the behavior is just unadulterated abuse. A boy I talked to from an inner-city school was similarly hurt and sore from birthday punches he had endured the day before.

The pressure to prove strength, agility, and power as a means of being accepted in school is perhaps most damaging to youth who are physically challenged. In most schools, students who are seen as disabled in any way are also targets of abuse. Barbara, from a poor northeastern rural area, said plainly: "There is a special education program in our school, and those kids get made fun of a lot." One girl who is in a wheelchair is unable to move her head or her arms and needs to push a button on her chair to get around. "When she goes down the hall, people start laughing at her." Instead of receiving compassion and support, the students who are not seen as the "fittest," in a socially Darwinian culture that values power and success, are shunned and degraded.

The pressure to succeed physically is so overly emphasized in our schools that activities unrelated to sports are frequently denigrated. In many schools, even academics become not just secondary but a potential social deficit.

Booing Academics

Mixed messages about the relationship between intelligence and social status frustrate students, who find that high grades register on some external barometers of success but are often scorned in school, where most of their social interaction takes place. Much of the criteria for status in the school environment—appearance, popularity, trendy clothes, or a nice car—echo those of the larger society. The same is not true of intellectual achievement. Even adults, who urge students to get good grades, often send different signals about what matters most to them. For instance, Columbine High School prominently showcased athletic awards but gave no visible recognition of students' academic successes, and my students from wealthy suburbs have said this is par for the course.

At Glen Ridge High School in New Jersey, where the infamous gang rape of a developmentally disabled female student by student athletes took place in 1989, display cases across from the principal's office were stocked with athletic trophies; and footballs, plaques, cups, bats, and gloves lined the walls of the school office and library. "Nowhere visible was last year's student honor roll," wrote Bernard Lefkowitz in his book, *Our Guys,* about the town and the incident.[38]

Murray Milner describes in *Freaks, Geeks, and Cool Kids* how "a combination of male preps and athletes and the most attractive females in the school" that he studied placed "geeks and nerds" at the bottom. "Sometimes a distinction was made between 'nerds' who were openly preoccupied with academic success and an even lower strata referred to variously as 'dorks,' 'trash,' or 'geeks' who were considered hopelessly inept when it came to social events, dress, and style."[39] At best, being smart, earning good grades, and showing interest in schoolwork may place students outside the popular crowd, while at worst it can make them downright outcasts. A 2006 study of gifted children found that 67 percent of them reported being bullied by the time they reached the eighth grade and that many had specifically been teased about their school performance.[40]

Rick, the student editor of his high school newspaper in a low-income northeastern rural area, said the kid that got picked on most in his school, Oliver, "is always reading. He loves books and you see him sitting in a corner reading, and he gets made fun of for that. They call him 'fag,' and 'Mama's boy.' 'What book are you reading? How far are you into it? Shouldn't you be studying and not reading?'" The comments are meant to convey disdain rather than interest, explains Rick. He thinks the problem is that Oliver makes them uncomfortable. "Oliver knows what he wants to do. He wants to go to college to be a chemist. He has a stable life compared to other people."

Shantique, the African American girl who also attended southern low-income rural schools, said, "I was the odd one out from very early. I was fat. I liked to read. I was nerdy." Because of relentless bullying, Shantique "spent a lot of time alone. I would just read. I was always picked last for stuff. No one wanted me on their team. I stopped trying and would just read, which just added to my nerdiness."

Children will go to great lengths—and even undermine their own achievements—to conform to the shallow values of the school pecking order and to prevent persecution by their peers. D. A. Kinney's 1993 study "From Nerds to Normals" found that smart students in many high schools would clown around or otherwise underachieve so as not to be labeled a nerd.[41] Another study found that boys with high scholastic aptitude, even those with other socially redeeming traits, often become reluctant to work up to their full academic potential for fear of exhibiting low-value behavior.[42]

Among boys, in particular, academic performance does not tend to count among the hypermasculine values that win status in the high school environment. This—more than any conservative notion of a "war against boys" promoted by feminism, or the popular explanation of differences in "learning styles"—may account for the fact that boys are perceived as flagging in academic environments, writes Michael Kimmel in *Guyland: The Perilous World Where Boys Become Men*.[43] Michael Thompson, coauthor of the 1999 book *Raising Cain: Protecting the Emotional Life of Boys*, says, "Boys hear that the way to shine is athletically. And boys get a lot of mixed messages about what it means to be masculine and what it means to be a student. Does being a good student make you a real man? I don't think so. . . . It is not cool."[44] Kimmel writes that boys are gay-bashed or nerd-bashed for achieving academically. Names associated with performing well in school—such as "Geek" and "Bookworm"—don't tend to confer masculinity status, and this contributes to boys' avoiding academic success in favor of demonstrating their burgeoning manhood.[45]

Many of the boys who perpetrated school shootings found that excelling at academics, which should have been a source of respect, became a social problem instead. Fifteen-year-old Thomas Solomon, who shot and wounded six classmates at his Conyers, Georgia, high school in 1999, a month after the Columbine massacre, was described by fellow students as a nerd and an outcast; students teased him because he didn't socialize in homeroom but instead sat by himself and did his homework.[46]

Luke Woodham was studying Latin and Nietzsche on his own. Eric Harris and Dylan Klebold were considered excellent students. Eric was said to be one of the smartest students in the class, intelligent and articulate. He was also recognized by major video-game manufacturers for the computer programs he wrote for Doom and Quake. Other members of their outcast group at Columbine also said they were harassed initially because they were smart.[47]

Dylan's friend Devon Adams remembers the day Dylan went up on stage at school to be recognized as a state champion for the national forensic debate qualifiers. He was booed by the football players. Devon was stunned. "It's really sad that academics are so low on our ranking, because it's something else to be proud of," she said.[48]

Eric and Dylan used guns to prove their worth in a school that seemed to value strength and power above other qualities. Yet even as the stories of the relentless bullying inflicted on them emerged, people across the country and the world continued to question why these teenagers became assassins.

Teaching Evil

Todd Calder, in his article "The Apparent Banality of Evil: The Relationship between Evil Acts and Evil Character," wrote that evil behavior takes place when someone acts in order to harm another person for bad reasons. When we want to harm someone for fun or because it makes us feel powerful, that's evil. According to Calder, "To have an evil character is to feel pleasure in the face of other people's pain and to feel pain in the face of other people's pleasure."[49]

Such descriptions call to mind Eric and Dylan laughing as they were shooting—smiling and giggling as they caused their peers—and countless others—unspeakable pain and loss. It also aptly describes scenes of everyday bullying, though of a different magnitude, where some students gain status and pleasure through the humiliation and suffering of others. Students standing around a fight or an episode of bullying are often seen laughing or egging on the aggressors. So, by Calder's definition, these children and adolescents are committing evil acts and exhibiting "evil character."

Evil behavior is rewarded when bullies gain status for their abilities to hurt other people. By not intervening, bystanders gain social credit too, dissociating themselves from the victims and identifying instead with the victorious aggressors. Further, schools that condone, encourage, or refuse to intervene in the status wars that confer power to some and mark others as abused pariahs sustain an environment that might well itself be considered evil.

Those who attribute evil acts to the inherent evil in human nature deflect attention from systemic social problems. They blame each incident of violence—in a country with the highest per capita rates of assault and homicide in the industrialized world—on the innate nature of the person who committed it. This ignores the fact that even if aggressive impulses are innate, how aggression is manifested and directed is still within the province of socialization.

In *Civilization and Its Discontents,* Sigmund Freud famously wrote that it is through society that our aggressive instincts are tempered or civilized: "Civilization, therefore, obtains mastery over the individual's dangerous desire for aggression by weakening and disarming it and by setting up an agency within him to watch over it, like a garrison in a conquered city."[50] Further, as evolutionary psychologists have found, tendencies toward destructive behaviors are activated in particularly negative environments and tend to lie dormant when people with such proclivities are nurtured and supported instead.[51]

Calder suggests that a social environment can create conditions where otherwise "normal" people may commit acts perceived as evil.[52] In many ways, then, in the way we teach boys to become men, and girls to become women, we are failing in the "civilizing" task to which Freud refers. Instead of helping young people to be responsible and compassionate individuals, we often encourage them to be violent and abusive.

When people act with cruelty on a regular basis, it is necessary to look at the social features of their environment.[53] In his famous experiment, Stanley Milgram instructed a research participant to be the teacher and in that capacity to deliver what appeared to be increasingly painful shocks to another participant, the learner; each time the learner got an answer wrong. Milgram reported that approximately 65 percent of his teachers obeyed the experimenter, delivering potentially fatal (450) volts of shock even when the learner screamed in agony. Milgram argued that people are inclined to follow authorities even when there are negative consequences and even when they feel that the behavior they are instructed to commit is wrong.[54]

Many people, however, equate bad behavior with an evil nature rather than seeing it as a product of negative social conditioning that encourages average people to act in ways that are hurtful, callous, or even cruel. Partly as a symptom of our overemphasis on individualism, we tend to attribute evil behavior to individual disposition rather than to social environment. Lee Ross and Richard Nisbett call this the perspective of "lay dispositionism," suggesting that people have a tendency to underappreciate the power of situational factors.[55]

In the book and film *The Smartest Guys in the Room: The Amazing Rise and Scandalous Fall of Enron*, Bethany McLean and Peter Elkind use the Milgram experiment as a backdrop to explain how Enron became an environment where making money and being powerful trumped other values. Much as bystanders express pleasure in schools as they egg on the likely victor in a fight, Enron traders rejoiced when a forest fire threatened a major electrical line in California, a disaster that would increase their financial gains: "Burn, baby, burn," they were heard laughing on tape. Alex Gibney, the film's producer, explained: "These weren't bad apples. But within a corporate culture that rewarded this behavior, they were suddenly allowed to run amok." This was a culture that mixed raw capitalism with fierce machismo. Gibney continued: "If you go into a lot of trading floors, they all have this kind of macho culture. It's part of the trading culture." Tapes were found of brokers laughing about the millions of retirees who had lost their pensions, California residents who had lost their electricity and suffered through numerous blackouts, and "grandmothers" who were lost in the dark and left penniless: "All that money you stole from those poor grandmothers in California . . . Now she wants her fucking money back for all the money you charged her up her ass."[56] (Stockbroker culture, like locker room talk around many school sports, uses language steeped in references to male sexual dominance.)

Kenneth Lay, Jeff Skillings, and the other high-level people who worked for Enron were by all accounts "normal" individuals. This was a culture, though, where being selfish and self-absorbed was normal, even (or especially) if it would lead to other people's demise. As the 1980s Wall Street criminal Ivan Boesky famously said, in a 1985 commencement speech at the University of California's School of Business Administration: "Greed is all right, by the way . . . I think greed is healthy." Evil behavior was normalized and normal people became evil. Of course, not all people in high schools (or businesses) are evil. Many, however, are unaware of the painful circumstances that surround them, whether willfully or less consciously.

Those in cliques perceived as more popular are sometimes cushioned by their social status and then find that they have the luxury of being unaware of how other students are treated. Some of my students have insisted that there are students who "just like to be alone," while others in the class have protested that many such students have been so brutally excluded they have given up hope of making social connections at school. In 1907 G. W. F. Hegel famously articulated the master-slave relationship in his book *Phenomenology of Spirit*, explaining that those in power are more likely to refuse or be unable to recognize those that are oppressed because the latter have little impact on their lives, whereas those who are "enslaved" find that they need to be aware of every move of those in power lest they become the next victims. Those who are teased and harassed at school often stay out of the cafeteria, try not to take the bus, or otherwise avoid the people and places where bullying might take place; those who are more likely to be bullies or bystanders have no reason to recognize that this elaborate avoidance is taking place.

Hannah Arendt famously observed that perpetrators of horrific deeds are often ordinary individuals without any history of physical violence or specific psychological malaise or any guiding ideology. Instead, their evil acts rise from a culture that produces morally unreflective individuals and then places them in situations where evil behavior is encouraged and expected.[57]

In schools, bullying behavior often becomes normal, and many students get used to it. On a New York City private school tour, one parent asked: "Does this school pressure the students? I don't want my daughter to get anorexia when she's eleven years old." The earnest parent tour guide explained: "Well, this is a New York City private school and we are part of a particular social stratum, so you have to expect certain behaviors. We try here to mitigate them as much as possible." The parent guides talked about cliques and hazing as common behavior and even positive lessons for young people to learn regarding their roles in a given hierarchy. The parents communicated that while some efforts were made to temper the worst extremes, hurtful behaviors were essentially normal and tolerated there.

In fact, many schools have become resigned to the hazing, bullying, or "rough play" that takes place among students. Books like Peggy Tyre's 2008 *The Trouble with Boys* and Christina Hoff Sommers's 2000 *The War against Boys* actually suggest that boys in particular should be encouraged to be combative and that "cooperation games" undermine boys' learning.[58] Sommers rails against empathy exercises recommended in a well-known antibullying curriculum, "Quit It!"; Tyre writes plainly: "Why are we so paranoid about boys and aggression?"[59] Such statements ignore or underestimate what Freud, again, identified as the fundamental task of civilization. It is the role of society in general, and schools in particular, to temper aggressive proclivities and help people live cooperatively in a peaceful society. Freud wrote: "The fateful question for the human species seems to me to be whether and to what extent their cultural development will succeed in mastering the disturbance of their communal life by the human instinct of aggression and self-destruction."[60]

Schools that believe they have to cater to boys' aggressive needs and decrease their cooperative expectations, à la Tyre and Sommers, do so at the expense of boys' (and girls') humanity. Freud wrote: "Human life in common is only made possible when a majority comes together which is stronger than any separate individual and which remains united against all separate individuals. The power of this community is then set up as 'right' in opposition to the power of the individual, which is condemned as brute force. This replacement of the power of the individual by the power of the community constitutes the decisive step of civilization."[61]

Similarly, when administrators, teachers, families, students, or other community members resign themselves to the fact that bullying will always exist and that it is unreasonable to expect otherwise, they actively fail in the civilizing task Freud cautioned society to accept in his classic works. Whether the tendency toward violence is innate or socialized, schools and families can be instrumental in eradicating rough or other forms of bullying environments by teaching compassion and by working hard to create communities in which members are responsible for creating, maintaining, and developing relationships of respect and empathy with one another.

Instead, teachers and families sometimes ignore, encourage, or even play a role in shaping aggressive and uncompassionate behavior because it has become such a social convention; rather than question and challenge it, adults further condone it, believing they are somehow teaching appropriate limits to what they consider otherwise inevitable behavior. The acceptance of such behavior, however, serves to undermine the humanizing influence that schools, parents, guardians, and other adults were otherwise meant to exert and inadvertently promotes a bully culture.

Schools that don't take responsibility for creating compassionate communities, in individual classes as well as the larger school environment, render it more likely that it will be "ordinary," and "normal," for many young people to hurt and to be hurt on a daily basis—or increasingly, for school shooters to respond in such a heinous fashion. Misguided school faculty and families play one role, and unsupervised peers, who mimic adult social structures, often recreate destructive dynamics in authoritative social cliques.

Pecking Orders

Students in every stratum of society, from staid upper-class communities to inner-city gangs, describe school cultures that not only reward cruelty but demand it. Students quickly learn that they must ostracize certain classmates—stop talking to them, harass, or even assault them—or they will face the same abuse themselves. Of course, it is not the experience of all students, but it is a reality with which students contend across all demographics.

In *Queen Bees and Wannabes*, Rosalind Wiseman writes about the chain of command the average girl feels compelled to follow if she wants to be a member of her school's social community rather than one of its pariahs. "On a daily basis, she'll learn what kind of girl she has to be to be accepted by her group, and this will influence everything from her choice of boyfriends to the classes she takes, her after-school activities, her clothes, her hairstyle, the people she talks to, the people she doesn't talk to, her beliefs and values, and her overall sense of self." With these and other rules regarding how girls should act and dress to prevent their social annihilation, as well as by some threats of physical as well as mental abuse, girls often feel pressured to follow the orders of the more powerful students; "Group cohesion is based on unquestioned loyalty to the leaders and an us-versus-the world mentality," writes Wiseman.[62]

Thirteen-year-old Vanessa spoke to me about her seventh-grade school experiences in the honors program of an urban northeastern school in 2008. Lauren was a popular girl in the school who befriended Vanessa—but at a high cost. "When we were friends, she made me think of other things, made me act differently to my other friends. I started acting like her because I thought it was cool, but it made me feel terrible." Vanessa found herself being much less nice to people—snapping at them and treating them less respectfully. Lauren used a familiar tool to make Vanessa admire her: Lauren's family had money. "She would drone on about places she went to—Alaska, Hawaii, Venice—and things she was getting; it made me feel bad—like I wasn't cool, since I didn't go anywhere, I just felt terrible—like she was much better than I was." Lauren used her financial advantages as capital she could flaunt to win the admiration and subservience of other less wealthy girls. When that failed, Lauren wasn't above using violence to maintain Vanessa's obedience: under the guise of giving an innocent "nuggie," "she dug her hand into my scalp," said Vanessa. "I thought I was going to bleed."

Among boys, varsity players often have the most power to declare who should be "saved" from daily harassment and who should become the school's targets of abuse. The "weaker," less athletic, more academic, "nerdy" boys and girls are often excluded and assaulted, while the varsity players and their followers become the executioners.

Boys are frequently presented with the stark choice of whether to be the tormenters or the tormented. Tommy, a boy from a wealthy suburban community who had been so badly bullied that he had to change schools, and Lenny, a bullying victim from an inner-city school, both told me the same thing, and I heard it repeatedly: the only way to keep from being targets for bullies would be to become bullies themselves.

Students forced to fend for themselves in destructive school environments often find that their unsatisfied needs lead them to seek refuge in cliques, where they tend to abandon their own values and notions of appropriate behavior. By following the orders of their seemingly more popular peers, students see some hope of being included and appreciated and becoming part of a group where they might be accepted. They also recognize that going against the wishes of the students perceived as popular may cause them to be permanently excluded from the social connections they deeply crave. These powerful yearnings and fears of reprisal cause many students to objectify classmates who have been targeted for exclusion and harassment; following the wishes of perceived student leaders becomes all-important, and isolating others to win some popularity and recognition becomes seen as a social necessity rather than as cruelty. The students referred to as popular often feel compelled to objectify other students to maintain their power and recognition and to sustain an "us versus them" mentality in a competitive school environment that does little to promote community and positive relationships in any other way.

Thirteen-year-old Kate, from an upper-class northeastern suburb, went from being popular to becoming a target to being marginally accepted again. The powerful girls in her school gave orders and Kate complied. "If they ask me to sit at their table, I don't want to say no because I don't want them to be mad at me," she explained. She said she was "pressured into doing stuff" to stay in the good graces of the popular girls. The group that everyone wanted to be part of was called "The Five"—a group of white, wealthy girls, perceived as attractive, who created a powerful clique. Anyone they felt was different or too much competition, too unattractive or too pretty, was objectified and in danger of being socially destroyed.

This capacity to objectify fellow human beings and see them as less than human is potentially in all of us. A version of this everyday evil is clearly present in our schools, where social expectations too often teach children to dehumanize one another. Rather than developing empathy, they learn to see their peers as "other." Without constructive alternatives, students view one another as dispensable objects, if such behavior might advance their own social needs for connection and recognition.

Natasha, who suffered years of bullying in her northeastern middle-class suburban schools, recalled that a boy named Eric had suddenly attacked her as she was daydreaming in school one day. "Why are you staring at me?" he demanded. "I'm not staring at you," Natasha, tried to explain. Eric cut her off curtly: "Stop looking at me. Stop talking to me. I didn't give you permission to talk to me." Then, raising his voice, he went on: "I didn't give you permission to breathe. You're not cool enough to look at me. You are taking up my airspace." The boy threw paper and pens at Natasha and didn't stop until she walked out of the classroom.

The pernicious social hierarchies and everyday violence that exist among boys and among girls (and between boys and girls) are too often accepted as a normal aspect of adolescent school life. This climate could not exist without the sanction or even encouragement of this behavior by peers, families, and faculty in the community, or without the larger social acceptance of these relationships. "Bystanders" in schools, then, include all the people who commit crimes of omission by allowing this abuse to take place.

Schools where students are ostracized can become training grounds for perpetrating prejudice. "Cliques are self-reinforcing," writes Wiseman in *Queen Bees and Wannabes*. "As soon as you define your role and group, you perceive others as outsiders, it's harder to put yourself in their shoes, and therefore it's easier to be cruel to them or watch and do nothing. It doesn't matter if we're talking about social hierarchies, racism, sexism, homophobia, or any 'ism,' this is the way people assert their power, which really translates into discrimination and bigotry."[63] Cliques are often perceived as harmless adolescent social networks, but can also thinly mask the same adult bigotries that sometimes manifest in vicious hate crimes.

Many of the school shooting perpetrators were persecuted partly because they were academically as opposed to athletically successful. Yet while many of the perpetrators were smart and excelling in honors programs, they were not able to imagine a different social structure where their qualities and strengths might be more appreciated. Their failure in imagination is, at least partly, explained by the fact that so many adults also accepted the social structures that found them wanting.

In their efforts to demonstrate masculinity through their shootings, the perpetrators effectively accepted the values that deemed them inferior in the first place. Their resistance to the social order in their schools was actually an act of acquiescence to the social hierarchies they despised (and that despised them). They didn't seek to change the values in their schools; instead, they meant to win at the same game—to become the biggest bullies, and therefore the ones with the highest status.

Destructive Forms of Resistance

Students perceived as popular make up a small minority of the school population. One estimate finds that among middle-school boys about 15 percent are popular, 45 percent are widely accepted, 20 percent occupy an ambiguous status, and 20 percent are outcasts.[64]

Most students fall in the middle of the social hierarchy. In seeking ways to avoid pariah status, though, many still uphold the status culture. A study of bullying on an elementary school playground showed that children other than the primary bully were involved in bullying 85 percent of the time. "Their involvement ranged from joining in the bullying, to observing passively, to actively intervening to stop the bullying. When students are asked what they usually do if they witness bullying, many (50% or more) admit that they do not try to intervene."[65]

This shared reticence serves to silence resistance and perpetuate obedience. Again, in schools where little is done to address these issues, status flows to those who comply with the dominant values of the social order and is withheld from those who oppose or resist. Thus prevailing norms in many schools and communities reinforce the rule of the few over the majority of students.

Some students develop alternative groups as a form of resistance and refer to themselves (or are referred to by others) as Goths, burnouts, greasers, or the like. Yet these groups often mimic the groups from which they attempt to differentiate themselves. They may define themselves as a mirror of those who exclude them, taking their outcast position as an unconventional kind of status symbol. Some are drawn to ideologies that affirm evil or racism (such as Satanism and neo-Nazism), and thus embrace an even more destructive, violent, and hierarchical view. Yet they still live according to and within the prevailing power structure, rather than finding new ways of being.

For every action there is an equal and opposite reaction. Isaac Newton recognized this law of physics more than three hundred years ago, and it often applies equally well to human interactions. There are always, though, multiple ways to react. In their most extreme expressions, responses to vicious bullying took the form of school shootings and suicide. The perpetrators who were harassed and losers in the social status wars finally bullied back, but with overwhelming lethal force. By shooting their enemies and trying to blow up their schools, the boys who killed tried to destroy the people and the physical structures they blamed for maintaining their oppression—the preps and jocks who tormented them, the girls who rejected them, the adults who condoned or supported the brutal status system, even the school buildings that had served as the settings for their suffering. Yet the way they reacted affirmed, rather than challenged, the very system they claimed to despise.

The French sociologist Michel Foucault, a seminal thinker, points out that fighting power directly reproduces similar power in a different form. Foucault argues in *Discipline and Punish* that power is not the "privilege" of a dominant class exercised on a passive, dominated class but rather something that is exercised through and by everyone involved. Power is not binary. Thus it is not just the top-down structure that the boys perceived and protested. It cannot be resisted or undermined by reversing the positions of the oppressor and the oppressed—by the bullied becoming bullies. Foucault wrote that power operates through an infinitely complex network of micro-power relations, expressed through the daily social relationships among individuals and groups. Every day, people observe their own and others' behaviors and assess whether they are measuring up. They carry out a surveillance on one another, policing "their everyday behavior, their identity, their activity, their apparently unimportant gestures."[66] Foucault provides an accurate description of how average students and adults in schools become the gender police operating in today's schools.

When the school shooters pushed back with brutal violence, they missed the connection between their own ordeals and how society values and imposes gender and social status. In his discussions of how power works, Foucault criticizes the "coercive, centralized Normality . . . imposed on education."[67] The tentacles of this coercion are varied. In today's schools, many students enforce it via codes of dress and behavior. Boys fight to maintain an image of themselves as hypermasculine, an illusion in constant need of defense and protection, since they are always in danger of being exposed as fallible humans, like anyone else. Low-status boys often perpetuate the same standards by accepting hypermasculine values, internalizing hatred of their own "feminine" attributes and using violence and domination to prove that they too can conform to social expectations. Girls have their own parallel set of markers by which they assess their own and others' feminine "normality," as well as conformity to the more recent expectations placed on girls to display qualities and behaviors associated with masculinity.

Both the oppressors and the oppressed are victims of social values that are not effectively questioned or challenged. The sociologist A. N. Oppenheim wrote that many young people are unable to go against the expectations of their given clique; this takes a bravery that that is not particularly encouraged or supported in many schools.[68]

Individual students are not necessarily the ones who create the attitudes that confer prestige on some and humiliation on others within a given school social hierarchy. In developing these values, they receive cues both within the school and outside it—in the larger economic system, in the consumer culture, and from adult role models who accrue status based on similarly troubling criteria. By exposing the oppressive power structures endemic to most American schools, families, faculty, and other adults can begin to transform the conditions that students otherwise battle by themselves.

2

Masculinity and
White Supremacy

On December 1, 1997, in West Paducah, Kentucky, a skinny, short, bespectacled, fourteen-year-old Heath High School freshman named Michael Carneal rode to school with his seventeen-year-old sister, Kelly. Unbeknownst to her, he placed in the trunk of her Mazda two shotguns, two rifles, and a .22 caliber semiautomatic pistol.

When Kelly dropped him off, a large group of students was gathered in the lobby of West Paducah High School to say their prayers and sing hymns, as they did every morning before the bell rang. While they prayed, Michael showed a group of boys a gun. He hoped they would be impressed and think he was tough. The gun didn't seem to have any impact, though—so Michael decided he would have to do more. Calmly, he waited for the students to say "Amen." He then pulled out the pistol and started shooting. He killed Nicole Hadley, a tall, fourteen-year-old girl who played in the school band with him, as well as fifteen-year-old Kayce Steger and seventeen-year-old Jessica James. Five other students were injured—including one girl who was paralyzed from the chest down—before Michael surrendered his weapon.[1]

In eighth grade, Michael had written a gruesome story where the main character, Mike, killed the students called "preps" as revenge for the abuse his character endured; his younger brother in the story (who did not exist in real life) helped Mike shoot them down.

In middle school, someone had once pulled Michael's pants down, Michael told psychiatrists after the shooting. He also told them that he had been enraged when students called him "queer" and "faggot," and that he had cried when the gossip column, "Rumor Has It," in the student-run newspaper implied he was involved sexually with another boy. The public humiliation had become unbearable for Michael; he was taunted even more mercilessly after the column was published and called all kinds of derogatory names associated with homosexuality. Classmates hadn't listened when he insisted that he was not gay. The incident had escaped the eye of any authorities in the school, and the ridicule had persisted in full view of most school members. Michael had been a boy unwilling to fight back when he was harassed. "I get mad, but I won't do anything," he once said. "When I'm mad, I do nothing but think about things people have done to me, and it makes me real mad."[2] Michael couldn't sustain his passivity in this particular school environment, where he found no one who would help him stop the bullying he endured every day.

At the same time, he had no success with girls. The mother of Nicole Hadley believed that Michael was in love with her daughter. For a few weeks before the shooting, he called her almost every night, ostensibly to discuss chemistry. She didn't dislike him necessarily, but she didn't return his affection. Nicole was Michael's first target.[3]

Michael's classmates couldn't remember him being particularly bullied. The teasing was such a normal part of their day that it didn't register as harassment. But when principal Bill Bond reviewed Michael's school essays, he found a theme of feeling "small and powerless, that the world had teased him and he was going to show the world how powerful he was."[4]

Michael said after the shooting that he had only intended to do a show-and-tell when he brought the guns to school. He had stolen the five guns and seven hundred rounds of ammunition from a neighbor's garage in the week of Thanksgiving prior to the shooting. When he sneaked the guns into his house through a bedroom window, he told the psychiatrists, he felt "proud, strong, good and more respected. I accomplished something. I'm not the kind of kid who accomplishes anything. This is the only adventure I've ever had."[5]

A few days before the shooting, he took the "best guns" to a friend's house, where they shot targets. On Sunday, after church and homework, he wrapped the guns in a blanket to take to school the next day. He was hoping the guns would help him gain the recognition and connection he craved. He thought "everyone would be calling me and they would come over to my house or I would go to their houses. I would be popular. I didn't think I would get into trouble."[6]

But when he arrived at school and told his friends what was in the blanket, they were unimpressed. In western Kentucky, firearms are a common part of life, nothing to brag about. Frustrated by the lack of attention, Michael stuck earplugs into his ears and rammed the ammo clip into the pistol. Still, nobody paid him any mind. So he started shooting. "I had guns," Michael explained. "I brought them to school. I showed them to them, and they were still ignoring me." Michael told the prosecution psychiatrists that when he took out the guns he thought "his friends would say 'Wow!' or 'Cool!'" Indeed his friend Cory Giles saw the guns and said "You've got the biggest balls here."[7]

Be a Man, but Don't Be a Hu-man

Many of the school shootings that took place between 1979 and 2009 attracted high-profile news coverage. The shooters and some of the victims made many statements that should have shed light on the perpetrators' motivations, just as they did in Michael Carneal's case. Yet few reports considered the idea that gender norms in our society—and especially its masculinity prescriptions—encourage a subtle and pervasive pattern of violence against boys who are for any reason associated with femininity. Boys perceived as being too gentle or kind are often brutally attacked in an effort to demonstrate the requisites of manhood in school. Michael explained that he was first bullied in school because he was considered "too nice" to the girls in his class.[8]

As discussed further in the methodology section, an analysis of hundreds of reports on these cases—television, radio, newspapers, online news sources, scholarly journals, and books—reveals significant patterns. Boys who committed school shootings were trying to conform to accepted ideas about what makes "real" boys and "real" men.

As a result of the women's movement, girls have more access to what have traditionally been considered both masculine and feminine aspects of their personalities. Boys, on the other hand, are allowed only a small part of their human spectrum. Boys and men in our society have been taught to view violence as a requisite of masculinity. They are encouraged to be aggressive, passive-aggressive, or otherwise hurtful to others as a means of protecting their image as men. This training begins early, when boys are pressured to behave in a host of essentially superhuman or nonhuman ways. They are discouraged from showing weakness, sadness, or any form of dependence.[9] Men, as well as women, suffer as a result of these pressures. Many men (and women) feel ashamed of their own vulnerable feelings, including being sad, lonely, or uncertain. Rather than accept themselves and allow others to see their fallibilities, many men go to great lengths to hide these human qualities and portray instead a hard, violent, or otherwise disengaged exterior. They end up having difficulty developing relationships with others—connections that they nonetheless crave.

William Pollack, in *Real Boys: Rescuing Our Sons from the Myths of Boyhood,* writes that society expects boys to wear a "mask of masculinity." Instead of the range of emotions (marginally) available to girls, boys are permitted to feel only anger and are encouraged to control their other feelings behind a calm and cool front. The lack of intimate relationships and friendships, combined with societal pressure to suppress emotion, can result in an uncontrollable and even lethal rage.[10] On a daily basis, it contributes to a cycle of abuse that damages boys and girls, perpetrators and victims.

In *Sadomasochism in Everyday Life: The Dynamics of Power and Powerlessness,* sociologist Lynn Chancer writes about how destructive these prescriptions are for men as well as women. She quotes Simone de Beauvoir, who writes in *The Second Sex* that little boys are gradually denied the "'kisses and caresses they have been used to. . . . [A boy] is told that "a man doesn't ask to be kissed. . . . A man doesn't cry." He is urged to be a "little man" and to win "adult approval by becoming independent of adults."[11] As Chancer writes, a boy must renounce his dependency needs "*in order to gain approval* within the patriarchal world dominated by men, so as to feel he is not deviant or feminized (a form of intimidation containing implications both sexist and heterosexist)."[12]

While "the process of achieving socialized masculinity cannot erase the reality of his quite human vulnerabilities and insecurities," Chancer writes that the boy learns never to admit his vulnerability: "He must deny it at all costs, to himself, to others, to women who little by little come to represent this displaced and alienated part of himself. . . . He will have to project confidence, to premise his association with others on a macho indifference and bravado, to appear invulnerable."[13] The gender system convinces him that privileges related to masculinity—power, domination, violence—are "so intrinsic to masculine identity that he fears he will cease to exist without them."[14] According to Michael Thompson, coauthor of *Raising Cain,* "Boys measure everything they do or say by a single yardstick: does this make me look weak? And if it does, he isn't going to do it."[15]

James W. Messerschmidt writes in his essay "Schooling, Masculinities, and Youth Crime by White Boys" that school is the primary place where gender is learned and reinforced.[16] Many schools, it seems, have become training grounds for young men (and women) to become sexist, racist, and otherwise violent. Thus many young boys try to prove their manhood in these hurtful ways, and then strike back violently when their masculinity is challenged. It is worth remembering that some of the school shooters killed themselves, as well as others, rather than endure continued threats to their masculine identities—which according to Chancer, may have felt like attacks on their very existence. Boys, as well as girls, crave intimacy, compassion, and care, and as most boys grow up they are told these human needs must be denied. In fact boys can be teased and ridiculed if they exhibit vulnerable qualities. Being human is in fact not being a man, they are told in one way or another—and many try as hard as they can to live up to these impossible and largely unfulfilling imperatives.

Theories of Masculinity

It is hard to understand either the school shootings or the everyday bullying and hazing that takes place in our schools without analyzing how "normalized masculinity" disguises and conceals certain types of violence. In her groundbreaking work *Masculinities*, R. W. Connell identified multiple forms of masculinity that, in one way or another, boys get pushed into performing.[17]

"Hegemonic masculinity" refers to the form of masculinity most legitimate in a given society; today, military heroes, successful businessmen, and powerful politicians tend to represent this type. Men who have this kind of power are likely to embody stereotypical masculine traits, such as being unemotional, tough, authoritative, and/or controlling. Boys who exhibit these qualities also fit into this category. They are perceived to be at the top of the masculinities hierarchy, and they often rule their school hierarchies. They tend to reinforce their own fragile positions by eschewing anything that might be seen as feminine or "gay."

"Complicit masculinity" is intimately connected to hegemonic masculinity in that it includes most men who do not necessarily meet hegemonic expectations of manhood but who benefit from the subordination of women and gay men and related sexist and heterosexist value systems. Even though they are not on the highest rung of the social masculinity ladder, they receive a "patriarchal dividend," according to Connell, in that they can claim status and power just by virtue of being men.[18]

"Subordinated masculinity" applies to men and boys who are openly gay or perceived as gay and thus fall to the bottom of the hierarchy of normalized masculinity. Connell writes that heterosexual boys who are perceived as feminine can be subjugated in ways similar to the way women and gays are persecuted. "The process is marked by a rich vocabulary of abuse," writes Connell. "Here too, the symbolic blurring with femininity is obvious."[19]

In *Slow Motion: Changing Masculinities, Changing Men*, Lynne Segal writes that homophobia keeps all men in line, not only because it oppresses gays, but also because it creates contempt for men who express emotional qualities associated with femininity. Boys learn to despise the "feminine enemy within themselves" and to destroy any person who draws attention to these rejected aspects of their personality. At the same time, they are being taught to despise women.[20]

"Oppositional masculinity" is another form of masculinity that grows out of the subordinated experiences of boys who are continually put down by their more traditionally masculine peers; they may seek other ways to demonstrate their masculinity. In *Nine Lives*, James Messerschmidt defines oppositional masculinity as the manifestation of alternative masculinities when access to hegemonic behavior is somehow restricted.[21] Messerschmidt suggests that in schools, for instance, hegemonic masculinities are demonstrated by the "jocks and preps" and subordinated masculinities by those referred to as "gay," "wimp," or "nerd." In turn, "freaks," and "tough guys" tend to rebel against authorities in school, demonstrating oppositional masculinity. While they may not exhibit hegemonic masculinity in the traditional sense, they act tough and intimidating as a way to gain masculinity credit in another form. Messerschmidt notes that in seeking to "correct the subordinating social situation" boys may turn to what are usually considered antisocial behaviors, including crime.[22]

For Connell, such masculinity might be covered by what she terms "marginalized masculinity," which refers to men within stigmatized groups. Lack of power as a result of racism, classism, or other forms of discrimination may cause some men to seek alternative means to claim their patriarchal dividend.

Men and boys who are denied full male privileges and status because of their race or their social class tend to still feel pressured to demonstrate extreme male behavior to overcompensate for their diminished social position. Insults imbued with racism, classism, and other prejudice are often used to humiliate and degrade targets. Harassment related to different forms of bigotry may then also trigger a hypermasculinity retaliatory response—often violence—to prove manhood and reinstate a sense of power and strength in the face of these cutting attacks.

A member of the Los Angeles gang the Crips, Sanyika Shakur, a.k.a. Monster Kody Scott, started shooting at rival gang members when he was eleven years old and earned the name Monster for committing acts of brutality that repulsed even other Crips. He explained in his book *Monster* how feeling powerless in his urban community drove him to murderous rage. Following the pummeling of Rodney King by police officers, Shakur wrote: "What it boils down to is an overwhelming sense of inadequacy: the invisible man syndrome. . . . This incident also brought the realization of my powerlessness crashing down upon me, and with it, my rage and appetite for destruction rose."[23] His words illustrate how much gang violence has in common with other forms of reactive male violence. When boys are told they must be powerful and dominating and then instead find themselves marginalized—harassed, assaulted, and tormented—many will turn to violence to demonstrate the more hegemonic masculinity expected from them.

Marginalized Masculinity and the White Male Dividend

Marginalized masculinity may indeed be the best way to explain why the perpetrators committed school shootings. Most of them were white and middle to upper middle class, yet they did not receive their patriarchal dividend as Connell describes it—power, prestige, and material advantages conferred on men simply by virtue of their being men. They heard the message—that they should be strong and powerful, like the "jocks" and "preps" perceived as manifesting the epitome of hegemonic masculinity—but the expected means of proving manhood were not accessible to them. For the most part, they weren't big and muscular, particularly good at sports, or successful with girls. The cultural capital that many of them did possess—unusual intelligence, creativity, or computer savvy—was not particularly valued in their school communities. In fact, access to basic respect and recognition was consistently denied to them, since according to typical gender expectations these qualities rank low. The gender police in most schools tend to find boys lacking when they exhibit less typically hegemonic masculinity traits.

In addition to picking up guns to respond to the masculinity challenges they experienced in school, many of the school shooters gravitated toward powerful ideas and icons that might offer them a way to make up for what they were told were their masculine shortcomings. White supremacist ideologies became a means of demonstrating oppositional masculinity. These were a quick fix—a fast track to the feelings of power and dominance that they felt compelled to achieve by whatever means necessary.

Thus some of the shooters identified with fascist dictators and Nazi icons as a way to identify themselves as dominant rather than denigrated. Luke Woodham and his friends in Pearl, Mississippi, were reading Hitler's treatise *Mein Kampf*; they called their group the Third Reich before changing it to the Satanist Kroth.

At Jokela High School in Finland, an eighteen-year-old student shot eight people before killing himself. After the incident, YouTube removed eighty-nine videos linked to his account, many of them featuring Nazi imagery and Nazi war criminal footage.

Eric Harris and Dylan Klebold were said to be obsessed with Nazi history, shouting "Heil Hitler" periodically and wearing swastikas; they planned their massacre at Columbine High School for April 20, Hitler's birthday.

Other shooters showed some interest in Nazi history, or in current neo-Nazi and white supremacist groups, philosophy, and music. Several associated themselves with other icons that represented power and domination, like Nietzsche and Satan.[24]

There is a grim logic to the fact that these boys were attracted to Nazi attitudes and symbolism, which are associated with dominating, subjugating, and dehumanizing others. As boys deemed "not man enough," they were routinely objectified and dehumanized. In their schools, these boys suffered losses to their essential status as human beings. It was within this context that some of the school shooting perpetrators turned to white supremacy, a time-tested means of achieving status in America's racially, socially, and economically unequal society.

Indeed, of the perpetrators who were interested in white supremacy, few translated their ideas into action with any consistency when they carried out their massacres. The Columbine shooters murdered people regardless of their race. They targeted a black student using racist slurs, but they also taunted students for being fat and for having glasses—anything that might make them feel superior. Most of the other shooters also seemed not to discriminate by race when they chose targets in their mostly white schools. They seemed, though, to be attracted to ideologies that offered them a direct route to power, countering their degrading situations.

When the boys donned swastikas, they were literally wearing their race on their sleeves, perhaps hoping to finally reap the entitlements they had otherwise been led to expect. When they celebrated Hitler, they were relying on their whiteness to confer power on them and to counter messages that they were inferior; by engaging in racist attacks, they were striving to win masculinity credit.

Race and Marginalized Masculinity

The sociologist Katherine Newman, in *Rampage: The Social Roots of School Shootings,* and others have commented that the epidemic of school shootings is a phenomenon limited to suburban and rural white boys and that these rampages occur for entirely different reasons than those in the inner cities or among boys of other racial backgrounds. Yet the high-profile school shootings committed by boys from minority backgrounds (and increasingly by girls) reveal some of the same masculinity pressures as those experienced by the white shooters.[25]

In the cases where minorities perpetrated school shootings, the racist behavior of others sometimes served as another challenge to their masculinity. For instance, sixteen-year-old Nicholas Eliott, in Virginia Beach in 1988, wounded one teacher, killed another, and fired on a student who called him a racist name. He was one of only a few African American students in a mostly white private Christian school, and he was teased often as a result of his race.[26] Nicholas used two hundred rounds of ammunition and three firebombs to express his rage.

Derald Wing Sue introduces the concept of microaggressions to explain the daily onslaught of racist attitudes and behaviors that young people endure. Students experience outright racism, but they also contend with prejudice that is less immediately visible, including what Sue refers to as microassaults, microinsults, and microinvalidations through overt or hidden messages.[27] The more callous culture that develops as a result of persistent microaggressions has a devastating impact on all young people (and adults). It further aggravates the pressure on targets to demonstrate a violent masculinity to counter these challenges. Boys who are gay-bashed, race-baited, or otherwise challenged or marginalized often end up feeling that their manhood depends on retaliating.

In their chapter "Young Black Males: Marginality, Masculinity and Crime," Jewelle Taylor Gibbs and Joseph R. Merighi describe the dynamic in which young black boys are pressured to be masculine—powerful, wealthy, aggressive, and dominant—and then are marginalized through various forms of discrimination and exploitation that limit their access to mainstream sources of income, education, and social mobility. They note that "in a society that values wealth, power, and achievement, and measures adult males by these yardsticks, minority males recognize early that their marginal status creates nearly insurmountable barriers to success through traditional avenues."[28] Young African American males "often speak of feeling emasculated, of not feeling that they have achieved full manhood, and of being deprived of their masculinity due to societal oppression that denies them equal opportunity, equal justice, the right to develop their full potential, and to provide adequately for their family."[29]

Boys who have been told to achieve a certain level of status to be perceived as true men but who are then blocked from mainstream routes to this success may feel forced to find alternatives—"oppositional masculinity"—to achieve the power, income, and influence expected of them. These attitudes parallel those of the school shooters who, when marginalized in their schools because of perceived sexual identity, class, race, or other devalued status characteristics, become willing to do anything to confirm the masculine identity demanded of them.

Masculinity intersects with class, race, ethnicity, and sexuality. A boy's masculinity is effectively diminished to the extent that it is associated with anything other than being wealthy, white, heterosexual, and traditionally able-bodied. Hegemonic masculinity is further associated with a "misogynist and homophobic denigration of the feminine."[30] Boys who are not white Anglo-Saxon Protestants are already at a disadvantage in terms of their patriarchal dividend; then, any further deviation from this symbolic dominance undermines their masculinity accordingly. Boys who are less wealthy, who are from ethnically white or minority backgrounds, or who are perceived to lack body or social capital, associated with being heterosexual, are often belittled and degraded and made to suffer microaggressions as well as direct assaults on a daily basis. Such targeted boys may well feel driven to reverse these painful masculinity challenges.

The white school shooters who picked up guns in an effort to reclaim their manhood were playing out an other dynamic that takes place within slightly different parameters among African Americans and other minorities. Guns are associated with masculinity more generally, but when men feel demeaned as a result of marginalized status like race, class, or sexual orientation, the gun can be perceived as a restorative agent. Gibbs and

Merighi write: "Owning a gun is another potent symbol of masculinity for young black males, who are increasingly likely to use a gun in the commission of a crime and most at risk from being killed by a gun. Not only does the gun give them a sense of power and invincibility, but it also provides them with a sense of control in situations that are ambiguous or potentially dangerous."[31] Similarly for the school shooters, guns provided instant masculinity in an environment where their masculinity was otherwise questioned and attacked.

Nature or Nurture and the Potential for Nonviolent Masculinities

Whether perceived as subordinate, complicit, oppositional, or marginalized, young men experience extreme social pressure to achieve hegemonic masculinity in U.S. culture.[32] The gender scholar Judith Butler maintains that all people are forced to "perform" gender through a series of conventions and rituals that create the appearance that everything about gender is essential or natural, when in fact much about gender (and sex) is socially and culturally shaped. Society defines and imposes "compulsory heterosexuality" upon its members and punishes those who stray.[33]

Theorists such as Connell and Messerschmidt argue that pressures to prove heterosexuality often incorporate violence against girls as a means of demonstrating power, influence, and ability to dominate. As mentioned earlier, many boys feel compelled to demonstrate what I call a *"flamboyant heterosexuality"*—talking about their sexual exploits with girls, publicly commenting on girls' bodies, and differentiating themselves from boys who appear less conventionally masculine. Many high-profile crimes like the New Bedford, Massachusetts, and Glen Ridge, New Jersey, gang rapes are prime examples of the willingness of males (from both working-class and upper-class areas) to become criminals (or at least support the perpetrators) in order to prove their heterosexuality to one another. Men (in the New Bedford case) and boys (in the Glen Ridge case) were teased for being unmanly if they were unwilling to participate or otherwise support these brutal sexual assaults; many chose to commit the crime rather than endure any doubts about their manhood.[34]

Men, across demographics, independent of their place in a given adult or school hierarchy, are pressured to prove themselves. Even those situated at the top of the masculinity scale—those possessing "hegemonic" masculinity, according to Connell's scheme—often feel the need to prove their manhood again and again, lest they slip into a less respected position.

Messerschmidt makes an important distinction to explain why some men are more likely to commit violence when they are challenged. In his study of nine young boys (three who committed sexual assault, three who committed nonsexual assault, and three who did not commit violence), Messerschmidt found that the distinguishing factor among the boys was the way masculinity was defined by important people in their lives, especially school peers, fathers, and grandfathers. While all the boys learned that using violence was a way to demonstrate masculinity at school, the boys who committed violent acts found that their parents, especially their male relatives, supported this way of expressing masculinity as well. If they were threatened, their role models cautioned them, the boys needed to effectively show the offending person who was boss.[35]

The same was not true of the nonviolent boys. While they were similarly threatened, picked on, and provoked at school, they heard different messages from people who were important to them. For instance, their families suggested that the boys "walk away" from aggression and stated that it was "wholly inappropriate for a young 'man' to respond to any type of provocation with violence." Messerschmidt writes, "Although each (nonviolent) boy constructed a different type of masculinity, what they produced in common is that the different types rejected violence as appropriate masculine practice."[36]

"Indeed, gender has been advanced consistently by criminologists as the strongest predictor of criminal involvement," Messerschmidt writes— not race or class, as many suggest.[37] Would gender continue to be the greatest predictor of crime if men and boys felt more encouraged to demonstrate empathy and kindness as a means of expressing masculinity? Certainly boys who have nonviolent masculine identities are less likely to use violence in their lives and are less likely to engage in criminal activities. But for now, most young boys and men grow up associating masculinity with violence, sexism, and heterosexism. Consequently, a school culture of violence and bullying persists.

One obstacle to reversing such attitudes is the entrenched perception that boys have an innate, uncontrollable impulse to act in sexually (or physically) aggressive ways toward girls (and boys). Outdated science has been used to bolster these long-standing social assumptions. For example, some sociobiologists have linked domestic violence to "male reproductive striving." Primates, according to this argument, use aggression against females to intimidate and to secure reproductive advantage; the goal is to prevent resistance to the male's mating efforts and to reduce the likelihood that females will mate with other males. The implication, then, is that aggression, violence, and domination are "natural" masculine tendencies.[38] For example, David Barash has claimed that "violence may or may not be as American as cherry pie, but it is as male as male can be."[39]

Other scholars have challenged this notion of hormones as destiny and warned of its implications. Indeed, sociobiology has morphed into a more evolved science, now referred to as "evolutionary psychology"; it recognizes that the environment plays a significant role in influencing biological tendencies, which then reaffect the environment in a cyclical fashion.[40] Leda Cosmides and John Tooby's *The Adapted Mind: Evolutionary Psychology and the Generation of Culture* highlights these new concepts. Along with other evolutionary psychologists, including Sarah Hrdy, Terri Moffitt, and Avshalom Caspi, they illustrate that genetic tendencies are highly influenced by social factors.[41]

According to Lucy Bowes et al., there is a particular gene linked to antisocial behavior, but it is activated only if a child is treated badly; a more nurturing and compassionate environment would render the gene entirely dormant.[42] Maia Szalavitz, who writes on the relationship between brain and behavior, said in an interview that a more altruistic and kind society would increase genetic dispositions toward empathy, whereas a culture that encourages more aggression increases genetic tendencies toward violence. "Society is able to effectively turn up or down the dial on our genetic proclivities," she explained.[43]

This more recent scientific orientation is in sync with a sociological framework that blames cultural forces for promoting narrowly defined masculinities and a male-dominated social order and family structure. As Michael Kimmel has argued, "The belief that violence is manly is not a trait carried on any chromosome, not soldered into the wiring of the right or left hemisphere, not juiced by testosterone. (It is still the case that half the boys don't fight, most don't carry weapons, and almost all don't kill: are they not boys?) Boys learn it." They learn it, he says, "from their fathers, nearly half of whom own a gun . . . , from a media that glorifies it, from sports heroes who commit felonies and get big contracts, from a culture saturated in images of heroic and redemptive violence."[44] According to Kimmel, even those who may believe that "boys have a natural propensity towards violence and aggression" need to ask themselves, "Do we organize society to maximize that tendency, or to minimize it?"[45]

Another aspect of gender police surveillance encourages violence against women and girls. Popular commentaries often suggest that this too is a result of natural masculine inclinations that can't be tempered. The result of this resignation is that "low levels" of violence toward women and girls are often tolerated. When such incidents morph into more extreme forms of violence, people think they were blind-sided—when actually the antecedents were right in front of their eyes.

3

Violence against Girls

In October 1997, Luke Woodham beat and stabbed his mother to death before hiding a gun under his coat and making his way to his Pearl, Mississippi, high school, where he killed two students and wounded seven others. His main target, he said, was his first victim, his ex-girlfriend Christina Menefee. "I shot Christina," he later said. "I never really knew why the others got shot. It just happened."[1]

In a taped confession, Luke said that his mother had never loved him: "She always told me I wouldn't amount to anything. She always told me that I was fat and stupid and lazy." He cited the unrelenting bullying he endured at school, where "people always picked on me. They always called me gay and stupid, stuff like that." But a primary trigger for the rampage, he made clear, was his ex-girlfriend's rejection: "She'd always flirt with other guys. She always did that kind of crap, right to my face. She'd always tell me how cute other guys were, and all this kind of crap, and it just gets to you. I mean, I loved her, and she just didn't care."[2]

At his trial, Luke described the devastation he had felt when Christina Menefee broke up with him a year earlier. "I didn't eat. I didn't sleep. I didn't want to live," he sobbed. "It destroyed me." Luke acknowledged that he had been influenced by the leader of a group of boys who were into Satan—but even in that context he remained focused on the rejection. He told a psychologist that the older boy "said he knew I had been hurt by Christina, and that there was a way to get revenge. He said Satan was the way."[3]

In interviews following his shooting and in his own written manifestos, Luke conveyed his belief that by using violence he could stop being a tormented victim and prove he was strong and "manly," capable of making others quiver in his presence. "One second I was some kind of heartbroken idiot," he declared, "and the next second I had the power over many things."[4] He explained that he had been told too often that he was weak and ineffectual—not masculine, but "gay." He wrote, in an apparent effort to sound like Nietzsche: "I am not spoiled or lazy, for murder is not weak and slow-witted. Murder is gutsy and daring."[5]

Luke was not the only shooter who tried to prove his masculinity by shooting his ex-girlfriend. Perpetrators targeted girls who rejected them in many of the school shooting cases. Violence against girls has not gotten the attention it deserves as a dominant feature of these crimes. Examining this violence closely also reveals high levels of sexual harassment and dating violence as antecedents to the shootings. These behaviors are too often perceived as normal aspects of teenage life, but in fact they constitute some of the most devastating expressions of our students' surveillance of one another as members of the gender police.

Violence against Girls and School Shootings

Crime statistics have shown that boys under eighteen commit a significant proportion of sexual offenses, including 25 percent of all rapes and 50 percent of known child sexual abuse cases.[6] Sexual harassment is a norm in many schools, and dating violence is much more common than people realize. A 2001 national study, by the American Association of University Women (AAUW), of students in the eighth to eleventh grades documents the wide range of harassing behaviors students experienced, from sexual comments, jokes and gestures, to sexual rumors and graffiti, to flashing and mooning, to touching, grabbing, and pinching. Some students reported having their clothing pulled off, being physically blocked or cornered, and being forced to kiss or perform other sexual acts.[7] Adults in many schools often ignore or don't notice these practices.[8] The tendency to write off less extreme behaviors as "normal" may obscure many of the warning signs leading to serious crimes.

In the case of many of the school shootings, this attitude may have allowed the shooters' peers, and the adults around them, to explain away the many small incidents that preceded the shootings. Even after the fact, many were reluctant to view the shootings as intimately linked to dating violence and sexual harassment. A closer examination, however, shows that the shootings were part of a continuum of normalized masculinity sanctioning violence against girls.

In at least twenty-three school shootings, the perpetrators' stated motives related to relationship stresses: rejection, jealousy, a desire to protect girls, or frustration or perceived failure with girls. That the boys consistently offered these explanations is evidence of a prevailing mentality: they believed that the girls' behaviors were "triggers" that rendered their responses more understandable and perhaps even justified. In this, they exemplified a version of the disturbing but commonly held belief that boys' violence is natural and that girls' victimization is, at least in part, girls' own fault.

In numerous incidents, young boys targeted and shot girls who rejected them in one way or another. Luke Woodham's 1997 murder of his girlfriend who had broken up with him is just one example.[9] Fourteen-year-old Michael Carneal's first shot killed a girl who was the object of his unrequited love; he also killed another girl who had refused a date with him one month earlier.[10]

In Jonesboro, Arkansas, in 1998, thirteen-year-old Mitchell Johnson, angry after his eleven-year-old girlfriend, Candace Porter, "dumped him," targeted Candace in the shooting; five others were killed, all of them female, and of the wounded students, nine of ten were female.[11] Mitchell vowed to "shoot all the girls who had broken up with him."[12] He had been violent toward Candace prior to the shooting, but no one had taken much notice.[13] He had even told a few students of his plan to kill this girl, but they did not take him seriously. He also threatened to kill another girl who said she was going to tell other students that Candace broke up with him.[14] Clearly, Mitchell was not just upset about being "dumped"; he feared that others would think less of him when they heard about the rejection. Andrew Golden, eleven years old, had recently been rejected by his girlfriend, Jennifer Jacobs, who was one of those shot when he joined Johnson in the shooting.[15]

Many people remark that girls and women should "just leave" abusive relationships. Yet research explains why so many targets of family violence stay; and these shootings bear that out. Girls and women, in particular, who stay in abusive relationships are likely to continue being beaten, but those who leave are more likely to be killed.[16] Candace Porter left Mitchell because he was hitting her, so Mitchell shot her.

Students believed that fourteen-year-old Andrew Wurst was targeting his former girlfriend when he brought a gun to a dance at his school in Edinboro, Pennsylvania, in 1998. Three months before the shooting, she broke up with him. When she rejected him, Andrew replied, "Then I'll have to kill you." Still, he asked her to the dance, but she declined. Other students said that Andrew was looking for his ex-girlfriend, and also for a second girl who had laughed at him when he invited her to the dance too.[17]

In Lake Worth, Florida, in 2000, Nate Brazill killed his favorite teacher, Barry Grunow, when Mr. Grunow would not let Nate speak to the girl he liked, Rosales, who was sitting in Grunow's class. Nate, age thirteen, came back to school after he was suspended for throwing water balloons. He said he was upset about being suspended and particularly angry that he would not get to speak with Rosales before the summer break. The defense in Nate's trial said that Nate came to school with a gun to force Mr. Grunow to let Rosales out of class.[18] Rosales reported that Nate would send her flowers and had worked hard to get her to date him. He kept giving her gifts after she told him she was not interested. Under cross-examination, Rosales reported that Nate had made a common threat indicating the presence of, or foretelling of, dangerous dating violence: "If I can't have you, no one will."[19]

Nate also expressed concerns about his future. "I didn't want to leave school early," he told the *Miami Herald*. "I thought I'd never catch up at the beginning of next year. All my friends would leave me behind. I thought my future was ruined."[20] Nate had been an honor student, but his grades were dropping, especially in Mr. Grunow's class. He had been sent home with one other student, Michelle Cordovaz, who testified that Nate had told her he planned to get a gun, return to school, and shoot the guidance counselor, whom he blamed for getting him in trouble. "Just watch, I'll be all over the news," she remembered him saying.[21]

Nate, like most boys, had been told that he could be seen as a strong young man by being successful with girls and achieving financial success in his future. Thus he felt belittled and undermined by the suspension, which threatened his view of his future economic prospects, as well as his ability to prove heterosexual virility through success with this girl. Unable to feel power over the girl or over his own school plight, and subject to the will of the teachers and guidance counselors, he reached for a means to instantly achieve masculine power and status. He told Michelle he would bring the gun to school—hoping probably to impress her—and he referenced his desire to be recognized and to make an impact—"I'll be all over the news."

Rejection in some form also figured in a school shooting in Michigan in which a six-year-old boy, Dedrick Owens, killed his six-year-old female classmate, Kayla Roland. The two were arguing. Kayla told Dedrick that he was showing off; he said later that she had slapped him. The next day, the boy called out to Kayla, "I don't like you." "So," she replied. The boy swung around and shot her with a semiautomatic handgun.[22]

Some boys experience rejection by girls as an unbearable reversal of traditional roles.[23] If the rejected male does not have access to alternative coping strategies, or rather, alternative masculinities, he may use violence and aggression to defend his manhood. When boys murder girls who have rejected them, this can be explained, though not excused, as an effort to reverse the effects of their perceived subordination sustained through rejection.

Difficulties with girls were cited as part of the shooters' motivation in other cases as well. Some boys said they picked up guns because they were upset about a breakup, though they did not specifically target the girls involved.[24] In Bethel, Alaska, in 1997, Evan Ramsey's girlfriend broke up with him just before the shooting.[25] Kipland Kinkel, the 1998 Springfield, Oregon, school shooter, despaired over his unrequited infatuations with girls. Kip said of a girl he liked, "Every time I talk to her, I have a small—of hope [sic], then she will tear it right down."[26]

Dylan Klebold was so shy with girls that his parents paid him $250 to attend the Columbine High School prom. Another student who considered himself one of Dylan's good friends said that Dylan had not asked a girl on a date since one turned him down during freshman or sophomore year. The other shooter, Eric Harris, had asked three different girls to go with him to the prom; they all said "no."[27]

Additionally, perpetrators cited jealousy, or their efforts to protect girls from humiliation—which was perceived to be an insult to the assailant too—as a motivation for their shooting. In a combination of jealousy and territorial behavior, boys either punished or "protected" their girlfriends by shooting boys who appeared to threaten their relationships.[28] In Conyers, Georgia, in 1999, fifteen-year-old Thomas Solomon wounded six students and specifically targeted Jason Cheeks, a "jock" who along with other students had teased Thomas relentlessly at school. Thomas believed his ex-girlfriend had "turned her charms on Jason." Thomas and his ex-girlfriend had just had a serious argument the day before the shooting, one of Thomas's friends reported.[29]

Another shooting in New York City on January 15, 2002, was apparently meant to demonstrate masculinity in the face of what the shooter perceived to be a threat to his girlfriend's dignity, and therefore to his own status. Vincent Rodriguez wounded two boys at Martin Luther King Junior High School because he said he wanted revenge on two boys who had called his girlfriend names and pulled a bandanna off her head. Vincent came back with a gun because he didn't want it to seem that he had backed down from their challenge to fight for his girlfriend's honor when they referred to her derisively.[30]

In Fayetteville, Tennessee, in 1998, an eighteen-year-old honor student, Jacob Davis, killed Nick Creson because he had slept with Jacob's ex-girlfriend, Tonya Bishop. In a letter Jacob wrote to Tonya before the attack, Jacob said: "I bleed, and for that he [Creason] should bleed as well. Justice says he deserves it: i [sic] want to hear his skin sear and pop under fire while i stand in front of him and recite the lyrics to 'Soma' by Smashing Pumpkins. I want to put a 3 inch diameter hole in his chest from a 12 gauge slug." Jacob's attorney, Ray Fraley, sought to rationalize Jacob's behavior by explaining that anyone with common sense knew that Tonya's affair had caused Jacob to undergo a change.[31]

Vengeance correlates significantly with greater machismo—an exaggerated sense of masculinity.[32] Rick told me that most of the fights in his northeastern rural working-class high school were related to "you're hanging out with my girlfriend kind of stuff." Ms. Petrey, a teacher at his school, agreed: "Physical altercations between boys are almost 100 percent of the time over a girl. All of the fights that I am aware of, that's what they are about." Violence around girls was something Lenny, from an inner-city neighborhood, also came to expect: "You go to a bar and talk to a woman, a guy will bully you, try to take her from you. That's just how it is."

Normalized masculinity encourages men to dominate women, to compete for particular women, and to "protect" women who are perceived as "belonging" to a particular man. Men are taught to perceive such "challenges" as threats to their sexual adequacy and then to restore their manhood with violence.[33]

In one of the shooting cases, the perceived threat to the relationship came from a female friend. In Tempe, Arizona, two young women were killed in a double murder-suicide by a twenty-two-year-old male college student. Arizona State University student Joshua Mendel believed that one of the women, Carol Kestenbaum, had been undermining his relationship with his girlfriend, because Carol had told the girlfriend that she didn't approve of him.[34]

Nearly all the school shooters exhibited some warning signs, often in their dealings toward girls. Yet a lack of adult awareness and/or a reluctance to intervene in sexual harassment or dating violence allowed these behaviors to escalate with deadly results. The assailant in the 2007 Virginia Tech shooting, Cho Seung-Hui, had reportedly harassed two female students with threatening messages and had stalked at least one of his classmates.

Police and university officials did not take any steps to protect the women, and when Cho was sent for a psychiatric evaluation he was found to be a danger to himself but not to others. Even when he did strike out with deadly violence, dismissive attitudes regarding male violence against women may have had a revealing—and deadly—effect upon the initial response. Rumors spread that the first person killed by Cho, Emily Hilscher, was Cho's current or former girlfriend and the subject of his obsession or jealous rage, although it later became clear that the two had never had a relationship. As James Ridgeway, the Washington correspondent for *Mother Jones,* reported:

> Local police and university administrators appear to have initially bought this motive, and acted accordingly. In the two hours between the murders of Hilscher and her dorm neighbor Ryan Clark, and Cho's mass killings at another university building, they chose not to cancel classes or lock down the campus. (They did choose to do so, however, in August 2006, when a man shot a security guard and a sheriff's deputy and escaped from a hospital two miles away.) Virginia Tech President Charles Steger said authorities believed the first shooting was a "domestic dispute" and thought the gunman had fled the campus, so "We had no reason to suspect any other incident was going to occur." The assumption, apparently, is that men who kill their cheating girlfriends are criminals, but they are not psychopaths, and not a danger to anyone other than the woman in question. (Or, as one reader commented sarcastically at Feministe, "Like killing your girlfriend is no big deal.")[35]

Many boys and men in our society have been taught to view violence as a requisite of masculinity. Even though feminism has made significant strides in changing attitudes toward women, males are still encouraged by both peers and adult figures in their lives to be manipulative, domineering, and controlling toward girls and are often rewarded for displaying such "typical" masculine behavior. Boys who get attention from girls and are also able to dominate or victimize them directly can often improve their social standing in the competitive school masculinity hierarchy. But boys who are unsuccessful with girls, and even those who are "too nice" to the opposite sex, can quickly lose social standing and begin to topple toward the feared pariah position that awaits children and teens who fail to meet gender expectations. Many students and even adults in a school community—the schools' gender police—expect boys to make comments about girls' bodies, talk about them derisively with one another, and keep the upper hand in any sexual interactions. Perceived infractions against these kinds of codes can incur the wrath of a boy's peers (and even adult role models) and the boy may chastise himself as well.

Many of the shooters experienced rejection by girls as a source of unbearable humiliation—something that damaged their masculinity and contributed to their disintegrating social status. Newman writes that there is "a difference between feeling rejected and feeling emasculated after such rejection. Not all boys who are rejected by girls feel emasculated by the slight. Emasculation happens when a girl is seen in the boy's eyes primarily as a way of demonstrating his masculinity."[36] Newman implies that the latter interpretation is unusual and a feature of the school shooters' mental disturbance, but school cultures tend to perpetuate these kinds of masculinity barometers, and a school's gender police regularly enforces these codes. In this context, it is not so out of the ordinary that the perpetrators—who were often teased, harassed, and called gay and other words associating them with homosexuality—interpreted rejections by girls as a blow to their already assaulted masculinity.

The shooters understood these associations, which govern cross-gender relations in many schools today. Student and adult members of the gender police tend to ambush most often in boys' locker rooms, where boys spend at least some time before or after gym or other sports in which they participate. A few minutes there often reveals the extent to which boys feel pressured to brag about their heterosexual conquests in order to gain respect. Those who have nothing to share may feel pressured to make something up. Those known to be inexperienced or perceived to be "undesirable" are often brutally teased; similar contempt can be shown toward boys who speak less harshly about girls. Tender feelings tend not to be tolerated in locker rooms.

In this setting, a breakup wounds not only the boy's heart but his status in the school environment. Clearly, the normative belief that boys demonstrate manhood by dominating girls or making a sexual conquest is highly damaging. It warps young people's relationships and undercuts one of the few sanctioned avenues for personal intimacy. On a daily basis, it also contributes to a cycle of abuse that damages both boys and girls—a cycle that contributes to sexual harassment and dating violence in our schools.

The behavior often goes unnoticed by adults and unrecognized even by the girls (or boys) who fall victim to it. Toward the end of a school violence class I taught, one of my students raised her hand and said she had just realized that she had been a victim of dating violence; she had bruises and other physical scars from her relationship, but she had previously thought that was somewhat normal. In subsequent classes the same kinds of comments were made—girls thought a certain amount of violence in their relationships was common and not entirely objectionable. The high school and college women I interviewed also corroborated high statistics relating to dating violence when they said the incidents of violence in their relationships, however upsetting, were not "deal-breakers." In many ways, the acceptance of a certain amount of violence in relationships reflects the dynamics of the adult world. Amnesty International found that "violence against women is one of the most pervasive human rights abuses. It is also one of the most hidden."[37]

Research addresses violence against adult women in some depth, including its links to popular conceptions of masculinity.[38] Teen sexual harassment and dating violence, however, have historically received less attention from researchers.[39] While some researchers seeking explanations for school violence explore the role of bullying, fewer address the high incidence of dating violence and sexual harassment as specific types of bullying.[40] However, several pioneering researchers have focused on the role of normalized masculinity in these behaviors.[41]

Likewise, law and social policy now recognize sexual harassment and domestic abuse as unacceptable and even criminal when perpetrated by adult men, but similar behaviors are more widely tolerated when the perpetrators are minors. Many schools do have sexual harassment policies and violence prevention programs. They tend, though, to be consulted only in extreme cases of harassment and are ignored when it comes to the daily harassment so many students experience. Most schools exhibit a profound lack of consciousness about the extent and impact of everyday violence against girls. When I ask my students how many have seen or experienced sexual harassment in their schools, every hand goes up. The "normality" of sexual harassment in schools reflects the widespread acceptance of men's aggression against women and even the pressure men receive to demonstrate dominance over women.

Sexual Harassment of Girls

Like school bullying, violence against women has been referred to by commentators as an "epidemic," a term DeKeseredy and Schwartz suggest understates the problem. An epidemic implies that a disease peaks before subsiding, while violence against women, and bullying behaviors more generally, are instead "endemic" to our social cultures, pervasive, with no sign of ameliorating any time soon.[42]

Research shows that more than four out of five students experience some form of sexual harassment in school.[43] In the AAUW study, 83 percent of girls said they had been subject to sexual harassment at some point in their school lives, while 30 percent said they experienced it often. Nearly half of all girls said they had experienced a physical form of sexual harassment.[44] Meanwhile, 57 percent of boys said they had been perpetrators of sexual harassment.[45]

Sexual harassment is a common occurrence in American high schools. As a college sophomore, Tommy reflected on the culture he had experienced in his northeastern upper-class suburban public middle school: "Guys grabbed their asses and you could tell the girls weren't pleased. They felt uncomfortable, but nothing was done about it." In eighth grade, Tommy said, boys would publicly grab girls all the time, "slap their asses, try to kiss them, try to hug them." There was a lot of verbal abuse as well. When Tommy went on to a Catholic high school where the students wore uniforms, it wasn't much different. The moment students were on a field trip, the boys "would call the girls 'sluts' for whatever they were wearing."

Twenty-one-year-old Chris said he had seen the same kinds of harassment when he went to a different middle-class suburban public school in the same area: "In gym the guys would sit in girls' laps, and you heard about girls getting beaten by their boyfriends. Guys did get rough with girls, and the girls didn't like it. A guy would go out with a girl and then call her a whore if she didn't do what he wanted. Girls were expected to do what guys wanted them to do." A lot of this behavior came from the jocks, Chris said. "The kids who were harassing kids verbally or physically were involved in some sport or another."

Barbara, a student from a working-class rural area in New England, agreed that the worst harassment came from school athletes. "One of my friends was asking someone about a girl," Barbara reported, and a football player said, "'Don't do anything with her, she's a slut,' and not because of anything in particular." The boys who call girls "bitch" and "slut," Barbara said, "don't really know them. They are just judging them. People judge each other a lot, call each other names, and then it gets bigger."

Lola shared that girls in her northeastern white upper-class suburban school were harassed "all the time." "Boys refer to you as bitch, slut, whore, every day. Kids would say stuff like that to you all the time." Lola described a culture in school where boys would routinely grab girls and "put their hands all over them, slap their asses, call them sluts. In gym class some boys pulled this girl's pants down in front of everyone. She was hysterically crying in the middle of the gym class. She was embarrassed and mortified." Lola said parents were often told about these kinds of incidents and "it wouldn't matter. They would get notes about it," but no one did anything about it.

Such attitudes help ensure that victims don't receive the support they might otherwise expect from school leaders or other adults. Indeed, in one study only 40 percent of students said they would tell an adult if they experienced sexual harassment.[46] Even some purported efforts to take school sexual harassment seriously have little impact, perhaps because they are not backed up by meaningful programs of education and counseling.

In some schools, these behaviors are so common—and so "normal"—that students are not conscious that they are participating in sexual harassment or that their behavior is hurtful. "One time this girl came up to me," Lenny, from a northeastern inner-city school, shared with me. "She was a friend of someone I was dating, and she told me that when we were in high school she walked in my house and everyone sat there and laughed at her because she wouldn't have sex with them. I apologized for it, but I don't even remember that particular incident."

School sexual harassment did not even begin to gain attention until well after sexual harassment among adults reached public consciousness through Anita Hill's testimony during the confirmation hearings for Clarence Thomas in 1989.[47] In *Classrooms and Courtrooms*, Nan Stein writes that such assault is repeatedly "tolerated, even expected, and allowed to flourish."[48] Stein's research belies the typical portrait of girls as passive or encouraging these behaviors. Most harassment, she shows, takes place in public, in front of bystanders, including students and school employees. The victims often speak out against the harassment, even to school officials—but their stories are usually dismissed or trivialized.[49]

Girls can be intimidated by the widespread belief that harassment is "no big deal," even as it makes them feel self-conscious, uncomfortable, and otherwise distracted in their school environments. Worse still, a "blame the victim" mentality often continues to pervade the school culture. In my class on school violence, a student said: "They sent girls home for wearing a skirt that was too short or a strap that was too thin. A lot of teachers would pull a student out of class and they wouldn't be back. 'You need to come with me,' they would say. 'Your tank top is too revealing.'"

Lola shared a similar experience. One of the boys came over to her and pulled her underwear up since it was visible above her jeans. He "pulled it and ripped my underwear and I started to cry," Lola said. "It hurt, and then the teacher kicked me out. You asked for it, she kind of said. The teacher said, 'If you had your jeans higher, it wouldn't have happened.' He didn't get into trouble, but I got sent to the assistant principal," Lola continued. The teacher ignored the abuse and instead punished Lola for what she was wearing. Other adults are similarly dismissive of sexual harassment and even dating violence.

In terms of federal law, sexual harassment is generally considered a form of sex-based discrimination and is therefore covered by Title IX of the Education Amendments of 1972, which prohibits discrimination in activities receiving federal financial assistance. The U.S. Department of Education's Office for Civil Rights (OCR) says on its website: "Through its enforcement of Title IX, OCR has learned that a significant number of students, both male and female, have experienced sexual harassment, that sexual harassment can interfere with a student's academic performance and emotional and physical well-being, and that preventing and remedying sexual harassment in schools is essential to ensure nondiscriminatory, safe environments in which students can learn."[50] The law requires schools to take action to "prevent and remedy" sexual harassment. But schools are often at a loss as to what to do about "low levels" of sexual harassment, especially as so many school members expect it and enforce its practice. The less severe harassment often escalates and in the worst cases becomes fatal.

Both the boundaries of sexual harassment and the actions schools are required to take in response remain open to interpretation, and court decisions have not consistently been supportive of harassment victims. In February 1992, a 9-0 decision in the U.S. Supreme Court (*Franklin v. Gwinnett County Public Schools*) brought attention to the problem of sexual harassment in K-12 schools. Six years later, in another Supreme Court case, *Gebser v. Lago Vista Independent School District*, the school district was not held liable for sex discrimination because the authorities didn't have "actual knowledge of the sexual relationship between a minor female student and a male teacher."[51] Many school harassment complaints continued to be thrown out of lower courts in the 1990s. The Supreme Court did not take decisive action until 1999, affirming in *Aurelia Davis v. Monroe County Board of Education* that school districts may be held liable if school employees are deliberately indifferent to complaints of peer-to-peer sexual harassment.[52]

Some of the adults responsible for preventing and responding to student-to-student sexual harassment are themselves guilty of such behavior. In a *Cornell Law Review* article entitled "Note: Innocent Kiss or Potential Legal Nightmare: Peer Sexual Harassment and the Standard for School Liability under Title IX," Emmalena Queseda reported that 18 percent of students who experience sexual harassment said that their harasser was a school employee, such as a teacher, bus driver, or counselor.[53] In the AAUW study, 38 percent of students said they were aware of teachers or other adult school employees sexually harassing students.[54] (In this same vein, Anita Hill accused Clarence Thomas of sexually harassing her when she was working for Thomas in his post as chair of the Equal Employment Opportunity Commission—the organization charged with protecting Hill from the harassment in the first place.)

In many environments, adults and students alike seem to assume that a girl's appearance—the way she dresses, her body type, or anything that makes her look "different"—is fair game for commentary. The harassment isn't always explicitly sexual—any mention about a girl's appearance and body can be said to demonstrate dominance. Lola said that in fourth grade she had had crooked teeth. So boys "would throw wood chips at me. They would call me beaver. I was devastated and now I have straight teeth and I am still self-conscious about it."

Girls who don't possess the perceived appropriate body capital are often targets. Many students I talked with told me about the nasty names they were called if they didn't have the "right" body. Natasha, from a middle-class suburb, who was twenty-one when I interviewed her in 2008, was called "fat" and "cow." When she walked into class, she said, some students would "moo," and others would say, "Hold on, earthquake." Rebecca, twenty at the time of our discussion, also from a middle-class suburb, recalled a friend of hers being called a "dog"; the boys would bark at her when she walked by. Rebecca herself, who was also heavy, got called "thunder thighs" and "jelly roll," and people laughed at her when she walked down the hall.

Girls are also often singled out for having "too much" body capital, especially those who are considered too feminine, curvy, or sexy. Veronica, from a wealthy suburb in the Northeast, at age twenty-three in 2009, described a time in high school when a boy turned on his video camera "and put it in between my legs. He put it on the floor underneath me. I was embarrassed and creeped out about it. What the fuck is this guy doing with my body?" she thought. "He would talk about our breast sizes, 'great asses,' and how guys 'wanted to do them.'" Even when this treatment is passed off as "compliments," it can be disturbing. In an article she called "The Butt Remark Dilemma," teen Kristy Castora described how she felt when a group of boys yelled, "Nice butt" as she walked across the school gym.

> I felt angry. How dare they treat me like a piece of meat? I hated feeling powerless. My body and my privacy were violated, yet all I could do was shoot them a dirty look. When I realized that they were all staring at me, my disgust quickly melted into self-consciousness. I felt exposed, vulnerable—like some carnival freak. I covered my uneasiness with a sheepish smile; meanwhile my mind was racing. . . . I found myself thinking, "Maybe they're not making fun of me. Maybe they like me. After all, I do have a nice butt." I guess that's why I said, "Thank you." It felt good to get attention . . . to be noticed. . . . I left the gym wondering how a 10-second exchange that involved only seven words could make my head so screwy.[55]

This type of harassment is considered run of the mill. Yet research has shown that for girls (and boys) the physical and emotional ramifications of even "ordinary" sexual harassment and relationship abuse can be traumatic.[56] In the AAUW sexual harassment survey, most girls said that their experiences left them feeling upset and embarrassed, and a third also said they felt scared. But there were also more insidious effects: 32 percent said they felt less sure of themselves or less confident; 22 percent said they felt confused about who they were; and 25 percent doubted that they could have a happy romantic relationship.[57] More than half of those surveyed (2,064 public school students in eighth through eleventh grades) said sexual harassment made them avoid certain people and places at school, and 20 to 30 percent said it made them miss school, talk less in class, and have trouble concentrating or studying; some said it affected their grades. Other effects included trouble sleeping, loss of appetite, changing friends and activities, and getting in trouble with authorities.[58] Even when boys assault girls on school property many defend the boys and try to marginalize anyone who seeks to discredit the male behavior. Girls are conventionally called "bitch" when they are too vocal about their objections.

Students and adults alike assume that males will use violence to assert and defend themselves—and anyone who tries to get in the way can face negative consequences. Jessina told me about what happened to one of her friends in her lower-middle-class northeastern urban high school. "One of my really good friends was dating a popular kid. They got into a fight and he pushed her against the wall. We were all like—'What are you doing? You don't hit girls. You don't have to do that.' But then all of the girls who tried to defend her were called 'bitch.' His friends were upset that we talked back to him. And they called her a slut because she broke up with him afterwards. They talked badly about her." There was an assumption that girls were supposed to "take it" from their boyfriends and that no one else should interfere in this private matter—even as it was played out in a school hallway.

Dating Violence

Dating violence is another step on an escalating continuum of behaviors by which boys, schooled in traditional masculinity, demonstrate their power over girls. A staggering number of girls are victims in a cycle of violence resembling the experiences of adult women in domestic violence cases. In many of the school shootings, the targets were victims of dating violence. A 2001 study found that 20 percent of girls from fourteen to eighteen years old experienced physical or sexual abuse by a boyfriend, partner, or date.[59] And 8 percent of high school-age girls said yes when asked whether "a boyfriend or date has ever forced sex against your will."[60] Approximately 25 percent of undergraduate women experience some form of sexual assault on college campuses every year.[61] These statistics indicate a trend regarding violence against girls in dating relationships. As for adults, the sociologists Walter DeKeseredy and Martin Schwartz refer to a "war on women" where at least 11 percent of married and cohabitating women are physically abused by their male partners. Intimate partners kill 1,200 to 1,300 women every year in the United States.[62]

A 2006 survey commissioned by the Liz Claiborne Foundation found that "power and control actions and attitudes are pervasive in teen relationships," with young people reporting that their partners were jealous and possessive and tried to control where they went and whom they saw. Almost half said they had "done something that conflicts with their personal values or beliefs" to please their partners. A disturbing number of dating adolescents took this kind of dominating behavior to the next level: 16 percent of girls said their partners had threatened to hurt the girls or themselves if they broke up, and 9 percent said their partners had threatened to kill them or commit suicide. Almost a third of girls said they worried about being hurt by a partner, and nearly one in four said they had gone further sexually than they wanted to because of pressure from their partner.[63] A related survey found a high incidence of teens using new technologies—cell phones, text messaging, and social networking sites—as tools to monitor, control, and threaten their dating partners.[64]

Many people are unaware of the high numbers documenting dating violence and other forms of sexual violence; others claim that many accusations are false or merely "regretted encounters."[65] Yet studies show that of the campus rapes reported to the police, fewer than 2 percent prove to be false allegations.[66] More accurately, much more violence against women takes place than is reported. Women resist reporting these crimes because they often fear retaliation by their abusers; they are concerned about the lack of support they are likely to receive if they report sexual violence; and they understand that it is more likely that they will have to endure outright hostility if they make the abuse known. Alarmingly, some women don't necessarily even recognize that violence has occurred: they assume that a certain level of disrespect and rough handling is normal.

In one of my gender studies classes, a group of students did a presentation on dating violence. They made a list of typical dating violence behaviors and asked the class: "How many of you have experienced any of these behaviors?" All but three of the twenty freshmen raised their hands. Nearly every young woman I interviewed, ages eleven to twenty-six, also had some experience with dating violence. Rebecca, age twenty-two, who came from a southern middle-class suburban community, told me that her boyfriend had gotten upset one evening when she wanted to leave his house. "He threw me on the bed and he took my keys. He took a beanie bag that I bought for him and hit me in the eye. I'm asthmatic, so then I couldn't breathe. I started hyperventilating and he put his hand over my mouth. I pulled his hand away twice to say I couldn't breathe. He wouldn't stop, so finally I screamed as loud as I could and his parents came in," she said. Even so, she admitted that "we didn't break up after that." By one estimate, 20 percent of American teen girls are physically or sexually assaulted by their partners, and 80 percent of these young women continue to date their abusers.[67]

Many girls feel pressures to remain involved with boys even when it means enduring abuse. Rebecca told me about a friend of hers who was seventeen years old and regularly had bruises on her. "Those aren't sex bruises," Rebecca said, confronting her. "You're not letting this guy hit you?" Rebecca said her friend didn't try to deny it. "She acted like it was normal. She knew it was bad, and she was ashamed—but she admitted to me: 'This is my life and I'm accepting it.' Now they have a kid together."

Rosalind Wiseman starts her book *Queen Bees and Wannabes* by telling about how she once dated a popular boy to avoid becoming a target. In what is an all-too-common story, Wiseman escaped some bullying as a result of the status she gained by being associated with this boy but endured cruel dating violence from him instead. She said: "I craved validation from other girls. I had looked around and realized that I had to have an insurance policy that would keep my social status secure—and that the easiest way to do that was to have the right boyfriend. He was 'right' to the outside world, but behind closed doors he was mean and abusive."[68]

Lola had the same experience in her suburban schools. After years of bullying in elementary school, similarly traumatic experiences in middle school, and then largely keeping to herself, she met her boyfriend, Tony, in eighth grade. "That put me in a different group," she shared. "He was captain of the varsity lacrosse team and really good, and I wasn't exactly the most popular girl." She started to "hang out with the popular girls when we started dating," she said. "I knew where to go because of him. People hung out with me because of him." She was in with all the popular boys too, she said. "It changed my status."

It also hurt her: Lola started drinking and doing drugs with her boyfriend and doing other "risky things." One time Tony "choked me in school. I couldn't breathe. I started crying. I was scared. The other guys were standing there and didn't say anything afterwards. That was bad. It went to the next level. He would hit me and abuse me and it hurt." If she complained he would "laugh about it, and say I was too weak," Lola said. At parties "he would pull me away and yell at me if I was dancing with my friends. He would call me a slut, and say 'You're disgusting' because I was dancing with girls." Over and over again, Lola said, "he made me cry." "He would make me sit on the phone the entire time if I was at a party so I wouldn't talk to anyone. He would shake me, and if I got hurt he'd say, 'Well, you shouldn't have done that,' whatever it was."

Tony often said things like "Fuck you. No one likes you. You're a slut. If you break up with me, you'll lose all your friends." Lola told me that when they did break up, she did lose all her friends. "I got kicked out of the group. The other [varsity] boys called me names and wouldn't talk to me anymore. They called me a whore and a slut when we broke up. They slashed my tires in the parking lot. It hurt 'cause these were my friends. My best friend took his side," Lola shared, still seeming surprised. "They turned their back on me when I needed them most." These girls seemed to think they had more to gain by siding with the popular boys, even though they knew how Lola was treated.

Often girls fail to recognize their experiences as dating violence because it is considered so normal for boys to wield more power. Veronica described a jealous boyfriend who grabbed "my hand and crunched it. He took it and pulled it down from my face and crushed it in his palm. And I'm thinking, Is this normal? Is this what guys do? Is this dating violence? Sexually we would have rougher sex with each other, but this time he hurt me when he was angry."

Among teen victims of dating violence, only a small number turn to parents or other adults for help. Perhaps even more troubling is the fact that 68 percent of the teen victims of various forms of dating abuse said they felt what they had endured was "not serious enough" to warrant telling their parents.[69] Others may not report the abuse because, like many teenagers, they are in conflict with their parents, or want to prove their own independence and are reluctant to ask for help.[70] Some even say they don't tell because they are afraid their parents will make them break up with their partners.[71]

They may also be responding to attitudes around them. Some parents, like teachers, don't recognize the abuse students are experiencing because they too assume a certain level of violence in life is normal. The widespread acceptance of a culture of violence feeds a bully-victim cycle as well as the high incidence of dating violence; violence as a cultural norm encourages girls as well as boys to become hurtful to one another rather than compassionate.

Wendy, who was tormented for years after she moved from a northeastern working-class city school to a nearby affluent suburb, described how the experience changed her. "Because I had been bullied, I became the bully; in elementary school, I was the sweetest girl on the planet." Wendy says now she feels that she displays more aggressive tendencies even in her intimate relationships and sometimes lashes out at her boyfriend. "I'll hit him every once in a while. I'll slap him if he says something I don't like. I can't even hold myself back. I'll bite him and I'll say mean things. I've lost sympathy for people. I don't care. I've been treated so badly, so now if you're mean to me, that's it. If I feel I'm being taken advantage of, I flip a switch. I'm not standing for this." Wendy said her mother always encouraged her to fight back when she felt she was being attacked. Her mother seemed to support the same hypermasculine codes regarding violence that were prevalent in school. These two significant forces (school and family) in Wendy's life contributed to her resignation to violence in school as well as the prevalence of dating violence in her personal life.

Sometimes parents don't recognize the serious nature of teen relationships and then are less likely to be aware that they can produce difficult emotions—or even abuse.[72] At the same time, school officials often fail to act in response to revelations of dating-related violence in school, instead seeking to minimize the problem "despite public schools' statutory duty to ensure the safety of all its students on school grounds during school hours."[73] In addition to not always recognizing dating violence as such, schools are under pressure to compete with other schools; exposing dating violence could undermine their reputations and in some cases risk vital support.

Carlson wrote: "Whether in dating violence or domestic violence, an abuser's desire for control and power over his victim is at the heart of the abuse."[74] Society can either promote or discourage this will toward control and power—and current masculinity norms tend to encourage it. Numerous studies have shown high levels of peer support and acceptance for violence against women and girls, in forms that include sexual harassment and date rape.[75] "Men who abuse women tend to associate with other men who have the same beliefs, and who give them support for thinking in this way," write Schwartz and DeKeseredy.[76]

One study showed that men's belief in their own entitlement to possess and control their women is a factor in many of the homicides by intimate partners. Many such homicides are planned and were preceded by abusive behaviors.[77] Tolerance for lower levels of relationship abuse may also contribute to the alarming statistics on murders of women. One million women are stalked in the United States every year. In two-thirds of the cases where a female victim asks for a police protective order, that order is violated. One-third of female murder victims are killed by an intimate partner. Of these, 76 percent had been stalked by the partner in the year prior to their murder. Murder ranks second (after accidents) as the leading cause of death among young women, and murder is the number one cause of death of pregnant women in the United States.[78] At least nine students and four adults were killed in dating violence-related school shootings.

The U.S. surgeon general in 1992 declared domestic violence to be this nation's number one health problem.[79] In 1998, the FBI declared violent attacks by men to be the number one threat to the health of American women.[80] Moreover, the age of female victims has steadily declined.[81] In response, a series of Healthy People health status objectives, designed by the U.S. Department of Health and Human Services for the years 2000 and 2010, target women and girls as young as twelve for education about the risk of physical abuse and assault by partners.[82] The extension of such programs to teens and preteens acknowledges that many of our schools have become, in effect, training grounds for adult domestic violence.[83] Yet little has been done in the United States to transform the school cultures that sustain an active gender police intent on enforcing these destructive norms; instead, sexist and heterosexist values and behaviors too often prevail, tending to create and maintain high levels of sexual harassment and dating violence in schools.

Hypermasculine Cultures

Data collected about individuals and communities reveal that the greater the degree of inequality between men and women in a relationship, community, or society, the higher the rate of violence toward women.[84] In many studies, authors show that environments that value hypermasculinity—for instance, fraternities and male sports teams (especially football)—tend to breed inequalities that lead to violence against girls.[85] In such communities, violence against girls in schools is considered a common ritual, like the bullying or hazing often imposed upon new members of an athletic team or against other students who are different, young, or new.[86]

Fraternity members, football players, and other elite students are virtually encouraged to flout the law. As a result, only 5 percent of victims tend to report crimes by these students, since the campus social order virtually guarantees that the claims will not receive fair consideration.[87] Schwartz and DeKeseredy conclude that many crimes perpetrated by fraternity members are ignored because administrators have an economic interest in not drawing attention to what might be perceived as unpleasant activities. The vast majority of reported cases do not result in serious penalties.[88]

A 1997 case in California, *Krengel v. Santa Clara Unified School District*, illustrates this trend. The Teddie Bears were an all-female sports club that attended boys' varsity football games and compiled statistics for the players. When the girls alleged sexual harassment, verbal insults, and assault by the football players, they were ignored by the football coach, vice-principal, principal, superintendent, and school board. Even when the young women resigned in protest, the football players largely escaped discipline.[89] This case and many others like it highlight how privileged male athletes are often allowed or even encouraged to use violence against girls without fear of reprisals.[90]

This dynamic played out in upper-middle-class suburban Glen Ridge, New Jersey, mentioned briefly before, when a group of high school athletes raped a seventeen-year-old developmentally disabled girl—a classmate who idolized them—with a broomstick and a baseball bat while others cheered them on; three varsity football players were eventually convicted of aggravated sexual assault in the case, although they received what were generally considered light sentences. In his 1997 book *Our Guys: The Glen Ridge Rape and the Secret Life of the Perfect Suburb*, Lefkowitz noted that before the rape the Glen Ridge High School jocks gained social status partly by seducing and demeaning girls, bragging to other boys, and passing girls along. Girls who were available were called "animals."[91] As one girl's father later reflected, the boys who participated most enthusiastically behaved as if they were gaining more legitimacy and authority as a group each time they victimized a woman. "If I think back about that period, I can see the group getting stronger, closer, every time they got together and humiliated a girl. . . . For them this was what being a man among men was."[92]

At Glen Ridge High School, according to Lefkowitz, football stars were given carte blanche by faculty. Peers, fathers, and coaches encouraged them to act disrespectfully to women, showing off their prowess and their ability to get away with anything. Boys got more status for displaying how much power they wielded in the school—over girls and within the school environment more generally. In her book *Fraternity Gang Rape: Sex, Brotherhood, and Privilege on Campus*, Peggy Reeves Sanday documents how degrading women becomes an endemic feature of many fraternities and violence against women becomes a norm.[93]

In *Guyland*, Michael Kimmel writes that much of the dating violence perpetuated by fraternity members and varsity sports players is institutional. At Southern Methodist University, "It was revealed that football boosters had paid sorority women up to $400 a weekend to have sex with high school football recruits." When one woman was gang raped during a recruiting visit, a recruit said, "I thought the young woman was one of the team groupies who hang out with team members and do whatever [the team members] want." Kimmel wrote that coaches "fear that if they *don't* do it, all the schools that *do* will gain a competitive advantage by getting all the good football players." One former coach said: "It's very difficult for any institution, or even any conference, to react unilaterally . . . because the competition is so fierce."[94]

Studies consistently find that members of fraternities have higher levels of participation in sexual coercion.[95] Studies also show that male college athletes are more often perpetrators of battering and sexual assault.[96] This research and related interviews convey that all-male communities tend to reify hypermasculinity norms and expectations, and the perception of girls as objects. One female teacher I interviewed from an elite all-boys' school said that in general her students "are arrogant, they kiss and tell, and they are disdainful of women." In private conversations that she overheard or that other boys shared with her, they referred to women as inferior; "There's a lot of posturing," she said.

In many co-ed schools, as well, these hypermasculine values dominate not only the "jock" or "frat" culture but the school culture as a whole. Sexual harassment is often so common that boys can be teased if they *don't* engage in this abusive behavior. At Kentucky's Heath High School, site of the 1997 shooting by Michael Carneal, football players teased girls in front of teachers with no consequences. They often made lewd remarks about the girls' bodies. Michael was called "gay" because he wouldn't "be mean to the girls."[97] He later killed three of the girls—presumably to prove a point.

In such environments, being "mean to the girls"—including subjecting them to harassment and abuse—becomes a prerequisite to proving manhood and achieving status and popularity. For some, violence enacted in company is the social glue that knits together the community of young males.[98] Male batterers or boys who perpetrate dating violence often feel entitled to exercise control and believe that their peers support their right to inflict abuse.[99] The connection between conventional masculinity and such violence legitimizes it as a male response.[100]

In a culture that demands constant demonstrations of masculine power, domestic violence becomes a daily norm that is passed on from parents to children. Rick, the editor of the newspaper at his working-class northeastern rural school, reported that there were "lots of fathers beating mothers" in his town. "You see that every day." Rick told me that the violence his peers experience at home seeped into the school. Boys may feel powerless and even emasculated when they see their fathers hurting their mothers; then they often feel pressured to demonstrate their masculinity in some other context. One student whose mom had just been beaten up came to school and "lost it on a kid and beat up a kid he didn't like. He just couldn't take it anymore."

The problem becomes complicated when it is argued that boys are "naturally" aggressive and when boys who perpetrate harassment are cast, as Stein puts it, as "sufferers of hormones run amok, or as playful creatures engaging in harmless fun that is misunderstood by adults and by girls, while the victims are portrayed as 'frail and whiney.'"[101] Even when interventions are finally directed at boys' violence against girls, they tend to focus narrowly on behavior, often on punishment, while failing to scrutinize, or address the underlying masculinity expectations.

The school shooters picked up guns to conform to the expected ethos dictating that boys dominate girls and take revenge against other boys who threatened their relationships with particular girls; their actions were incubated in a culture of violence that is largely accepted and allowed to fester every day. Transforming these hypermasculine school cultures and dismantling this faction of the gender police are essential to preventing not just school shootings but also the more "mundane" violence that girls (and boys) regularly experience at school. Instead, violence against anything perceived as feminine—and especially gay—is disturbingly common in U.S. schools.

※ 4 ※

Gay Bashing

On the morning of February 2, 1996, fourteen-year-old Barry Loukaitis dressed in the clothing he had laid out the night before:
black pants, black shirt, black cowboy boots and cowboy hat, and a
long black trench coat his mother had bought him. He strapped on
a holster with two handguns, western style, and slung eighty rounds
of ammunition across his body. Through a hole cut in the pocket of
his coat, he carried his father's rifle. Barry then walked a mile and a
half to Frontier Junior High School in Moses Lake, Washington. He
headed for his algebra class, entered, aimed his rifle at Manuel Vela
Jr., and fired.[1]

Barry also killed a second boy and the teacher, severely injured a girl,
and held the class hostage before another teacher wrestled the gun away
from him. His primary target, though, was Manuel, whom he considered the ringleader in the gay bashing he endured. At his trial, classmates
would testify that Barry had pledged to kill Manuel after the boy repeatedly taunted him, calling him a "faggot."[2]

An honor student who liked to read and write, Barry was described
in the *Seattle Times* as "gangling bordering on wispy, with long, thin
arms and outsized feet" and a "little-boy face." He was also diagnosed as
depressed, and his mother had talked about killing herself. Locals were
shocked and mystified by the shooting, as indicated by a piece in the *Seattle Times* after the crime:

> A task force was created; the task force became a focus group; the
> focus group splintered into committees. The chief result: the posting
> of two security guards at each of the town's two junior-high schools.
>
> Town meetings have been held. Civil suits have been filed. Pub-
> lic-health counselors, dispatched like SWAT teams, have introduced
> "closure" into the town vocabulary, even as its citizens struggled to
> figure out what happened.

"We like to think of ourselves as 'Mayberry RFD,'" said county deputy prosecutor Robert Schiffner, referring to the 1960s television show about an idyllic rural town. "Obviously, we are not that."[3]

But one blogger who grew up in Moses Lake and still lived there (and who wrote that his "opinions sometimes get me into trouble" with his neighbors) had a different reaction. On the tenth anniversary of the shooting, he wrote of Barry: "He was a screwed-up kid, to be sure, but not a psychopath. He knew right from wrong. He knew, for example, that bigger kids beating up and humiliating a smaller one is wrong. Barry was assaulted, called names, swirlied, wedgied and (so I've heard) even held down in the school locker room and urinated on. Combined with the troubles he had at home, he simply reached a point where he couldn't take any more, and he snapped in a huge way."[4]

Masculinity expectations in the form of heterosexism are a crucial but underexamined motivation for school shootings and school violence generally. While gender norms have presumably relaxed in some ways, they remain oppressive, and gay bashing is still one of the most prevalent and devastating forms of school bullying. It affected most of the school shooters. They were called "queer" and "faggot" as they walked through the school halls; they were tormented emotionally and in many cases threatened or roughed up physically. Luke Woodham in Mississippi announced that he was "tired of being called gay" to help explain his shooting. Columbine's Eric Harris and Dylan Klebold made it clear that they were enraged at preps and jocks who had gay-bashed them, and the students referred to as jocks in the school confirmed the boys' reports. Michael Carneal was taunted and physically assaulted and called gay in the school newspaper.[5] Charles Andrew Williams, who in 2001 killed two male students who taunted him and wounded thirteen others in Santee, California, was called "pussy" and the like.[6] This occurred even though all of the shooters considered themselves heterosexual.

Gay bashing includes abuse against people who identify themselves as gay; it can also involve any abuse that is based upon its victims' perceived lack of hypermasculine qualities. This kind of bullying yields a particular type of humiliation and related response. The school shooters' peers, their schools' gender police, gay-bashed the perpetrators for failing to meet their masculinity expectations. The perpetrators responded by picking up guns to prove their manhood using a time-honored method—extreme violence. The social expectation to prove manhood in the face of constant, emasculating degradation is so strongly conditioned that the perpetrators seemed to feel they had no other options.

It takes violent responses like these shootings to make headlines, but gay bashing, and the culture that produces it, are everyday facts of life in schools across the country. In some schools, such words as *gay* or *faggot* are used for anything that is perceived as "stupid" or "uncool"—a fact that does nothing to lessen the impact on the victims of the abuse. Homophobic and heterosexist remarks are the most common type of biased language heard in today's schools, according to a 2005 survey.[7] More than three-quarters of the students surveyed for the report said they heard homophobic slurs "often" or "frequently" in their schools.[8] In fact, 44 percent said they heard these types of remarks from "most of their peers," and 19 percent said they heard them from teachers and other school staff.[9] In another poll, of thousands of America's highest-achieving high school students, almost half admitted prejudice against gays and lesbians.[10]

Such comments and attitudes are a fact of life for most U.S. students. The direct link between the constant gay bashing in schools and the shootings and other dramatic school violence it incites begs for more attention and intervention, yet progress in this area continues to face challenges. Everyday bullying behavior so often involves gay bashing that some fundamentalist groups in the United States actually resist bullying prevention programs because they fear the interventions will promote a "gay agenda."[11] The same prejudice that incites this violence serves as a barrier to ameliorating it.

In addition to condoning homophobia, such reactions ignore the fact that heterosexual students are gay-bashed as much as, if not more than, gay-identified students. Indeed, allowing gay bashing to fester in schools torments most students, not just gay-identified ones. One study found that the average high school student hears twenty-five antigay slurs a day.[12]

The gender police have strict expectations for how a boy should demonstrate and display his heterosexuality. Boys who do not exhibit the perceived all-important body capital—being strong, big, and muscular—are at a particular disadvantage. Boys are also in danger of being persecuted by their school's gender police if they are perceived as being too short, too skinny, or overweight. They are abused if they are thought to be bad at sports or if they are involved in school activities or clubs that are considered "nerdy." Boys who excel academically and those who are shy or insecure with girls are also at risk of being gay-bashed. In a 2001 report called *Hatred in the*

Hallways, Human Rights Watch estimated that two million U.S. students a year were bullied because they were, or were thought to be, homosexuals. But in reality, three-quarters of the students targeted as "gay" identify as straight. The Safe Schools Coalition reported similar proportions of abuse against homosexual and heterosexual students: for every gay, lesbian, or bisexual youth who reported being harassed at school, four heterosexual students were targeted because they didn't conform to the expected stereotype embodying masculine or feminine qualities.[13]

These facts suggest a disconnect between how people identify their gender and sexual identity (gay, straight, bisexual, transgender) and whether they live up to socially defined standards of masculine and feminine behavior. One survey, by the Gay, Lesbian and Straight Education Network (GLSEN), notes that "sexual orientation, gender expression and appearance may be inextricably linked" for many students. Students who were seen as insufficiently masculine or feminine, the survey found, were more likely to be bullied for a variety of reasons, including general physical appearance, race or ethnicity, or disability.[14] In the end, what seems to put boys, in particular, most at risk for becoming targets of bullies is a perceived lack of "manliness"; boys often see others as potential victims if they detect weakness or passivity. The gender police look for deviations from a traditionally hegemonic demonstration of masculinity and punish transgressors severely.

The distinction between sexuality (being gay) and gender expression and perception ("looking" gay or "acting" gay) may explain why there has been little discernible decrease in gay bashing, even though young people are more likely to be familiar with and accepting of the idea of homosexuality. In a 2005 survey, more than half of teens reported knowing another student who was gay, lesbian, or bisexual, and two in ten said they had a close personal friend at school who was lesbian, gay, bisexual, or transgender (LGBT).[15] LGBT teens are far more likely to come out to both family and peers than in past generations.[16] Yet half of these LBGT students say that they feel unsafe at school.[17] Boys who, regardless of their sexuality, do not conform to typical masculinity expectations also seldom feel—or are—safe in most school environments. Whether they identify as heterosexual, homosexual, or other, the boys targeted for gay bashing are often told that they are not masculine enough, and in this culture that can make you a target.

"I was called 'faggot' three to five times a day," confided Gregg Weinberg, who as an adult served as the director of Health Informatics and Knowledge Development at Gay Men's Health Crisis. Gregg grew up in a middle-class area in New York City, always identified as heterosexual, and offered to use his real name in this book. One day on the bus in junior high school, "These guys got on and gave everyone rubber bands and they shot rubber bands at me" while calling him "faggot." "That was my name," Gregg said matter-of-factly. "The whole thing was mortifying. I was close enough to my home so I got out, but I felt angry, upset, alone, powerless, and enraged." Gregg was picked on from age five through age eighteen. His persecutors would "steal my book bag, throw snowballs at me, push me; it was constant torment." Students would threaten Gregg and call him "gay" everywhere—"on buses, outside school, inside school. I never felt safe, never comfortable, never happy, and very much alone," he said.

Tommy, from a wealthy northeastern suburb, told an all-too-common story of his buddy Albert. "He was shy and quiet, and didn't have a deep male voice," Tommy began. "Every day of the week he was harassed—he was called 'homo,' and they were pretty evil, they would throw a condom at him and say, 'Here, use this for your boyfriend, you faggot.' They'd throw him against the locker and shout at him, 'I don't want to catch what you have. I'm going to kill you.'"

There is considerable research about how gay bashing affects students who identify as gay. One recent study found that lesbian, gay, bisexual, transgender, and questioning youth are up to four times more likely to attempt suicide than their heterosexual peers, while another found that lesbian, gay, and bisexual young people who come from a highly rejecting family are over eight times more likely to attempt suicide than their LGB peers from families with no or low levels of rejection.[18] Gay bashing also contributes to the low self-esteem and social alienation that drives students to abuse drugs and alcohol; one report found distinctly higher levels of lifetime drug abuse by people who had identified as LBGT while in their teens. And an estimated 40 percent of street kids are lesbian, gay, bisexual, transgender/transsexual, questioning, or intersexed; many of them having left or been thrown out of their homes because of their sexual orientation. There is every reason to believe that when heterosexual boys are repeatedly put down as "fag," "sissy," or "homo" because they don't exhibit traditional masculine behavior the effects are similar. A 2002 survey by the National Mental Health Association, which studied both gay teen and teens "perceived to be gay," found that students who are gay-bashed are at higher risk for depression, eating disorders, and suicide. In many cases, gay bashing has incited not only violence against the self but also violence, even murder, against others.[19]

The Punitive Gender Police

Gay bashing preserves and promotes the exaggerated gender roles that prevail in high school (and adult) culture. By engaging in name-calling, bullies distance themselves from what is perceived as feminine or homosexual, reinforcing their status as top males. The boys derided as "gay" suffer an intolerable loss of status, which serves as an example for the other boys: unless they "act like men" within the narrow definitions of masculinity, they, too will be tormented. As Gregory Lehne, a medical psychologist at Johns Hopkins who studies children's gender issues, notes: "The fear of being labeled gay is a threat used by societies and individuals to enforce conformity in the male role, and maintain social control. . . . [It is] used in many ways to encourage certain types of male behavior and to define the limits of acceptable masculinity."[20] In fact, if a boy fails to join in gay bashing, he risks being gay-bashed himself.

Latoya, from a largely African American northeastern middle-class urban school, told me that boys and girls both were often teased if they were suspected of being gay. "If you didn't make fun of someone, you were perceived as gay: 'Oh, that's your boyfriend,' they would say." Students often feel pressured to choose sides: appear tough and bully others, or get labeled gay—and thus goes the bully-victim cycle. Silent bystanders are in danger of being heaped in with other targets, though they can sometimes slip under the radar.

Adolescents of minority ethnic groups can usually find support within their families and their peers if they are being singled out, but students who are put down as "fags" by schoolmates often have no supportive options. Parents and siblings may subscribe to the same homophobic feelings. Latoya, a gay-identified woman, said she had seen terrible prejudice from parents as well as other youth about her friends' sexuality, whether they were girls or boys. "My friends would come out and their parents would say: 'I'm not having this. This isn't possible. It is someone else's fault.' They were upset if their daughter even associated with a lesbian." Teachers and other school faculty and adult members of the community may themselves voice disdain for homosexuality. A child who faces gay bashing every day may literally have nowhere to turn.

According to the 2001 report by the American Association of University Women Educational Foundation on sexual harassment in schools, *Hostile Hallways*, 73 percent of all students reported that being labeled gay or lesbian would cause them acute distress. Among boys, the report found, no other type of harassment provoked as strong a reaction, not even physical abuse.[21] Yet parents and teachers are far more likely to shrug off this type of name-calling than they would racial, ethnic, or religious slurs. Gay bashing, along with the sexual harassment of girls, is so common in schools that it is considered everyday behavior.

Hypermasculinity is often cultivated as compensation when men or boys are told their masculine identity is in one way or another, inadequate. The sociologist R. W. Connell describes how boys can become more aggressive and violent in an attempt to heal a damaged sense of manhood. She explains that relations of domination operate between men and women and among men themselves and that teasing is one of the deadliest blows to a boy's self-image, devastating to his sense of himself as a man. According to Connell's hierarchy, set forth in chapter 2 of this book, men who are gay or perceived as gay are pushed to the bottom of the masculinity ladder. Their masculinity is subordinated.[22]

As discussed earlier, campus fraternities, team sports, military combat units, and various forms of gangs tend to breed an exaggerated conformity to traditional male behavior. In addition to hosting cultures that tend to be hurtful toward females and males perceived as weak, these institutions often practice hazing, involving the humiliation and abuse of their own members. One strange phenomenon found in some of these hypermasculine environments is a prevalence of men and boys acting out homosexual acts—a kind of homophobic homoeroticism. In the high-profile 2003 Mepham High School football team hazing case, in Long Island, the male victims were anally raped and forced into simulated enactments of gay sex.[23] As part of the torture that took place at Iraq's Abu Ghraib, naked prisoners were forced to simulate gay sex and were sometimes photographed doing so by their captors.[24]

In addition to the actual rape that takes place in so much hazing, it is a disturbing reflection on our culture that forcing "weaker" students, athletes, or prisoners to perform such simulated acts is considered a way to humiliate them. It may also have to do with more complicated feelings on the part of the abusers and the culture that produces them.

The scientist Alfred Kinsey became a household name in the 1950s for his research published in two volumes on the sexual mores of men and women. He believed that most people are at least somewhat bisexual; developing a 1-6 scale, Kinsey sought to show the "many gradations" of sexuality. Only a minority of people are completely 0 or 6, heterosexual or homosexual, respectively. Everyone else exists in the middle, with more or less bisexual proclivities.[25]

On a cultural rather than a biological basis, men and boys certainly feel a range of emotions deemed "feminine" that they are forced to suppress.[26] In a society that considers such feelings a threat to masculine identity—and especially in hypermasculine institutions—men with such inclinations may force others to simulate homosexuality in order to at once satisfy and punish their own desires. Homophobic homoeroticism then becomes a cultural norm in many all-male social spaces. A member of the gender police can be particularly punitive when he uncovers an infraction against expected masculinity norms in himself. In such cases, the gender police demand and often then receive some demonstration of violence to put to rest the given masculinity challenge.

Flamboyant Heterosexuality

In thirty-six of the school shootings, the perpetrators are known to have been gay-bashed or otherwise attacked because of a perceived lack of masculinity. In most of the cases, they were specifically called "gay," "faggot," and the like. Even when they were not explicitly taunted as gay, the harassment and name-calling tended to imply a lesser manhood, some inability to exert power, domination, or influence.

It is striking, for instance, that so many of the boys who committed school shootings were described as skinny, fat, or small—physical characteristics that were considered unmanly in their schools and that brought them further disdain. As discussed earlier, in addition to their looks, they tended to come from (sometimes just moderately) less privileged backgrounds and to excel more in academics than in athletics. In other words, they were in some way lacking typical masculine characteristics. Thus within their schools' bully cultures, when the perpetraters endured insults that implied they were "effeminate" or "not masculine enough," they seemed to feel, effectively, invited to counter with violence.

Eric Hainstock killed the school principal in Weston High School in Cazenovia, Wisconsin, in September 2006 because he was repeatedly bullied and often called "faggot."[27] One of Eric's relatives testified that Eric had brought the guns to school only to scare people. "He didn't actually want to hurt anybody," said the relative. "He was sick of people making fun of him and I guess he decided to take things into his own hands."[28]

In some cases, the school shooters were tormented by students referred to as jocks and preps, who were not only more powerful and popular but also often wealthier. Luke Woodham, for instance, was consistently called "faggot" not only because of his appearance—he was an overweight student with thick glasses—but because of his lower economic background. Luke's father and mother had separated when he was seven, and his mother had raised him and his brother by herself, working as a receptionist.

After the shootings, few media reports recognized that the boys' desperate effort to reverse their humiliated masculinity was a significant trigger for their violent acts. Even among those who acknowledged its damaging effects, few identified it as "gay bashing" or linked it to the narrow and oppressive view of masculinity that reigns in today's schools. The words of other students in the targeted schools, however, show that students had less difficulty making this association. Ben Oakley, a soccer player at Columbine, knew that Eric Harris and Dylan Klebold were mercilessly "teased and humiliated." He thought nothing of it, though, until the shooting. Referring to the group branded by their tormentors as the Trench Coat Mafia with whom Eric and Dylan were associated, he said: "Nobody really liked them. . . . The majority of them were gay. So everyone would make fun of them."[29]

A few observers, apparently taking this word that Eric and Dylan were gay, had a similar response, taking their perceived homosexuality as evidence of their general depravity: "Right-wing leaders were quick to light on the possibility that the Columbine killers were gay, with little or no prompting. The Westboro Baptist Church in Topeka, Kansas, sent out a media alert saying, 'Two filthy fags slaughtered 13 people at Columbine High'; the Rev. Jerry Falwell described Klebold and Harris as gay on *Geraldo Live*."[30] Many adults and students alike thought it made sense that these mostly more academic and less athletic boys would and should get gay-bashed; they also assumed deductively that they were then in fact gay. It takes a lot for students to demonstrate to their schools' gender police that they are heterosexual even if they are. The gender police expect constant proof of heterosexuality in the form of aggressive acts, sexist behaviors, and repeated public displays of heterosexuality—regardless of whether others involved in such performances are willing participants.

Boys of all backgrounds then feel pressured to use violence to prove their manhood and heterosexuality. Lenny, who was in an inner-city school, was heterosexual, but that didn't prevent him from getting gay-bashed. "I had a couple of bullies my whole life. I grew up very little. They take your lunch money, ridicule you in front of your friends, beat you up, pick out your flaws and attack," he said. "It started the first day of school" and continued relentlessly. "The minute you walk in there, everyone's going to go after you like you're fresh meat." "It's just a common thing," he explained, "if you're upset or you dress a certain way you get called gay. If you wear anything out of the ordinary you get called fag; if you wear something too tight, they call you fag; or too colorful, they call you fag." They picked on his nose "because I have a big nose," Lenny explained, and "made fun of my mom" because she was disabled. Lenny learned that the only way to stop the abuse was through violence—"The minute I threw a punch it was over"—but only for that particular incident.

Many people speak derisively about "flamboyant homosexuality," but in reality, far more common is the pressure for boys to demonstrate on demand a *flamboyant heterosexuality,* a term I introduced in an earlier chapter. Dress "masculine," talk "trash" about girls, beat up on smaller guys, tell everyone about your sexual exploits—or make them up—talk and brag about violence; these are often the imperatives to which boys feel forced to conform at the average school. Boys are pressured to do all sorts of things to avoid being teased as gay. "At one party, I got attacked by a girl," Lenny said. "She wanted me, but I didn't do anything with her. I didn't want to. So then she told people I was gay; it took a while to recover my name again. I was getting called a fag." A girl he broke up with "told them all these rumors about me. I tried to explain—she's lying. If I have to prove it, I'll take you to my house right now." Lenny was punished for not demonstrating a flamboyant heterosexuality that would exploit any opportunity to have sex with a girl, even if he wasn't interested. A perceived pause in a boy's demonstration of flamboyant heterosexuality invites merciless abuse from the gender police; the inflicted cruelty is even worse if a boy is indeed gay and actually chooses to express his authentic self.

"Coming Out" Still Unsafe

Gay and lesbian students take a big risk if they come out in the majority of schools, which are generally homophobic. Natasha's friend Sean came out to his friends in a northeastern middle-class suburb, and by the next day the news had spread like wildfire to the four hundred students in the school. One day in a criminal justice class, a student named Charlie, who was sitting behind Sean, was "kicking him in the butt." When Sean asked him to stop, Charlie said: "You know you like it, you faggot." Sean tried to ignore it, but his face got ashen white, he was so upset. He was relentlessly tormented then. They called him "rainbow bright" and "doll" and taunted: "Where is your boyfriend?" "You take it in the butt." In the face of such abuse, most gay students choose to keep their sexuality hidden. One teacher at an elite all-boys school told me, "No one is out of the closet." She believed that "a boy who came out as gay might find himself isolated"—or worse.

After the Columbine shootings, one former Littleton student later spoke about what had happened when he came out in eighth grade at a local middle school that feeds students to Columbine High School.

> "One year everyone loved me," he said. "The next year I was the most hated kid in the whole school." Jocks were his worst tormentors, he said. He described one in particular who pelted him with rocks, wrote "faggot" and "we hate you" on his locker and taunted him in the hallway with: "I heard the faggot got butt-fucked last night."
>
> "It gets to the point where you're crying in school because the people won't leave you alone," he said. "The teachers don't do anything about it." The boy attempted suicide several times that year, and eventually spent time in a mental hospital. "It can drive you to the point of insanity. What they want to do is make you cry. They want to hurt you. It's horrible. I hope that the one thing people learn out of this whole thing is to stop teasing people."
>
> In the interview, the boy didn't condone what Harris and Klebold did, but said he understood what drove them over the edge. "They couldn't take it anymore, and instead of taking it out on themselves, they took it out on other people. I took it out on myself. But it was a daily thought: 'Boy, would I really like to hurt someone. Boy, would I like to see them dead.'"[31]

As an openly gay middle school and high school student in Ashland, Wisconsin, Jamie Nabozny suffered years of relentless verbal, physical, and sexual abuse. He was called antigay epithets, urinated on, and made to suffer repeated assaults and indignities, including a mock rape. Eventually he was beaten to the point of requiring surgery, and he and his family began to receive death threats. Despite frequent meetings with school officials, the identification of his attackers, and the intervention of his parents, the schools took no meaningful disciplinary action against Jamie's abusers.[32] "After the mock rape in eighth grade," Jamie said in an interview, "I went directly to the principal's office and told her [Ashland Middle School principal Mary Podlesney] what happened. Her response was, 'If you're going to be openly gay you have to expect this kind of stuff. Boys will be boys.'"[33] In high school, after several boys knocked Jamie down and urinated on him, Principal William Davis's solution was to send Jamie to a guidance counselor, who tried to change his schedule so that he would have less contact with his abusers. No action was ever taken with the boys who harassed and assaulted Jamie.

Asked why he thought the abuse became so bad, Jamie said, "I definitely believe with all my heart it's because the administration did nothing. Every single time they refused to do anything they were saying it was OK to harass me. . . . Optimistically, I kept going back [to administrators] and every time it was still ignored. The assistant principal said I had to be provoking it." He also believed that "if I would have denied that I was gay from seventh grade on, if I had played the role I was supposed to play and did the things I was supposed to do, I probably could have avoided the abuse. That doesn't mean I deserved it."[34]

Jamie dropped out of school twice, suffered post-traumatic stress disorder, ran away from home, and tried to kill himself several times. In eleventh grade, he left Ashland and moved to Minneapolis, where, with his parents' support, he lived with a gay foster family and earned a GED.[35] He also filed a lawsuit in federal court against those who had ignored and, in effect, permitted his abuse, accusing them of violating his Fourteenth Amendment right to equal protection. In November 1996, the U.S. Court of Appeal for the Fifth Circuit ruled that the abuse Jamie had suffered was indeed a crime and that school officials could be held individually liable for failing to address the gay bashing and discrimination.[36] This has been upheld, but it continues to be difficult to prove, as gay bashing is considered so normal it often continues unnoticed. In a landmark settlement reached after that verdict, Jamie received nearly $1 million in damages.[37]

At least one student who chose to come out at school paid for it with his life. Fifteen-year-old Lawrence King had told classmates that he was gay, and had begun to wear makeup and jewelry, shortly before he was shot to death in an Oxnard, California, school in February 2008. The day before his death, Lawrence had an argument about his sexual orientation with his killer, fourteen-year-old Brandon McInerney. The shooting was labeled a hate crime.[38]

Abuse and harassment help enforce the antigay norms that prevail in many American schools. Rebecca recalled the abuse boys experienced in her middle-class southern suburban school if they were perceived to be gay. She had a male friend who claimed to have a girlfriend back in Texas, but students in the school were convinced he was gay. "He got tortured," said Rebecca. "They wanted him to come out and admit it, but it was in his best interests to do what he did—if he came out he would have gotten bashed." Another boy who wore tight clothes experienced it even more directly, said Rebecca. "People threw things at him—apples, anything— and yelled out 'faggot' when he walked by."

Chris spoke about his experiences being gay-bashed in tenth grade. He had been heterosexually identified at the time (later he identified as bisexual). Students would call him derogatory names, he said, all the time. He was called "faggot," as well as "gay," "weak," "woman," "homosexual," "loser," and "queer." The other students seemed to think he acted feminine in the way he walked and talked—a serious offense according to the gender police. One day "some boys paid a few kids to beat me up," Chris said. On another occasion, in twelfth grade, two students were paid twenty dollars each to mock "hump him"—just as Jamie had experienced. Chris said he always followed the rules, did what teachers told him to do, and didn't cut class. "I went where I was supposed to go and followed the guidelines—some kids called me a 'pussy' for that. Every hour I hear something antigay. I lived my life being harassed." "Anyone else would have brought in a weapon," Chris admitted, with some compassion for the school shooters who had experienced similar abuse.

Chris and other students at his university told me that boys in their middle- to upper-class high schools were so worried about being called gay themselves that they came up with a phrase to ward off any such accusation. "Gay people were seen as weird, but if a guy said something that might be perceived as gay"—maybe something that revealed a more vulnerable or fallible aspect of themselves—"they would say, 'no homo.' That was supposed to protect them from being perceived as gay," explained Chris. Boys have to go through a lot to express the full continuum of their humanity when so many common emotions and behaviors are labeled "gay." Most of the time they just don't bother; and girls often find they are expected to harass others and police themselves to make sure they are not perceived as vulnerable human beings either. Empathy for others sadly tends to invite gay bashing and other forms of abuse.

While Chris's persecutors were usually male, girls would sometimes join in the gay bashing, Chris reported. "They would pretend that they liked me. But if I asked them out, they would say 'Hell no, get away from me, loser.' Sometimes a guy would say a girl liked me or a group of girls liked me," but this would become another opportunity to laugh at him when he tried to make friends. "I may have been what some people called a nerd because I always did my work, but I didn't deserve all that," Chris said sadly.

Chris's reaction to these experiences was to become depressed; Wendy's reaction to similar experiences was to transform herself from being what she considered "sweet" to being mean and defensive. Jamie Nabozny tried to commit suicide; Michael Carneal in Kentucky picked up guns and murdered his classmates. This kind of bullying is dangerous to the target of abuse and to the perpetrator, as well as to innocent students who may find themselves in harm's way when the target unleashes his or her reactive wrath.

Few legal measures specifically address gay bashing. However, on the federal level, laws such as Title IX that prohibit discrimination on the basis of gender, as well as the Fourteenth Amendment's equal protection clause, have been applied in several cases, and some states have other applicable laws as well.[39] In one Minnesota case, *Montgomery v. Independent School District*, the court found that a student who had suffered through eleven years of relentless gay bashing with no meaningful response from school officials had a claim under Title IX because "he suffered harassment due to his failure to meet masculine stereotypes."[40]

In some cases, lawsuits have not only awarded damages to students but also forced reforms within schools. For example, in a 2003 case in California, *Flores v. Morgan Hill Unified School District*, the court awarded a record $1.1 million to six students who suffered harassment and physical violence "on the basis of their real or perceived sexual orientation and gender." It also commanded the school district to amend its antidiscrimination policy, including adding sexual orientation and gender identity in the policy's language, and instituting mandatory trainings for teachers, school officials, and students to prevent further discrimination.[41] These interventions are useful, and students need to be protected from abuse when it occurs, but the most effective way to prevent gay bashing in the first place is to teach students to accept and appreciate one another regardless of their differences.

Legal victories are important, but by themselves lawsuits will not eradicate gay bashing in schools. Legal cases tend to develop when students have the courage and support to seek justice, sometimes only in the more extreme instances of abuse and, worst of all, only after the fact. Some schools admirably try to teach tolerance of students perceived as different, but these efforts are still largely ineffective in that they rarely seek to foster actual acceptance and appreciation of gay and lesbian (as well as other) students. Putting up with one another is unlikely to create the kind of compassionate communities students need to thrive.

Efforts to address incidents of harassment and violence infrequently look at the wider culture that feeds them—the culture that subjects students to subtle and not so subtle pressures to practice "normal" masculinity and gives them tacit permission to "discipline" those who violate these norms. The first step in violence prevention is to acknowledge the pressures boys are under to exhibit hypermasculinity and to avoid any behavior that can be read as "feminine" or "gay." Interventions that focus on expanding what it means to be masculine will allow students a wider array of reactions and behaviors that don't entail violence. Such efforts need to be directed at all students, not just boys. The terrain girls navigate is just as painful, unsupportive, and alienating as the one for boys; it is also increasingly dangerous.

5

Girl Bashing

Elizabeth Bush was fourteen years old on March 7, 2001, when she took her father's gun to the cafeteria at Bishop Neumann High School in Williamsport, Pennsylvania, and started shooting. Her only victim, a thirteen-year-old girl whom Elizabeth had once considered a friend, was wounded in the arm but survived. Elizabeth, described as a "serious, introverted, religious" girl, later said in an interview: "There was a deep part of me that just exploded."[1]

Among the many students who carried out rampage shootings in their schools in the last three decades, Elizabeth is one of the few (eight are known for sure) female perpetrators. Yet her story closely resembles those of many male school shooters. She described a long history of bullying, which had reached brutal proportions by the time she was in junior high school: "They'd just call me an idiot, stupid, fat, ugly, whatever," she said. "One incident was I was walking home from school and five or six kids were behind me and they started throwing stones at me. . . . They were just kind of laughing and I don't know why they were doing this but they were barking at me."[2] Like many kids who endure bullying, Elizabeth initially turned her pain inward. She began to skip school, became depressed, and started "cutting," a form of self-injury that is now common among teenagers.[3]

Elizabeth said she cut herself because "I was angry at myself for being different. . . . People express their anger different ways. Crying helps, that didn't help me. So I thought maybe I'd try this and maybe it will help. The pain just takes away all your depression and for a minute you're not depressed anymore." Her parents moved her to a small Catholic high school, but the bullying continued.[4]

In Elizabeth's new school, she was befriended by a girl considered popular, Kimberly Marchese, who was a cheerleader and played soccer and basketball. According to Elizabeth, she confided in Kimberly and even told her about the cutting—but her friend told her secrets to other students and made fun of her. "She was laughing. She was calling me a freak and all this stuff," Elizabeth said. "I was very hurt that she'd do that to me. . . . Those feelings, those thoughts that I told her, they were never supposed to be revealed to anybody; and that's what she did." Elizabeth said that when she brought her father's revolver to school, "I was thinking of shooting myself because I wanted to show her this is what you made me do." Instead she turned the gun on the friend she felt had betrayed her.[5]

Like most of the male shooters, Elizabeth suffered at the hands of the school's gender police, who pressure students to present themselves as "perfect" boys or girls. She was declared "fat" and "ugly" and therefore an unacceptable girl. Consequently she became one of the pariahs—her vulnerabilities were made into fodder for gossip and ridicule. Elizabeth was also attacked for being "weak"; she then looked for ways to grapple with the painful feelings she experienced as a result of the bullying. When she cut herself, she may have longed for compassion and support, but instead she endured more harassment. Like the boys who were brutally bullied, she was expected to "just take it."

Girls are in a new double bind. They are expected to be "feminine"—demure and attracted and attractive to boys—but also "masculine," as the larger bully society demands—tough, hyperaggressive, excessively self-reliant, and able to fight for themselves if it comes to that. Girls (and boys) find that making and sustaining authentic connections with themselves and others is difficult in most school environments, which expect and encourage students to be tough rather than caring. Instead of forming meaningful friendships, girls often do whatever they can to prevent social annihilation.

In fact, the bullying that girls endure is not wholly different from that with which boys contend. Contrary to popular belief, girls engage in as much dating violence as boys, and boys use as much relational aggression, if not more—gossip, social exclusion, ridicule—than girls.[6] What we learn about violence among girls also contributes to the important knowledge we need to prevent violence among boys, and vice versa.

Use Violence if Necessary

Many of the girls I spoke with experienced or observed bullying. Like boys, they were expected to prove their heterosexuality; they were also expected to demonstrate femininity, which lately has become even more complex and difficult to both define and obtain; and just as the school shooters were often harassed because they were perceived to be too skinny or heavy, girls suffer abuse relating to their bodies.

Wendy, from a wealthy suburb, said, "They called me 'Miss Piggy' in high school. I was 165 pounds. My friends would make fun of me. 'Wendy, you shouldn't be eating that. Why are you eating that?' they would say." Wendy was eventually encouraged to fight her aggressors, by other students and by her mother too. "One girl called me fat, and I had it. I pulled her by her hair and said 'I want an apology.' She wouldn't give it to me, so I pushed her and shoved her, and she ran away." Wendy, like many others teased in school about their bodies, lost the weight and developed what she calls "an eating problem."

Kate, from a wealthy suburb, had two close friends in a group of girls considered popular and referred to as The Five—introduced in an earlier chapter. Kate described how the group targeted and socially destroyed one girl after another. They called one of her friends a "slut" because they thought she was too confident with boys. Kate believed she herself became a target because she was seen as "too pretty" and too attractive to boys; the very qualities that had allowed her to become a member of this powerful clique later caused her to be kicked out. Yet Kate still worked to be accepted by these girls.

It may be difficult to understand why Kate would continue hanging out with them, but she explained, "They pull you in and they are so much fun." She also thought it would make her safe from the abuse they hurled at other students. "But it wasn't safe," she said sadly. "Everything I told this friend of mine would be spread all over the school—even if I said, 'Please don't tell.' And we had told each other everything!" She added, "They would not just talk about me behind my back, but even right in front of me."

Sometimes the abuse from the group became physical: "Gayle knocked into someone in the hallway and yelled in her face, 'You're really ugly. I can't believe I was ever friends with you,'" Kate said. "They knock into people going on their way to class all the time. And they choose to be mad at someone just for entertainment. They would accuse someone of talking to their boyfriend, even if they knew it wasn't true," and then they would exclude the person from their group. "She can't sit with us anymore," Kate would hear.

Girls are tormented for not being "girl enough," and the barometers against which they are measured tend to be overwhelmingly hurtful and mean. Rachel Simmons, in her book *Odd Girl Out,* likens the popularity contest prevalent among girls to the concerns society has more recently recognized regarding the impact of ubiquitous images of girls as thin and "flawless." That everyone must be liked or even worshipped by their peers at the expense of authentic relationships fuels dynamics where girls sometimes work to socially destroy one another. "This makes popularity, and the race for it, as dangerous an issue for girls as weight, appearance, or sexuality," writes Simmons.[7]

Psychological bullying often breeds physical violence, even though sociobiological theories tend to argue that boys are "naturally" aggressive and that girls are not. When girls turn to physical violence, the popular assumption is that they do so primarily in self-defense, in response to harassment or domestic or dating violence. Recent research, however, indicates that girls often initiate violence as well.[8] In one study, girls identified a number of offenses as deserving of a violent retaliation, including verbal attacks, gossip, or efforts to steal another girl's boyfriend.[9]

My female university students often report increases in fighting among girls in their precollege school years. Young women of all different ethnic and economic backgrounds say that as girls they felt compelled to "defend their honor" and often had mothers and fathers who told them to "do what it takes" to stand up for themselves and "protect what is yours." Girls, like boys, also report that to avoid being targets they become bullies. Rebecca recalled one time when she made fun of a girl that other students teased often. "That was me getting something out because so much was done to me. It made me feel better because it wasn't me being teased for once. I made something up. The joke wasn't on me and that made me feel better."

For girls, the gender police are always on duty—girls watch themselves and one another and punish each other and themselves severely for perceived infractions. They get chastised by their parents as well as by both their male and female peers if they have gained weight, for instance. Body capital among girls is made out to be more precious than gold. Even mothers become victims of a school's gender police and hear from their children as well their children's peers if they are perceived as being overweight or otherwise less than perfect physically. The cruelty boys are encouraged to use against one another to display hegemonic masculinity parallels the vicious behaviors girls are pressured to use in order to enforce some of the same gender codes.

Ms. Thomson, a guidance counselor implementing a bully prevention program aimed at girls in her southern middle-class urban school, told me that in her experience girls are mean in many of the same ways boys are: "They will throw the ball too hard at another child when playing a game; they won't pick certain kids for pickup games," she explained. They will leave each other out, not pass the ball to certain kids—anything to exercise power and establish dominance.

Stories of girls engaging in physical violence are not difficult to find and often echo stories of adolescent male violence. In 2003, a touch football game in Northbrook, Illinois, that was supposed to be an initiation for Glenbrook High school junior girls turned into a terrifying street fight; a bystander videotaped the scene, which was subsequently shown on news channels all over the country. "Basically it started out as a fun hazing like our initiation into our senior year," one girl who had been injured told CNN. "About ten minutes into it, everything changed—buckets were flying . . . people were bleeding. Girls were unconscious." Girls slapped, punched, and threw objects at other girls who were cowering on the ground. One girl reported that a pig's intestine was wrapped around her neck; another girl said she was forced to eat mud; and witnesses said they saw the girls throw urine and feces at each other. Students who came to watch the game, including some boys, joined in, and five girls had to be treated at the local hospital.[10]

In a few cases, violent bullying by girls has turned deadly. In a suburb of Victoria, British Columbia, in 1997, Reena Virk, a fourteen-year-old South Asian girl, was attacked by seven girls and one boy in a Gorge Park, while dozens of bystanders watched. Reena managed to crawl away, but one of the girls and the boy went after her, beat her again, and drowned her in the Gorge Waterway, where they left her body.[11] Reena was reportedly lured to the park by two girls, "to teach her a lesson" after she called up boys using numbers she had gotten from a phone book belonging to one of them.

Like many incidents of girl bashing, the Reena Virk case involved competition over boys. But it also reflects issues of race and class, which join with gender in determining the "codes" enforced by the gender police. Reena was slightly overweight and dark skinned, the child of working-class immigrant parents, and she had spent time in foster homes. In her 2004 essay "Racism, 'Girl Violence,' and the Murder of Reena Virk," Sheila Batacharya argues that these qualities are central to understanding this crime: "She was not thin, white, and middle class which is the dominant definition of a 'girl' in Western culture."[12] The white girls who attacked Reena appeared to be outraged that Reena had considered having sexual or other relationships with "their" boys. This kind of "competitive heterosexuality," Batacharya writes, often "frames white women's violence against women of color."[13]

The media frenzy that followed this crime highlighted the shocking nature of white middle-class girls committing atrocious violence. This response, though, ignores the hierarchies of power that exist among women and girls. Racism, sexism, classism, ableism, and heterosexism place girls in dominant and subordinate relationships to one another. Just as boys who are not necessarily the biggest and strongest get what Connell calls a "patriarchal dividend" and wield dominance over girls just by virtue of being boys (and race and class become factors determining which men get the biggest dividend), white girls get a similar "dividend" on the basis of their whiteness—a "white girl dividend." Girls who are white, wealthy, able, and flamboyantly heterosexual are encouraged to assert their dominance over girls who score lower on these measures. The white girls in this case believed they had a "right" to the white boys, upon which girls like Reena were not permitted to impinge. Girls' violence is often framed around these hierarchal prejudices, which girls see demonstrated in the adult world as well. Girls then feel tremendous pressure to prove that boys are attracted to them (and only them). Other girls seen as threatening this sought-after perception are often called sluts.

More recently, fifteen-year-old Phoebe Prince in South Hadley, Massachusetts, was brutally slut-bashed before she committed suicide in March 2010. As an Irish immigrant, Phoebe was targeted because she had dated a popular senior football player in her first weeks at the school as a freshman. Other girls believed she was invading their territory and called her "Irish slut" and "whore."[14]

Such racism and ethnic prejudice, mixed with gender violence, comes from values in the adult world, as discussed further in subsequent chapters. In fact, the bully society in schools is similar to the workplace bullying that adults sometimes face. In the absence of alternative values, the cutthroat competition and discrimination prevalent in the larger society among women and men infiltrate schools and recreate similar power plays among children.

Girls (and boys) desperately want authentic friendships and connections. Too often, though, they find that their relationships in school are largely instrumental—students trade each other's secrets as information capital, exploit their sexual interactions to try to become popular, and compromise their former values to be accepted. Where students look for friendship, intimacy, and self-acceptance, many find it "makes more sense" to mistrust. They learn quickly that punishment for going against the expectations of those students perceived as popular may well land them at the bottom of their school's hierarchy and render them a target. Thus slut bashing (and gay bashing) become normal aspects of children's days as they vie for dominance rather than seek connections. Prejudice regarding race, class, ability, sexuality, and other differences can become the glue that cements student relationships rather than their more intrinsic interests and passions. When girls call each other "slut," class and race, and an effort to establish relationships of subordination, are often implied aspects of these insults. Leora Tanenbaum writes: "The slut label carries a set of class associations. . . . Regardless of her family's actual economic status (or even the girl's sexual experiences), the slut is thought to be low-class and trampy."[15]

Girls, like boys, attack each other within every racial and economic group. Shantique recalled relentless bullying by the other African American girls in her working-class southern rural school. She endured taunts and harassment that often crossed over into shoving or hitting. "It was six days a week, because I had to go to church with those girls, too," she said. "They had planned stage fights. Girls would organize fights, and the only way I could negotiate getting out of the fights or not getting beat up or being in a fight was to play lookout. I would tell them if a teacher was coming. The ringleader would rotate and she would decide: 'You two have to fight each other.' And the girls would go into the bathroom and scratch each other. It might be about 'You looked at my boyfriend and now you have to beat her up,' and you had to or you would get beat up yourself." The popularity contests and backbiting among cheerleaders were similar to those described more often among white suburban kids in wealthy schools. In her school, said Shantique, "The cheerleaders were the popular, pretty girls, and they were the ones who did the name-calling, and threw the spitballs, and made me a butt of a lot of jokes." Finally, "I got used to it. It was just the way it was."

Lots of students get used to violence as a norm in their lives. While the research is controversial, recent studies show that girls are committing more violence on all levels, from bullying in school to crimes that bring them into the criminal justice system at higher rates.[16] The Harvard University professor and child psychologist Alvin Pouissant estimates that girls commit 25 percent of the violent incidents in schools.[17] Statistics show a significant rise in girls' acts of criminal violence in the 1990s. According to the U.S. Department of Justice, from 1990 to 1999, aggravated assault committed by girls under eighteen increased by 57 percent; arrests for using weapons increased 44 percent for girls; and girls committed 157 percent more offenses against people, as opposed to property.[18] James Garbarino writes that "the official arrest data indicate that girls today assault people and get arrested more often than did girls of generations past."[19] One 2003 news report stated that the juvenile justice system used to be approximately 95 percent male and 5 percent female. Now, it is 80 percent male and 20 percent female, and the female percentage is still climbing.[20] Deborah Prothrow-Stith and Howard R. Spivak's 2005 book *Sugar and Spice and No Longer Nice: How We Can Stop Girls' Violence* is among a series of new books noting that girls' violence is increasing and needs to be more effectively addressed.[21] Why are girls committing so much more violence?

Masculine/Masculine

The high level of girls' violence today may, at least in part, be due to a cultural shift such that girls, like boys, are driven by masculinity values dominating our cultural landscape. Girls are expected to compete for power, financial resources, and status, just like boys. Some second-wave feminists, in particular, believed that women tend to be more conciliatory and relationship oriented, whereas men are more competitive and aggressive; it was reasoned that a more peaceful world would develop if more women were in leadership positions.[22] Carol Gilligan explained these gender differences in her best-selling book *In a Different Voice*, arguing that women are more empathic and men more rule oriented.[23] In *The Reproduction of Mothering* Nancy Chodorow writes that women are more relationship oriented because of familial dynamics when the mother tends to be the primary caretaker. Little boys feel pressured to differentiate themselves from their mothers as a way to figure out what it means to be a boy. Since in the traditional family fathers are less present as role models, little boys instead define themselves as "not mother." Boys may then believe that to be a boy they need to embrace the opposite of the maternal qualities their mothers exhibit—being emotional, supportive, or loving, for instance. At the same time, girls, according to Chodorow, do not feel pressured to separate as much from their mothers. They instead model themselves after their primary caretaker as a way to define themselves as a girl. Hence girls are encouraged to accept the more vulnerable, empathic, and relationship-oriented aspects of themselves that their mothers may embody.[24]

Chodorow's psychoanalytic insights, however, could not have accounted for the hypermasculine, competitive, and power-focused economy and society in which girls would find themselves during the twenty-first century—nor how these forces might affect earlier psychological tendencies (nor the more complicated familial dynamics that have developed as fathers are increasingly more involved in child rearing). Girls are encouraged to be less relationship oriented today (just like boys) and are pressured instead to seek domination and control. As women assume more leadership positions, their otherwise feminine-associated values—compassion and empathy—become subordinated to the current economic, political, and social climate, which tends to demand more masculine-oriented, winner-take-all qualities from men and women alike. Growing up in this climate, both boys and girls are encouraged to be tough and independent rather than emotional, supportive, and compassionate. Earlier feminists hoped and predicted that women's presence in the workplace would make for a more compassionate society. Contemporary times reveal instead the extent to which the economic system defines and drives gender identities. Women are expected to embody the same hypermasculine values endemic to contemporary workplaces. Neither men nor women are particularly encouraged to be compassionate, supportive, or cooperative in our cutthroat economy. Empathy, therefore, has become less common among men and women alike.

In schools, girls are pressured to fight, to humiliate others, and to show their dominance and power. Across economic, racial, and ethnic demographics, girls are encouraged to act tough and to try to intimidate others. Jody Miller writes in *Getting Played: African American Girls, Urban Inequality, and Gendered Violence* that girls in urban environments tend to use typically masculine-associated behaviors to respond to the daily onslaught of sexual harassment they endure—expressing anger and hostility or using threats.[25] Girls in mostly white and wealthier communities are also responding with more violence-oriented strategies when they are challenged.

"The most traditional or classic example of bullying that I see," said Ms. Willis, a teacher in a middle- to upper-middle-class northeastern suburban high school, "involves athletics. I still can't believe the hazing I see on soccer and football teams; and girls are even more aggressive in this type of hazing. One time at a pep rally, the senior and junior female soccer girls handcuffed and taped the freshman girls and made them go out to the gym floor. They drew all over them. And the older girls thought it was funny to make them prove that the freshmen were loyal to the team. We told the girls they weren't allowed to do this, but then they just did it outside of school."

Another time, Ms. Willis said, "the younger girls were made to show up in a ridiculous outfit at a party and they were pressured to drink and do sexual activities with boys. Rampant rumors around school conveyed that this included the infamous lipstick parties. Each girl used a different color lipstick and they gave the boys blow jobs so everyone could see how far they could go when doing oral sex. Eventually the staff hears about what happened and the gossip spreads via e-mail and text messaging. Someone may have taken an embarrassing photo and then it is all over the Internet."

Girls are also increasingly expected to engage in sexual activities with the same emotional distance and cavalier attitude that have heretofore typically been more characteristic of males. Historically, it was understood that women were more interested in relationships whereas boys more often wanted sex. Andrea Dworkin and Catharine MacKinnon famously declared their indignation that in pornography women are portrayed as wanting sex as much as men.[26]

Today many feminists and nonfeminists alike assume that females want sex as much as males and that there is nothing wrong with that. But earlier feminists had hoped for a day when men would approach sexuality with the same intimacy more commonly associated with women's interests. Instead, boys and girls are both more likely to engage in a sexuality more traditionally associated with men. Terms like "friends with benefits" (friends with whom you are sexual) and "hooking up" (having casual sex) grow out of this new teen culture, where serial sexual relationships replace the more intimate and monogamous relationships associated historically with women's priorities.[27] This more popular "masculine" attitude toward sexuality is also prevalent in lesbian communities, according to Ariel Levy in *Female Chauvinist Pigs*. Levy writes that in the eighties lesbian separatist trends identified as "not male" and even spelled the word *woman* without the "man" in it—*womyn*.[28] Today, she writes in her chapter "From Womyn to Bois," there is a growing trend among lesbians to call themselves bois and identify themselves more like male teenagers. "Bois just get to have fun and, if they're lucky, sex," Levy writes.[29]

James Garbarino writes that girls' increased aggression is not wholly a bad thing precisely because girls are more open with their sexuality;

they also seem to be more active in sports and to enjoy what he refers to as "normal" aggression in rough-and-tumble play; girls are feeling more confident, according to Garbarino, with their physical prowess and power.[30] Yet girls also contend with the same gender pressures to win male approval. The more casual attitude toward sexuality does not necessarily reflect actual casual feelings. Levy writes about the "Girls Gone Wild" series of videos, in which girls and young women voluntarily expose their breasts, French-kiss one another, and perform other sexual acts for the camera. After interviewing many who participated in these activities, Levy concluded that many young women do so not for their own pleasure but again to please and attract boys. According to Levy, girls continue to view themselves as they believe males are viewing them; they see themselves through the "male gaze." Levy cites other examples of what she calls "raunch culture"—from sex-soaked reality TV shows, to ordinary women learning to dress and dance like strippers, to the boom in breast augmentation surgery—and argues that it isn't about sex or sexuality but rather about a kind of narrowly defined "sexiness" that doesn't necessarily satisfy or bring pleasure to the women themselves.[31] Raunch culture, Levy continues, "isn't about opening our minds to the possibilities and mysteries of sexuality. It's about endlessly reiterating one particular—and particularly commercial—shorthand for sexiness."[32]

In this context girls' openness with their sexuality is twofold, demonstrating new boldness *and* exhibiting a new form of subjugation. Indeed, some girls do feel strong, powerful, and comfortable with their sexuality. According to Levy, however, too many just look that way and are still trying to do whatever it takes to win male attention (and therefore male and female social approval). They may look confident, but they often feel insecure and pressured to do things sexually and otherwise that they don't want to do; then violence becomes more common as a by-product of these activities, since girls still feel pressured to defend their reputations even as they are also pressured to appear sexier and more sexually willing. The sexual liberation that third-wave feminism (1990s) hoped for and that was also prevalent among some second-wave feminists (1970s-80s)—as evidenced in works by such writers as Ellen Willis—appears to have arrived. Yet while female sexuality is more visible today, the outward manifestation may actually more thinly disguise the same sexual subservience women have historically experienced and protested. In such cases, the more "open" sexuality tends to translate into less intimacy, less connection, and less authenticity. It is unclear how much young women authentically embrace the ubiquitously casual attitudes toward sexuality and how much they are pressured to do so—to win the approval of men and to gain status in a society that rewards being tough, unemotional, and independent in so many realms of our social lives.

In any case, the trend toward prioritizing traditionally masculine relationships undermines young men and women alike, who find that when they do seek intimacy they are met with increasing social isolation and loneliness instead. Research shows that between 1985 and 2004 the number of people who had no one to talk to about important matters in their lives tripled. Trends toward increased loneliness and a decrease in friendships have been widely documented;[33] these statistics are surely related to the more common casual and less intimate relationships among young people. They also reflect greater popularity of values associated with masculinity—being tough, unemotional, and fiercely independent.

Further, when schools leave conflicts up to students to handle on their own, or intervene only reactively once something severe has occurred, or even encourage a certain level of rough play, violence in schools becomes increasingly the norm, and a more traditionally masculine attitude of handling things "by yourself," not caring, and talking and acting tough saturates school cultures. When schools do act, they tend toward similarly "masculine" approaches, including more punishment, greater surveillance, higher suspension rates, and increased police presence, as discussed in later chapters and addressed in Aaron Kupchik's 2010 book, *Homeroom Security: School Discipline in an Age of Fear*.[34] Many of the new school bullying programs that have sprung up across the country continue to focus only on the individual—helping individuals stand up for themselves and develop the confidence to talk back to bullies in presumably more effective ways. Few programs work on creating better relationships among students and others in the school community in the first place.

Thus there is a masculinization of self, a masculinization of sex, a masculinization of relationships, and a masculinization of school cultures and related policies, in an increasingly masculinized economy—or to put it another way—all yang and no yin. Girls and boys alike are encouraged toward conventionally masculine ways of being—casual and noncommittal, disconnected and unemotional, and cutthroat competitive and power driven, backed by violence and serious threats. Boys and girls both find that their more "feminine" desires for connection, intimacy, emotional self-expression, and cooperative and compassionate ways of being are discouraged at many turns. With this new emphasis, perhaps unsurprisingly, there is also a rise in violence among girls, not least in the form of slut and other girl bashing—as prevalent a torment as gay bashing tends to be for boys.

Slut Bashing

Rebecca's best friend Lila got called "slut," "whore," and all kinds of other derogatory names at school. "She wasn't doing anything different than a lot of the popular girls were doing, but she was getting tortured for it," Rebecca told me. "My friend slept with one guy and all of a sudden it was ten." Lila met her husband at the school where all these rumors got started. "He had a hard time getting over that," Rebecca shared. Whether it was true or not, he didn't necessarily want to marry a girl with a reputation. Even though he married Lila, the issues still plague them.

Rebecca remembers that one girl, Mindy, was particularly brutal toward Lila, and Rebecca decided the best route was to slut-bash back. She wrote on every bathroom hall in the school: "Mindy is a whore. Mindy is a slut. Mindy is a 'ho.'" Rebecca wanted the abuse of her friend to stop but could only imagine doing so by effectively turning the gender police back on Mindy. Rebecca got in trouble for doing it, but she said she didn't care.

The minefield girls tread is explosive and difficult to cross safely. While girls are pressured to appear sexy and sexual, and to expect sex to be less emotionally oriented, they are also penalized if they are perceived as stepping outside more traditional boundaries. Rebecca, Lila, Mindy, and Lila's husband all suffered unnecessarily because girls are expected to stay within these complicated sexual parameters. They are harassed if they are perceived as engaging in what might be perceived as "excess" sexuality (though boys are still mostly congratulated for the same behavior). Girls are still pressured to at least appear to be not "too sexually" active, and even teachers and administrators tend to discipline girls who express themselves and wear clothes in a manner they perceive as too sexual. Yet girls who are perceived to be "not sexual enough" are also tormented by other students where more sexually explicit clothing is considered de rigueur.

Girls' sexuality is policed by almost everyone, and girls are seldom allowed to find their own sexual identity and expression. Arbitrary rules governing girls' sexuality then become fodder for rumors, gossip, teasing, harassment, and even assaults. Then girls are largely left on their own to deal with the abuse. Rebecca used graffiti in the girls' bathroom to retaliate and was unmoved by the potential punishment her actions might engender.

Though teens' burgeoning sexuality could be an opportunity to connect authentically with another human being, sexuality is more often used as a tool of torture and abuse by the gender police. In this environment, young people quickly learn that trust and emotional engagement are risky and unwise.

"I was so shy in ninth grade, but I was forced into kissing a boy," said Wendy. The other girls "thought it was weird that I never kissed a boy and they were doing all these things, and then it became a question about my sexuality: 'Oh, do you like girls or something? Why are you so scared?'" The guy they wanted her to kiss was "so gross," she told me, but she did what the other girls suggested because she feared ridicule and didn't have a strong enough sense of self to do—or even know—what she really wanted. "All day they said, 'Tom thinks you're cute, you should kiss him. You should do it. He really likes you.' I felt special, but then at the end of the day, they literally dragged me over to a house and pushed us into a bedroom. We kissed and I freaked out and ran away."

Wendy was mortified. The pressure to prove her heterosexuality felt violating, but she conformed to the random expectations of her school's gender police to prevent further attacks. She escaped the wrath of her peers by obeying their rules—and then, like many students, veered further from understanding and expressing her own authentic self. She started to see movies she didn't like, listened to music like Justin Timberlake, the Backstreet Boys, and Britney Spears, even though "I never really liked it, but [the other girls] did, so I would pretend."

Later, Wendy met a boy she actually did like, "and being so young, I broadcast it," she said. "I told my friends. Someone overheard and they ganged up on me. They told the guy to ask me to be his girlfriend so I would think the guy liked me. I went home actually happy for the first time. But the next day he had a new girlfriend and he was holding her hand. He was like 'Oh, sorry.'" Wendy felt devastated, and the other girls taunted her: "'Did you really think he would be your boyfriend?'" they said, as if the idea were implausible. Whatever Wendy did, she never succeeded in living up to the standards of the gender police at her school. Sadly, she now talks about "trust" as a childish value. She, like many students, learned early that she couldn't trust other people in a culture that values domination and that deemphasizes compassion, kindness, and empathy.

Wendy's experiences caused her to lose an authentic connection to herself as well as her potential to have meaningful relationships with others. She also turned from what she considered being a "sweet girl" to someone who would "turn a switch" at the slightest provocation. Violence is an expected result in a culture that encourages students to be mean to one another.

Adults tend not to be adept at discovering, preventing, or intervening in girl-bashing challenges. The problem is bigger than each individual incident implies: competition for status and wars waged for popularity are extensive. While many people suggest that bullying is essentially adolescent, generally it is the adult world's values that infiltrate students' social environments in the first place, often to devastating ends. There is little motivation or external reward, in either student or adult worlds, to connect to oneself, others, and one's work. Neither women nor men tend to have access to the avenues, or even the time, in a fast-paced bottom-line economy, for the authentic relationships most crave.

These difficulties persist face to face but also in cyberspace, where too often young people (and adults) retreat to try to find safer, more fulfilling social connections. Sadly, though, many children (and adults) find instead that they are by themselves in a room, with a computer, experiencing even more hurtful bullying.

6

Cyber-Bullying

"**B**ullying for our parents was getting beat up, stuffed in a locker, getting stuff stolen from you," said Austin Charles, a junior at South Carolina's Socastee High School. "I don't know that physical bullying happens very much around here. Cyber-bullying happens a lot." He continued: "Some people go as far as to creating entire pages devoted to making fun of somebody. I think they call them hate books and hate spaces."[1] In September 2010, a school resource officer was shot and wounded at Socastee, and several pipe bombs were found planted at the school. The alleged perpetrator, fourteen-year-old Christian Helms, had been bullied for nearly half his life, according to his lawyer.[2]

Accounts suggest not only that this bullying extended to cyberspace but that the accused shooter himself turned to the Internet in the days leading up to his violent act. A day before the shooting, a Twitter account believed to belong to the alleged shooter included the statements "One more week and I get my shotgun shells" and "Things are going great. Should have 6 or 8 pipe bombs and 4 molotov cocktails soon." On the morning of the shooting, tweets on the same account read, "Haha wow, this is ganna be so much fun" and "Alright, I'm past the point of no return. No turning back now. Excited, but also scared." Several other students were apparently following the account on Twitter but said nothing to adults.[3]

Every type of school bullying—from status wars to slut bashing and gay bashing—extends beyond face-to-face encounters and into the 24/7 world of cyberspace. "Today, bullying doesn't even end at the school bell," President Barack Obama said at the White House Conference on Bullying Prevention in March 2011. "It can follow our children from the hallways to their cell phones to their computer screens."[4] When students are bashed on the Internet, the abuse can go on around the clock. Cruel dynamics that were previously played out predominantly in classrooms, hallways, and playgrounds in front of adults increasingly take place in cyberspace, behind anonymous identities.

Ms. Willis, a social studies teacher from a middle- to upper-middle-class northeastern suburban school, said: "Years ago a lot of this was done in the vicinity of adults. When the kids were interacting, there was an adult at arm's length." Today, she said, "I see less classic bullying in my classroom. They think they will get in trouble if they do it in school. Rather than call a person a nasty name, the student thinks, 'I'll send a text message.' Then I'm out of the loop." Ms. Willis told me that while she may not witness acts of cyber-bullying, the effects are palpable in her classroom. "I don't really know about it," she explained. "But it's affecting my classroom. I have no idea what went on on the Internet the night before. I walk into my classroom and I can tell something happened. No one will tell me. There is snickering at that one and it is affecting the class. Until it explodes, I'm not invited to this party."

Ms. Willis expressed multiple concerns regarding bullying online. "When I was in school, if I was angry at someone and something they said about me, I would be anxious. It's a big thing to walk up to someone and say, 'I don't like what you said,'" she explained. "But now they go behind these anonymous screen names. It's like 'I'm Oz behind the curtain.' It's easier for these children to bully and do nasty things to each other and no one knows who they are, so then responsibility and shame don't exist for them." Ms. Willis continued: "Because I am this screen name in the bedroom, they are not seeing it as something wrong. Everyone's doing it. Then I come in to teach the fall of the Roman Empire and all these other things are occupying them."

Jessina, from a lower-middle-class northeastern urban school, said the harassment in her elementary and middle school took place mostly on bathroom walls: "So and so is a slut; or slept with this person; or is a bitch; or this is so and so's phone number." But the ramifications weren't quite as terrifying and damaging as during high school, when people began texting and using instant messaging on the Internet. "In high school, texting became very popular, and instant messaging became the big thing—talking to people back and forth. People created screen names that you didn't recognize. And if you accepted them they wouldn't tell you who they were. And then you would get messages like 'I'm going to beat you up.' It was scary. You don't know who is doing it. Someone got your screen name and they wrote: 'I know where you live,' 'No one likes you,' 'You're a bitch.' They would paste your information in the message and say: 'This is your phone number and address. I'm going to have people call you.' These people had your information and you didn't know who they were. People were scared to go to school and believed that people would be waiting for them," Jessina explained.

Types of Cyber-Bullying

The organization StopCyberbullying.org defines cyber-bullying as any situation where a child or teenager is "tormented, threatened, harassed, humiliated, embarrassed or otherwise targeted" by another child or teen "using the Internet, interactive and digital technologies or mobile phones." In one survey, 42 percent of students in grades 4 to 8 said they had been bullied online, and 35 percent said they had been threatened. Fewer than half of these children had told their parents or another adult about the abuse.[5]

Cyber-bullying takes many forms, including "flaming," which involves posting provocative or abusive posts, and "outing," or posting personal information. Other forms of harassment include making threats or placing people's personal information and phone numbers in areas that endanger the victim—for instance, on sexual service sites. A Pew study found that some teens bullied others by forwarding private e-mails they had received to groups or posting them on social networking sites, while others spread rumors or made direct threats.[6] This kind of bullying has become common among adults and within workplaces too.

Much of the same cruelty that takes place face to face manifests in different forms on the Internet. For instance, students can be excluded from social spaces on the Internet just as they can be isolated from real-life social activities. "Blocking" is not allowing someone to communicate or be recognized anymore in a particular chat room or on a social networking site like Facebook. In one qualitative study of online relationships and cyber-abuse, the authors quoted a post revealing the feelings associated with being blocked: "I get sick of my friends rejecting me. Whenever I'm on msn, I try talking to people and they block me." Children who were blocked often said they felt distraught; one teen felt "alone, sad, and stressed, with no reason to live."[7] Some people block their Facebook "friends" to protect themselves from messages that they experience as hurting their feelings; then when that blocked person's feelings are hurt back, the cycle continues. To complicate matters, in cyberspace people don't necessarily see the impact of their actions on one another, and the empathy that might develop from witnessing a victim's pain becomes even more elusive.

In one of the most popular cyber-bullying trends, referred to as "sexting," students share compromising communication—including photos or videos of themselves or others—with other people via texts or other electronic media. According to a study by the National Campaign to Prevent Teen and Unplanned Pregnancy, one in five teenagers has participated in some form of sexting. Scholars, educators, and the popular media are particularly concerned about the impact of sexting on girls—especially where girls' reputations become precious commodities in school status hierarchies. Boys, though, are also devastated by this form of bullying, which is also often used to gay-bash. Sometimes students trade photos by mutual consent and do actually respect the privacy that trust implied; other times that trust is violated and the sender may find the pictures posted even internationally.

Ms. Willis said: "In the eighties if someone called a girl a slut, it ended with a slap across the face in the locker room. Today it is pictures being held ransom on the Internet." She said that students often are unaware of how permanent the pictures they circulate become. "You're at a party, someone gets drunk, and someone takes pictures. It goes up on a Facebook page. They don't realize that could be there for the rest of their lives. A prospective employer can Google it." She tries to explain this to her students, but it is a formidable challenge.

As new technologies develop, so do new forms of cyber-bullying. Students record fights or embarrassing episodes with their cell phone cameras and upload those on the Internet too. A special name, "happy slapping," has been given to incidents in which a victim is assaulted; bullies (or adult criminals) use mobile phones to take and distribute pictures of the humiliating event.[8]

In 2007, a video of two girls fighting in a school locker room in Ohio was posted on YouTube; two weeks later, more than six thousand people had viewed it. A news story on several NBC affiliates showed a long clip from the video, even as it reported on parents and school officials condemning it.[9] On her blog "Girl with Pen," Deborah Siegel noted that "the girl who shot the clip with the camera on her cell phone made no attempt to break up the fight or run to get adult help." Siegel, who wrote about the "Girls Gone Wild" video phenomenon in her book *Sisterhood, Interrupted*, continues: "The YouTube clip is part of a trend. There are entire sites now, like www.girlfightsdump.com and www.fightdump.com, virtual repositories of girls behaving badly."[10]

In 2008, an article titled "Are Mean Girls Getting Meaner?" described a brutal incident in Florida. A sixteen-year-old girl named Lindsey was pummeled by her female classmates, who intended to use the beating to make a video for YouTube and Myspace. Lindsey was beaten so badly by the six girls that she ended up in the hospital with a concussion, eye injuries, and other bruises.[11]

Deadly Cyber-Bullying

Cyber-bullying often involves enforcing the same strict gender codes online that dominate schools during the day. The Internet has thus become a primary site for slut bashing and gay bashing, sometimes with deadly results.

A ninth grader named Mary Ellen Handy reported that she got an e-mail calling her a slut; when she ignored the comment, assuming it was a joke, her instant messages increased. One day she received word that everyone hated her; then a doctored picture of Mary Ellen with horns appeared on a photo website; then her instant messages were altered to look as if she were spreading rumors about her classmates. Friends dropped Mary Ellen to avoid becoming targets themselves. Her grades dropped, and she developed an ulcer. When she and her family complained to school officials, Mary Ellen says, "they didn't take it seriously."[12]

"A big aspect of bullying is on Myspace.com," says Ms. Petrey, a teacher at a low-income northeastern rural school: "All of a sudden girls come to school and complain that someone wrote on their Myspace page, 'She's a fat bitch' or 'She's a slut.' Sometimes students complain that there are kids that keep texting them. A couple of our special education kids have been consistent targets."

One girl with multiple sclerosis found that students made fun of not only her weight but her illness and her potentially short life span as well. One anonymous writer mocked her struggle with MS, saying, "I guess I'll have to wait until you kill yourself which I hope is not long from now, or I'll have to wait until your disease [MS] kills you." Not long after, the girl's car was egged, and acid was thrown at her front door, injuring her mother.[13]

As early as 2003, young people were falling victim to what has since been dubbed "cyberbullicide." Ryan Patrick Halligan, a boy with speech and motor coordination difficulties, had been bullied in person since he was in fifth grade in Essex Junction, Vermont. In the summer after seventh grade, Ryan spent a good deal of his time online; that October, he hanged himself in his home. On a website dedicated to Ryan, his father, John P. Halligan, writes: "A few days after his funeral I logged on to his AOL IM account because that was the one place he spent most of his time during the last few months. I logged on to see if there were any clues to his final action. It was in that safe world of being somewhat anonymous that several of his classmates told me of the bullying and cyber bullying that took place during the months that led up to his suicide." One bully had started spreading a rumor that Ryan was gay, and "the rumor and taunting continued beyond that school day . . . well into the night and during the summer of 2003."[14] Subsequently, Ryan began exchanging IMs with a popular girl, building a relationship with her. John P. Halligan describes what happened when Ryan's eighth-grade school year began:

> Ryan approached his new girlfriend in person. I'm sure he was never prepared to handle what happened next. In front of her friends she told him he was just a loser and that she did not want anything to do with him. She said she was only joking on-line. He found out that her friends and her thought it would be funny to make him think she liked him and to get him to say a lot of personal, embarrassing stuff. She copied and pasted there *[sic]* private IM exchanges into ones with her friends. They all had a good laugh at Ryan's expense.
>
> Now certainly my son was not the first boy in history to be bullied and have his heart crushed by a pretty girl's rejection. But when I discovered a folder filled with IM exchanges throughout the summer and further interviewed his classmates, I realized that technology was being utilized as weapons far more effective and reaching then the simple ones we had as kids. Passing handwritten notes or a "slam" book has since been replaced with on-line tools such as IM, Websites, Blogs, cell phones, etc. The list keeps growing with the invention of every new hi-tech communication gadget.
>
> It's one thing to be bullied and humiliated in front of a few kids. It's one thing to feel rejection and have your heart crushed by a girl. But it has to be a totally different experience then a generation ago when these hurts and humiliation are now witnessed by a far larger, online adolescent audience. I believe my son would have survived these incidents of bullying and humiliation if they took place before computers and the internet. But I believe there are few of us that that would have had the resiliency and stamina to sustain such a nuclear level attack on our feelings and reputation as a young teen in the midst of rapid physical and emotional changes and raging hormones. I believe bullying through technology has the effect of accelerating and amplifying the hurt to levels that will probably result in a rise in teen suicide rates.[15]

In fact, young people have been driven to suicide by face-to-face bullying as well as cyber-bullying—but the latter is likely to become more common as children spend even more of their time in the online world.

In another shocking incident that took place three years after Ryan's incident, Megan Meier killed herself in O'Fallon, Missouri, a few months before her fourteenth birthday; she had become the victim of a cruel online hoax. Lori Drew, the mother of one of Megan's friends with whom she'd had a falling out, created a false profile on Myspace, reportedly to find out what Megan was saying about her daughter. Drew posed as a sixteen-year-old boy named Josh Evans and developed a relationship with Megan online. At first friendly, "Josh" turned menacing and mean. Some of Megan's messages were shared with others, and Megan began receiving messages saying, "Megan Meier is a slut" and "Megan Meier is fat."[16] On the day of her death, Megan received a message from "Josh" that read: "Everybody in O'Fallon knows who you are. You are a bad person and everybody hates you. Have a bad rest of your life. The world would be a better place without you." Megan was found hanging in her bedroom closet.

Fifteen-year-old Irish immigrant Phoebe Prince was incessantly slut-bashed in person at her new high school in South Hadley, Massachusetts. After she hanged herself in the stairwell of her home in January 2010, schoolmates told school officials that she had also been "taunted by text messages and harassed on social networking sites like Facebook."[17]

In September of the same year, Tyler Clementi, a student at Rutgers University in New Jersey, committed suicide after his roommate filmed him during a sexual encounter with another young man and streamed it live on the Internet. In a case of grim irony, Tyler's final act before committing suicide was to post on his Facebook page: "Jumping off the gw bridge sorry."[18]

Efforts to Curb Cyber-Bullying

These incidents have provoked national attention and debate; policy makers have struggled to find laws to prosecute bullies who harass youth in cyberspace, but this has proved to be a formidable challenge. Some of the cyber-harassment (slut bashing and gay bashing) with which children contend would invite clearer legal attention and protection if it were done by an adult. In January 2006, the United States made it a federal crime to harass people on the Internet—but the laws apply only to people over the age of eighteen.[19] In many situations students have to fend for themselves, without legal recourse and often without adult advice or support. Meanwhile, teachers, parents, students, and other concerned people are struggling to keep up with the latest forms of hostility becoming norms in our schools.

Laws are often impotent when it comes to cyber-bullying, and in many cases, statutes prohibiting harassment come into conflict with First Amendment rights to free speech. Lori Drew, the adult in the Megan Meier case, was convicted by a federal jury in Los Angeles on three misdemeanor counts of computer fraud for "having misrepresented herself on the popular social network MySpace." Myspace required "truthful and accurate" registration information; prosecutors said Drew's fraudulent identity was a "violation of the Computer Fraud and Abuse Act of 1986." But parents often encourage their children to use false identities to protect themselves from adult stalkers on the Internet, and others argue that they have good reasons to remain anonymous online. A federal judge later threw out the verdict.[20] Two students who bullied Phoebe Prince were among the first in the United States to be prosecuted for perpetuating school bullying; they received a year's probation and one hundred hours of community service.[21]

Other efforts to address cyber-bullying are more education oriented. Dan Savage and his husband Terry Miller launched a laudable program the "It Gets Better Project," in which more than ten thousand people around the world, including President Barack Obama, have posted inspiring stories on YouTube describing how they overcame their own youthful traumas. Savage and Miller were moved to create the project when they heard that Indiana teenager Billy Lucas had committed suicide because he was brutally gay-bashed.[22] The purpose of the project is to encourage beleaguered students, especially those who are being gay-bashed, to look forward to a better future after high school; the idea that school could itself become a compassionate and peaceful environment is considered inconceivable by the premise of the otherwise phenomenal project. The unintended message, it seems, is there is nothing anyone can do for you now.

Much of the information available regarding what to do about cyber-bullying is indeed conflicting and discouraging. The best-selling *Bullying beyond the Schoolyard: Preventing and Responding to Cyberbullying* (2009), by Sameer Hinduja and Justin Patchin, recommends handling cyber-bullying in the same ways as other infractions—including suspension and expulsion for the most serious offenses.[23] Schools are cautioned to educate students about the dangers lurking on the computer, and parents are told "to turn the computer off" when the abuse gets out of hand.[24] Schools are also told to handle complaints swiftly in order to prevent lawsuits; some schools try to block certain websites from faculty and students, but this is difficult to enforce "if the student knows where to go and how to do it."[25]

These recommendations, while well-meaning, are unlikely to change the social climate so that cyber-bullying is less common in the first place—especially when cyber bullies manage to remain anonymous. Chapter 10 suggests specific techniques for creating a kinder cyberspace so that bullying will be less likely to occur at all. Rather than assume that bullying will take place no matter what—and that perpetrators need to be disciplined, suspended, and expelled, and computers confiscated—we need to help students develop more compassionate relationships with themselves and others.

Internet Addiction and Social Isolation

Hinduja and Patchin write further that cyber-bullying leads to "school problems such as tardiness and truancy, eating disorders, chronic illness, self-esteem problems, aggression, depression, interpersonal violence, substance abuse, other forms of delinquency, and suicidal ideation and suicide."[26] Research shows, however, that students use electronic technology, including the Internet and cell phones, as a means of socialization more than any other medium. Children and teens report that they are afraid that if their cyber-abuse experiences are discovered their parents will revoke computer privileges and that they will then be isolated and disconnected from their peers even more. For many young people, such a prohibition is seen as more intolerable than enduring cyber-abuse.[27] Children literally would rather withstand the harassment than be cut off from their main means of socializing with one another.

Parents and teachers also often report that they are at a loss when it comes to helping children navigate these spaces. "Back in the day," says Ms. Willis, "teachers explained the history of problems that took place in school to the parents. 'We've seen it escalating and we want to talk with you about it.'" "Now," she says: "Parents know, but they think it is none of our business." Ms. Willis said when she is aware of text message harassment she tries to take the phone away. "If I take a cell phone away from a kid, I get a call from a parent. There's a school rule—no cell phones. But the parents tell them to keep it in their pocket. They want the kids to be able to call them. Then the kids become skilled in hiding it."

In an age of terrorism and a proliferation of school shootings, it is understandable that parents want their children to carry cell phones. Obviously, technology can be used in ways that promote connections, provide support and some measure of safety, and keep fluid the communication among loved ones. Why, though, does so much cruelty take place through these vehicles too? Technology has been blamed for increases in various diagnoses such as attention deficit disorder, inability to develop positive face-to-face relationships, reduced manners, poor writing skills, and sedentary lifestyles, as well as addictions to video games, texting, and the Internet in general.[28]

Surely, it is not technology itself that is at fault, but rather the values that dominate the social landscapes of young and old alike. In a culture that values independence and self-reliance to such extremes over connection, community, and interdependence, technology is more likely to be used as a means of escape from others. Indeed, my students talk about how they often pretend to text just to avoid potentially uncomfortable face-to-face social situations. This behavior has been named: "fauxting."[29]

Fauxting takes place because many young people are scared to appear lonely, bored, or in any way socially unsuccessful; an awkward encounter, for instance, could undermine one's reputation—and that danger is often perceived as worse than the possible benefits derived from having a potentially positive face-to-face interaction. Many youth don't want to risk undermining the images they've projected on their social networking sites by being caught off guard and appearing vulnerable and fallible in person. Instead, most socializing among youth takes place in cyberspace with carefully constructed personalities—and much of it becomes mean.

When people are encouraged to derive pleasure from winning in the face of another's loss, hurtful behaviors toward others makes some sense. When young people find that acting casual is rewarded more than expressing feelings, it stands to reason that technology will be used as a way to "tune out," rendering oneself unavailable to the human interactions that might otherwise create intimacy. Where people are judged negatively for their imperfections, it is likely that many will create false images on their Facebook pages, lie on their online dating sites, or attack others from anonymous user names in order to differentiate themselves from others' flaws. In a society that demands that people present perfected versions of themselves and that discourages authentic connections, technology is used as a means of escape.

Given these conditions, more teens are retreating to cyberspace for their social interactions. The Pew Research Center study "Teens and Mobile Phones" (2010) cites concerns that young people are talking to each other less and are instead texting one another. Over half of teens surveyed (54 percent) reported using texting on a daily basis to communicate with friends, while only 33 percent reported interacting with friends on a daily basis by talking to each other outside of school. The frequency of texting was also remarkable—half of those surveyed sent upwards of fifty text messages daily (1,500 a month), and one in three sent more than one hundred a day (3,000 per month).[30]

Indeed, one-third of Internet use by Americans takes place on social networking sites, and the amount of time Americans spend on sites like Facebook and Twitter grows dramatically every day. Teenagers who are thought to be addicted to the Internet are 2.5 times more likely to be depressed than those who engage in normal use;[31] but normal use, in contemporary America, is still "most of the time." While the research is still inconclusive, males are perceived to be more at risk for Internet addiction and related depression, replacing face-to-face intimacy and other relationships that could otherwise provide deeper and more fulfilling experiences.[32]

Scholars are also concerned that new technologies are not just interfering with face-to-face relationships but also preventing the development of emotional sensitivity, empathy, and reciprocity in relationships. Lauren D. LaPorta believes that young people who use social networking sites frequently create "alternative, solipsistic realities" where those who disagree with them are excluded. LaPorta writes that the result is isolation and alienation, as well as an increased tendency toward narcissism that may also lead to associated behaviors such as increases in violence and aggression. More than half the teen profiles on Myspace reference risky and violent behaviors.[33]

LaPorta further laments that youth escape to the Internet as a result of her curious belief that schools have made self-esteem a foundation of their missions. She suggests that this movement has bred a generation of young people who expect praise as their due and who have little motivation to work hard; she believes that young people turn instead to networking sites for the empty praise that they have become accustomed to, and that is otherwise less common in the reality they face after they finish their education. Yet online communication is not particularly affirming much of the time; instead, many people experience cyber-bullying, harassment, and other forms of negative interactions.

Rather than searching vainly for empty praise, it seems more likely that young people are anxious to find a connection that feels increasingly out of reach in face-to-face realities (as well as in cyberspace). Indeed, Americans of all ages appear to be starving for satisfying relationships. As noted in the previous chapter, the number of people with whom the average American discusses "important matters" has decreased significantly: three times as many Americans in 2004 as in 1985 said they had no one to talk to about important matters—25 percent of those surveyed. In 2004, most spoke about important matters in their life with two people; twenty years ago the average was closer to three.[34] Amid this increase in social isolation, the computer may create the false impression that love, friendship, and intimacy needs are being met—while emotional avoidance is actually the more dominant feature of both face-to-face and cyberspace relationships in contemporary times.

Friendship, on social networking sites, tends to be reduced to the number of people an individual can "collect"; this increases the person's status, as such "friends" are displayed on profiles for others to see and admire. A person can literally sport thousands of Facebook "friends" but have no more than one or two people (if any) that they speak to about important matters in their lives.

Like Keanu Reeves's character Neo in the 1999 film *The Matrix*, we are often sitting by ourselves, believing we are engaged in exciting adventures and involved in intimate relationships, when in reality our main companions are hardware. Many look for solace in these virtual worlds to escape the cruelty and/or banality of everyday life. Yet the harshness and anonymity in cyberspace can become even more daunting.

Additionally, the new Internet addiction phenomenon and its correlated increase in depression are problematic among teens as well as adults. Depression and addiction more generally are connected with decreased social connections and difficulty developing intimacy. Such symptoms are likely to develop when men and women alike are counseled to strive to be hyperindependent, self-reliant, unemotional, tough, and cavalier about their relationships.[35]

Enforcing masculinity norms to the exclusion of values relating to empathy and compassion is a recipe for violence, isolation, and despair.

To start to transform these dynamics, both face to face and in cyberspace, we need to clearly understand the culture of masculinity underlying our social interactions. Further, we need to know better how these masculinity norms come to saturate our schools, undermine our emotional health, and contort our behaviors toward one another—as well as why they persist in the larger society.

Many adults, (and youth) don't even recognize violence when they see it; others are integral members of the gender police themselves, both online and face to face, working hard to make sure "boys are boys" and "girls are girls" and often "disciplining" adults and young people alike if they are perceived as stepping outside their prescribed gender parameters. Adults come by their blindness fairly, however; the following chapters examine the relationship between our larger bully economy and the primary masculinity expectations it creates among adults as well as children, in a wide variety of U.S. social spheres.

7

Adult Bullies

In the suicide note found after the Columbine massacre, Eric Harris blamed the classmates who tormented him, but he also accused the adults who allowed it to happen:

> By now, it's over. If you are reading this, my mission is complete. . . . Your children who have ridiculed me, who have chosen not to accept me, who have treated me like I am not worth their time are dead. THEY ARE FUCKING DEAD. . . .
>
> Surely you will try to blame it on the clothes I wear, the music I listen to, or the way I choose to present myself, but no. Do not hide behind my choices. You need to face the fact that this comes as a result of YOUR CHOICES.
>
> Parents and teachers, you fucked up. You have taught these kids to not accept what is different. YOU ARE IN THE WRONG. I have taken their lives and my own—but it was your doing. Teachers, parents, LET THIS MASSACRE BE ON YOUR SHOULDERS UNTIL THE DAY YOU DIE.[1]

Eric and his friend Dylan Klebold were, of course, the ones who made the vicious choice to pick up guns and respond to bullying with murder. Like so many other school shooters, however, they were left largely on their own to deal with the humiliation, exclusion, and violence they faced daily at school. That's why many of them said they retaliated. In 166 school shootings between 1979 and 2009, recall that over 150 parents, teachers, administrators, coaches, and other adults were killed or wounded.

According to the memoir written by Brooks Brown, who said he had been one of Dylan's close friends since grade school, the abuse he and Dylan experienced came not only from other students but from teachers as well. In second grade, Brooks recalled, he and Dylan were playing in the mud and accidentally splashed a little girl's new jacket. They tried to explain that it wasn't on purpose, but their teacher glared at them and insisted they spend hours cleaning the jacket with a toothbrush as punishment for what was perceived as their malicious deed. "Don't you have any respect for other people's property?" the teacher yelled. Brooks said, "It was the first time in our young lives that we felt like an adult hated us." The teachers were no better than the kids, he continued. They picked on students for the smallest infraction, mocking them for picking their nose, ridiculing them in front of their peers. Some were especially cruel to the boys and others nastier to the girls.[2]

The mean-spirited hierarchy, writes Brooks, was replayed in one way or another by those who had the most power in school—teachers, coaches, and principals, as well as those referred to as jocks. They often seemed to take it for granted that the less popular students would be treated badly. According to Brooks, he and Dylan got into a special program for highly intelligent students and found themselves hit on the head by those sitting behind them, while the teachers looked the other way.[3]

Eric Harris's concerns about teachers were echoed in the online journal of Kimveer Gill, the twenty-five-year-old who wounded twenty people and killed one before committing suicide at Dawson College in Montreal in September 2006. This Canadian case contains some variations on most school shooting stories: Kimveer was not a student at the time of the shooting, and his friends said that in high school he had been quiet and introverted but not a target of bullies. Whether this was the case or not, however, this alienated young man identified with bullying victims, and he carried out his shooting in a school setting. He, too, placed blame on an adult society that created brutal hierarchies and then ignored their effects.

> I'm so sick of hearing about jocks and preps making life hard for the goths and others who look different, or are different. . . . Why does society applaud jocks? I don't understand. They are the worse kind of people on earth. And the preps are no better, they think they're better than others . . . but they're not. And all of society applauds the jocks and preps. As if we are all supposed to be like them. Newsflash motherfuckers: We will never be like them. NEVER.
>
> Stop Bullying It's not only the bully's fault you know!! It's the teachers and principals fault for turning a blind eye, just cuz it's not their job. You fuckers are pathetic. It's the police's fault for not doing

anything when people conplain *[sic]*. . . It's society's fault for acting like it's normal for people to be assholes to each other. Society disgusts me. It's everyone's fault for being so apathetic towards fucking everything that doesn't affect them personally.[4]

Kimveer, like all of the school shooters, made his own abhorrent choices. Yet he, like Eric, expressed a concern worth addressing: To what extent do adults contribute to school bullying—and especially gender-based bullying?

Some adults ignore, condone, or dismiss bullying even when it takes place among children and teens in their own communities, schools, and families. Others bully children themselves and subject them to humiliation and abuse, pressing them into the narrow gender roles that harm young people and sabotage school cultures. Often adults model these same behaviors in their treatment of one another too. Every disturbing behavior present in schools, from superficial status competition to sexual harassment and gay bashing to endemic racism, exists on a far larger scale in the adult world—buttressed by hypermasculine and hyperfeminine standards enforced by the gender police.

Parent Bullies

I heard about these issues when I interviewed a number of parents and students in one northeastern affluent suburb. Laura, co-president of the local parent organization, concluded that parents are so used to bullying behavior that they simply don't see it—and that when they do, many think that it is normal. "A parent will call another mother and say, 'Little Joey is picking on my son on the bus. He's calling my son nasty names and my son is very upset.' And it is not unusual to hear from that parent: 'Oh well, that's just kids, what's the big deal, it's just boys being boys.'" There isn't much a parent can do if the other parent refuses to recognize the problem, lamented Laura, who had had this experience with her own son.

Tiffany, a mother also in the PTA, encountered something similar with her daughter Amy. All of a sudden, Amy was targeted by Bethany, a girl who had a lot of power in the school. Bethany didn't want to be friends with Amy and convinced other people not to be friends with Amy either. Amy was so distraught that she attempted suicide. When Tiffany tried to talk to Janet, Bethany's mother, Janet "blew it off as 'Amy was just being oversensitive."' Although her daughter's bullying had caused another child such anguish that she tried to take her own life, Janet refused to take the issue seriously.

It is not surprising that so many parents deny or condone bullying by their children; they may practice the same behaviors themselves or fall victim to bullying by other adults in their lives. They may see this behavior everywhere and on some level consider it normal. Laura described her own experiences with adult bullying: "We've moved around a lot, and this is the hardest place we ever lived. You're not embraced, and if you don't have money you feel out of it. The worst cliques are around our children's sports. But even if your child is involved in sports, you have to be very outgoing or you tend to get left out." She continued, "The parents push the children really hard, but they also bully other parents to make sure their children get to play. The sports here are extremely competitive and aggressive."

As Laura talked candidly about her own difficulties, she might just as easily have been describing the cliques so prevalent in most high schools and middle schools. Even the criteria for popularity were the same: wealth, athletic achievement, superficial self-confidence, and aggressive behavior. Another woman I interviewed concurred: "Yes, it is very clear who is in the 'in' clique and who is not. Those that are 'in' have a lot of power in the community."

Another local parent, Susan, also agreed. Her nine-year-old daughter Alice was bullied by another girl the same age, Tina. Tina managed to get her daughter's computer password and used it to torment Alice. Alice enjoyed a website where she could acquire virtual pets that she virtually fed, groomed, and pet; Alice had six pets that she loved, and she took care of them diligently and proudly. Then she woke up one morning to find all her animals gone: Tina had wiped them out. Alice was devastated. Susan told me that Tina continued to manipulate Alice's emotions even after this incident occurred. "She would say, 'I'm your great friend,' and then, 'I hate you and I don't want to be your friend.'" Each rejection stung and upset Alice further. Soon she became afraid of the girl, afraid to go to school, afraid of what else Tina would do to her. Susan became concerned and got up the courage to call Miranda, Tina's mother. Miranda responded curtly: "We don't want to accuse anybody," she said.

"I'm afraid of the mom," admitted Susan. She knew Miranda was a trial attorney and a powerful member of the community, and she saw right away that Miranda was going to handle the situation contentiously. When she was president of the school's parent organization, "this mother blasted us because she didn't like the math curriculum. But we don't have anything to do with the math curriculum. The daughter is a lot like the mom. She is learning from her mother. I think her mom is mean to her . . . She intimidates teachers and principals and other mothers. She is charming one day and the next day very mean. When the mother decided she didn't like one of the teachers, she started bashing her left and right. I think it was because the teacher took a strong stand against the daughter's bullying behavior. But teachers and principals are also intimidated by her . . . When she threatens to sue, people get scared," continued Susan. "Parents of bullies are not willing to admit that their child is a bully, but we have to ask: Where does a kid learn this stuff?"

"Bullying behavior is modeled first at home," Laura agreed. It can also be modeled at school, according to another parent, Joanna, from the same affluent suburb, who worked as a teacher and saw it firsthand. The teachers "yell at them at the top of their lungs and single children out and call them dumb in front of the other kids. It's not the children that are the problem," she said.

Looking the Other Way

The sexual harassment, dating violence, gay bashing, slut bashing, and class and race hostilities that take place daily in our schools are often ignored or dismissed by adults—when they are recognized at all. Because there is so much bullying and harassment in our culture, so-called lower-level violence tends not to appear on the radar until it has reached an extreme level, so early interventions tend to be rare. Instead, abusive behaviors are left to fester in school hallways, playgrounds, classrooms and in cyberspace.

Children often do not tell their parents or teachers that they are being bullied. They may be humiliated or ashamed, reluctant to be seen as a "tattler," or afraid that it will only make the bullying worse. Adults inadvertently encourage this reticence when they teach their students not to tattle on others. It may make their jobs easier if they don't have to address every concern a child raises, but they might also miss something important. Young people need to talk about their concerns, whatever they may be, and to receive adult support and guidance on how to address them.

Sometimes children may not share their difficulties because they are not sure that adults will be willing or able to do anything about the bullying—and with good reason. According to a National Association of School Psychologists fact sheet, "Over two-thirds of students believe that schools respond poorly to bullying, with a high percentage of students believing that adult help is infrequent and ineffective." In fact, 25 percent of teachers "see nothing wrong with bullying or putdowns," and these teachers intervene in just 4 percent of bullying incidents, according to one study.[5]

A guidance counselor from a middle-class southern area told me that 50 percent of her students say they are bullied, but it is mostly just kids who "don't know how to handle other kids." She explains, "Kids get pushed around. They play too rough"—but that's not necessarily bullying, according to her. It begs the question regarding who defines what bullying is. If students feel they are being bullied, it makes it even harder for them if the adults in their community don't recognize it as such, and it becomes much less likely that students will get the support they need even when they ask for it.

Teachers and other school faculty too often are part of the problem rather than part of the solution. In an ABC News special called "The In Crowd and Social Cruelty," researchers found that an incident of bullying took place every eight minutes on the playground and that girls were as likely to bully as boys. When interviewed, teachers said they intervened in bullying "all the time." Yet the researchers observed the teachers intervening less than 5 percent of the time. Teachers and other adults in school often characterize what they see as "horseplay" and normal adolescent dynamics, while the victims find these same situations painful and overwhelming.[6] Alane Fagin, director of Child Abuse Prevention Services in Long Island, New York, says that adults sometimes allow bullying and hazing to fester. Many students believe that adults don't care because they do nothing when they witness bullying. This sends a clear message to children: if they become victims, no one will step up to help them. Bystanders to incidents often fear that they will become victims themselves if they try to intervene, and there is no mechanism for them to speak out safely.[7]

Andrea Cohn and Andrea Canter outline the multiple ways in which adults tend to not only condone but actually encourage bullying. Under "home factors," they write: "Bullying behavior is reinforced when it has no or inconsistent consequences. Additionally, children who observe parents and siblings exhibiting bullying behavior, or who are themselves victims, are likely to develop bullying behaviors. When children receive negative messages or physical punishment at home, they tend to develop negative self-concepts and expectations, and may therefore attack before they are attacked—bullying others gives them a sense of power and importance."[8] When school personnel ignore bullying, children get the message that intimidating others is acceptable. "Bullying also thrives in an environment where students are more likely to receive negative feedback and negative attention than in a positive school climate that fosters respect and sets high standards for interpersonal behavior," write Cohn and Canter.[9]

Bullied students do tend to remember the few times when a teacher stepped in to help them, however. Natasha, from a northeastern middle-class suburb, recalled a girl, Linda, in her gym class who was staring at her. When Natasha asked her to stop, Linda said: "I can look at you if I want to." Linda had been bullying Natasha throughout the year, and Natasha was wearing down. She went to the locker room to get away from her. "I was crying," Natasha told me, "and this teacher came after me." When Natasha explained what had happened, the teacher said to Linda, "Do you realize you made this girl cry?" Linda said, "I don't care." "You should apologize," the teacher instructed. "Whatever, I'm sorry," said Linda. The teacher recognized the lack of authenticity and communicated the need to make a sincere apology. "I'm very sorry Natasha," Linda tried again. "I didn't mean to make you cry." "That was the end with her," Natasha shared. "The teacher knew the situation and Linda didn't bother me again." It took very little to end what had been a pattern of targeted attacks.

Adults too often exacerbate rather than mitigate such difficulties, though. "Teachers play favorites," said Natasha, and look the other way when the favored students engage in bullying. When students make fun of others in class, she said, "the teacher will just say, 'It's time to be quiet,' and go back to teaching. It is rare for a teacher to grab it and try to fix the situation. When teachers hear the abuse and ignore it, it makes it worse. Very few teachers help." That's why it was so powerful when her teacher asked Linda to apologize. "It was so rare for a teacher to take action. So when they do, we know they mean business."

Alissa, from a northeastern urban area, told me that she had always thought of herself as different; being poor was difficult enough, but Alissa was also almost blind. It took a while before the school figured out she needed help with her vision. Once Alissa got glasses, she did better in school, but she remained self-conscious and awkward, and the harassment she had endured before she got the glasses persisted. Alissa remembers fondly the few teachers who "rescued" her from the isolation and bullying she otherwise experienced. "Kids wouldn't hang out with me—the normal kids. I was so alone I would count the little rocks in the pavement. I had nothing to do." Her science teacher told Alissa she could stay with him during recess. "We created a zoo for abandoned animals. Another teacher made me an editor of the school newspaper and let me hide in his little office until junior high school was over." As Natasha and Alissa recall the positive impact of these small efforts made by a handful of teachers acting on their own, it is possible to imagine how much better things might be if school policies focused on creating systemic support and respect in the school, where students could feel part of a safe community.

In my experience as a mediation coordinator in New York City public high schools, I found that for boys, who are taught that emotions are a sign of weakness and a threat to their manhood, simply providing a safe space where feelings can be shared often becomes an opportunity for them to express themselves and avoid violence. Thomas was a fifteen-year-old who came to me because he was being teased every day. Other high school students called him gay and faggot and other names that implied he lacked manhood; he was feeling isolated. Thomas was a smart boy, thin and serious-looking. He looked at me intently when he talked, as if he was trying to connect and show me respect. He looked very sad when he came to my office this time. He knew the boys who were teasing him, but he didn't want them to know that he'd told an adult about the teasing. Instead he stopped coming to school, and his grades dropped. I was having a hard time helping him because he was so rarely in school. With his permission, I managed to talk to the other students without mentioning how I knew that the teasing was taking place. I said that I had noticed it going on in the hallways, as I did after Thomas indicated to me when to look out for it. I asked one of them to come to my office and sit across from the table from Thomas. Thomas didn't say anything and didn't want to start. I initiated the conversation and expressed my concern about the teasing I had noticed. Thomas murmured that it upset him. The other boy, John, looked startled that Thomas expressed his feelings so openly in front of him. John said he was sorry and he would stop and would tell the other boys to stop too. We wrote an agreement that described this commitment, including a promise that both boys would treat each other with respect. We all signed the contract and kept a copy. Thomas started coming back to school and let me know that it seemed okay now. Creating an environment where expressing feelings was encouraged and supported made a big difference for these boys.

Mediation programs are much more prevalent in schools today, which can help—but they also need to be part of a wider school effort that promotes community and positive interpersonal relationships. Without institutional supports, it can be challenging even for teachers to step up, just as it is for students. Ms. Kahn, who teaches at an elite all-boys private school, told me: "It's hard for teachers to respond appropriately to bullying without further isolating the victim. They could easily be further mocked or talked down to in class, and it just embarrasses the student more." Worse, she said, "many teachers encourage or participate in it. . . . They laugh at it, repeat the jokes, allow it, think it is funny— some teachers will do anything to endear themselves to students. . . . It's hard to know where to draw the line." For bullying to be addressed effectively, teachers need to know that the administration will back them up and that the school promotes and prioritizes a positive school climate. Yet often schools are concerned that their reputations will suffer if they address bullying too openly, and/or they worry that trying to temper the competitive aggressive proclivities among students will undermine their athletic or academic achievements. Many experts believe, however, that the opposite is true: coaches, for instance, who focus on cooperation and helping all team members bond with one another are often more effective in racking up wins for their schools than those who depend on more hierarchical cultures, which include hazing.[10]

Coach Bullies: Masculinity and Hazing

When adults promote hypermasculine behaviors, they inadvertently or even directly play a role in creating the bullying behavior that pervades so many schools. Some teachers have the same attitudes as the bullies in their classes and encourage the bullying toward students who are perceived as less "masculine." In fact, studies in American schools reveal that most school administrators perceive that less mainstream students (e.g., "geeks" and "Goths") are violent, even though the football players ("jocks") are the ones who are more likely to beat up the less conventional students.[11] Even among adults, the jocks' high social status tends to legitimize or even encourage their abusive behavior especially toward boys considered less masculine.

Students referred to as jocks represent the epitome of American manhood and success; they tend to be competitive, dominant, and powerful, exhibiting Connell's hegemonic masculinity. Adults are often unable to see beyond this social conditioning. Likewise, adults are less likely to intervene when girls who are perceived to be pretty, well-dressed, and popular engage in similarly cruel behavior.[12] School faculty also may overlook hurtful behavior if the perpetrators are white and wealthy.

Gay bashing is perhaps most likely to be ignored or even condoned, since so many adults are themselves homophobic to one degree or another; some teachers and school administrators are more likely to condemn openly gay students for "flaunting" their sexuality than they are to punish their tormenters.[13] The same adults rarely intervene, however, when they see flamboyant heterosexuality—boys bragging and speaking contemptuously about their sexual exploits with girls, for instance. Adults also often judge girls according to their own beliefs about "appropriate" sexuality for females, and then girls get slut-bashed by adults as well as peers. The adult gender police is sometimes more scrutinizing and more punitive than the child and teen versions, partly because adults often have institutional power to enforce their gender expectations and to discipline perceived transgressors.

Within the sports culture of many schools, bullying is an institutionalized practice as well as a rite of passage—so much so that it has earned its own term, *hazing*. Hank Nuwer, author of multiple books on hazing, is concerned about the pro-hazing message in sports. At a National Conference on Hazing at Adelphi University in 2006, Nuwer pointed to two precepts that he finds particularly troubling: "To be a woman is to be less than a man" and "Hazing is fine to role-model for youngsters." Nuwer believes that coaches and senior team members consistently encourage hypermasculine, homophobic values that are hurtful, sometimes violent, and even deadly. Young boys are taught to reject their empathic, compassionate, emotional, or "feminine" parts of themselves and to prove their manhood by hurting others and showing off their dominance and power.[14]

New students expect to get hazed as part of their initiation onto a given team—and they anticipate coaches' looking away or approving of the time-honored rituals. Then all sorts of degrading and humiliating acts are performed on them. For instance, in one working-class rural area, Coach Lang found that his senior football players made the freshmen lick the urinals;

they also taped the freshmen up and shaved them in the locker rooms. Hazing expert Hank Nuwer reports at least 95 deaths related to hazing in the last three decades (1979–2009). According to the University of Connecticut, since 1970, there has been at least one hazing related death on a college campus each year; almost 25 percent of high school students on sports teams report being hazed.[15]

These kinds of behaviors are often anticipated by coaches. The game is being tough and sacrificing everything to win—even if, ironically, what boys are asked to sacrifice in hazing is their manhood itself. When coaches approve and encourage these activities, boys get the message that treating others with a lack of respect is normal and appropriate—and those boys who are victims of violent hazing get the message that they cannot report the abuse to their coaches. Instead, targets of hazing are expected to seek their revenge on the next set of new recruits.

Elizabeth J. Allan and Mary M. Madden, from the University of Maine, report on faculty complicity in their national study of student hazing. They write that 25 percent of the students who reported being involved in hazing behaviors said that a coach or organization advisor was aware of the activity, and 22 percent reported that the coach or advisor was actually involved in the hazing itself. Students suggested that they did not see their coaches as sources of support for hazing prevention because the adults were directly involved in the hazing and because there would be retribution by other students if it was revealed that they had shared the information. As one student explained, "I don't know anyone I could go to [to talk about hazing]. . . . I don't think there is anyone you could really turn to. If you turned to your coach and your team finds out, then good luck dealing with your team."[16]

Yet it is not entirely the fault of individual parents, teachers, administrators, or even coaches who support, ignore, or promote this behavior. All these forms of hurtful and harassing activities are reified in a hypercompetitive economic, political, and social culture that serves to normalize these behaviors and render them effectively invisible. Coaches who may not even approve of their teams' hazing cultures, for example, may come to believe that it is the only way to win games and keep their jobs.

As program director of the former Sports Leadership Institute at Adelphi University, working with the successful program Athletes Helping Athletes, Paul Grafer said that sometimes coaches consciously create or enable a hazing culture on their sports teams. "They do what they can to promote this kind of environment . . . It's a wins- or losses-focused business." It's less about education and more about how to get more wins, Grafer told me in a 2007 interview. "Even coaches who have great intentions find that the current system is not set up for them. There's tremendous pressure on them to win. High school coaches have to win or they are going to lose their jobs, and sometimes what they think they have to do to win can compromise their educational goals and the social part of the process."[17]

Thus, the coach may use bullying and hazing to support team hierarchy and to execute power plays that the coach thinks will help win games. Grafer says these coaches "directly or indirectly promote a system that benefits the hierarchy in their team. They have a student to go to when they want to address certain issues." Parents often support this environment as well. They too are focused on winning; they have a lottery mentality, Grafer explains. Many parents think that youth sports will pay off in college. Winning is everything because there are a few sports scholarships at stake. It's a zero-sum game, because someone will win and everyone else will lose. Grafer says there are actually more academic scholarships available than sports scholarships, but parents often focus on winning big in sports—partly because of the lottery mentality but also because sports success tends to confer masculinity status on both the teen players and, often in particular, the fathers. In many communities, the whole family wins greater recognition when their children win in sports, yet these kinds of accolades and acknowledgments are less often given when students are successful academically.[18]

As a result of the emphasis on these kinds of values in many communities, and the presence of the gender police enforcing these priorities, parents often cling to their own status as high school jocks. Mr. Lang said that football is so revered in his small rural town that there is effectively a "club of adults who played up to twenty years ago, and other adults who are still excluded if they didn't play football." Some of these parents, who appear to be trying to recapture their own days when they felt idolized, then pressure their children to excel at sports. Parents who came to believe that the only way to get recognition in school, particularly as a male, was to win in sports and bully others are sometimes anxious to make sure their children learn these difficult lessons early.

Parents bully kids all the time at sports events, said Rick, who was from the same working-class rural area. "It's the biggest pressure parents put on kids." A common comment by fathers on Rick's baseball team was

"Hit a home run and I'll buy you a supper." "A few of the kids on my baseball team don't get any hits and they commit errors on the field. Parents will give them hell. They take the kid behind the dugout and yell at them: 'Don't you know that this is your fuckin' life,' they say. They want their kids to be star athletes. 'You've got to do better than this,' they threaten."

Such aggressive behavior can be found among sports parents in all economic groups. Chris said that in his middle-class suburb he heard parents bully their sons in particular. "Be tough. Show them who's boss," were common refrains. "The sentiment is that if he doesn't perform in sports, if there is the tiniest weakness, he gets penalized by his parents," Chris continued. "They want their kids to be perfectly tough. You hear them say: 'You're not focusing hard enough. You're not kicking enough field goals or you're letting yourself get tackled too much.' There's reinforcement from parents that they have to dominate everyone else. The stress parents put on athletes cause them to lash out at others. They let their anger out on someone else because they feel harassed by their parents. You hear them being called 'failures,' or 'worthless.' Then these kids turn on other people, call them 'loser,' and lash out the way they are taught by their parents."

In one article looking at the most extreme incidents from 2005 alone, Regan McMahon reported that a "father in Philadelphia had pulled a .357 Magnum on his son's football coach, enraged that his son wasn't getting enough playing time—in an Under-7 Pee Wee football game." In another incident, during warm-ups, a "T-ball coach from a suburb of Pittsburgh, Pa., was sentenced to one to six years for offering one of his players, an 8-year-old boy, $25 to throw the ball at a teammate, a mildly autistic 9-year-old." The coach was hoping the less competent player would get injured and become "too sore to play" in the playoff game. Finally, McMahon mentions an "assistant coach for a San Joaquin County youth football team [who] ran onto the field during a game . . . and rammed his big adult body into the back of a player who was guilty of a late hit on his 13-year-old son." Violence among parents involved in children's sports increased fourfold between 2000 and 2005.[19] In the most famous case of sports parent bullying, a Massachusetts father beat another father to death after an argument at a teen hockey game while both their sons looked on.[20] Adult men driven by masculinity codes and expectations can be particularly dangerous members of the gender police. Some will do anything to prevent a challenge to their son's masculinity, which, they have also been told, throws into question their own.

Adults also participate in the scorn and social exclusion that often accompanies hazing incidents. One mother who helped organize Mothers against School Hazing talked about her son's experience of being hazed. Karen Savoy's son Jake was stripped nude, taped to a bench, beaten until he bled, and sexually assaulted in the football locker room. It was the ritual at this high school that children were hazed on their birthday; Jake had turned sixteen the day it happened.[21] At first, Jake didn't tell his parents what happened because he didn't want to ruin his birthday for them, but his parents saw the bruises. There were fifteen coaches on duty and in the vicinity of the hazing incident. No one saw anything and no one did anything. Jake fell into a deep depression and quit the team. He loved playing baseball, but the costs were too high. Their family had been well known and liked in the community, but "after the incident, we were considered dirt. We were spit at," said Karen Savoy. People told her, "Why don't you just let it go." But she insisted, "Letting it go is not letting it heal, letting it go is to forget."[22] Such reactions from the community are unfortunately typical, as people rally to support their star athletes and even blame the victims for their own abuse. The masculine code "You should be able to take it" is used to excuse or condone many of these crimes, whereas the support and compassion that targets of such abuse sorely need are, in such cases, hard to find.

A whole community may even become complicit in the gender police's dirty work; people will isolate and attack both the victim and his or her family, as the family's wounds are sometimes seen as throwing cherished masculinity codes into question. If people in the community recognized that the hazing behaviors were wrong, then what does it say about other time-honored traditions that few people want to question? Wedded to masculinity "truths," a community can render themselves unable to be the kind and caring neighbors so needed in such a situation, and instead collude with the young perpetrators of the crime.

Such ritualized bullying sometimes continues into adulthood. When a drunken New Year's Eve brawl at a Staten Island firehouse in 2003 left one firefighter maimed for life and another facing criminal assault charges, some questioned the "firehouse culture"—but others rushed to defend it. In a *New York Times* op-ed called "Hazing and Heroism," Tom Downey acknowledged that new recruits were forced to "earn the respect of veterans by enduring the silent treatment, tolerating jeers about their masculinity and bravery, and performing menial tasks like taking out the garbage and cleaning bathrooms."[23]

Adults are cruel toward one another in many of the same ways as students are. In fact it is likely that young people learn these behaviors from the adults in their lives—who are themselves enduring all kinds of damaging and painful abuse too.

Bullied Teachers

In a pattern that parallels behavior among schoolchildren, powerful school faculty often bully teachers. New teachers are expected to tolerate these conditions. When they become veterans, if they make it that far, many turn around and treat the next batch of new teachers badly too.

Like most workplaces, schools traditionally organize their adult faculty and staff in strict hierarchies, where those with more status are more powerful and better paid than those with less. Teachers are usually at the bottom of the hierarchy, after principals, assistant principals, and deans. In schools where sports define the town and the school, coaches are sometimes ranked above teachers. While veteran teachers may rank below administrators and coaches in such cases, they tend to be higher on the hierarchy than new instructors.

These conditions—and not just curricular demands or low pay—can drive many promising new teachers out of the profession, according to a 2005 article by the teacher Mary Patterson. When she joined the Longfellow Middle School faculty in Berkeley, California, Patterson was disturbed by how new teachers were treated. She saw the problem as comparable to hazing, which she defined as "institutional practices and policies that result in new teachers experiencing poorer working conditions than their veteran colleagues." Many veteran faculty are simply too busy in their daily teaching jobs to notice that their new colleagues' decisions to leave their positions might result from unfair institutional practices rather than inexperience, writes Patterson. The least experienced teachers, she found, nevertheless routinely had the most difficult jobs. These attitudes extended beyond the classroom. When Patterson once proposed that their scarce staff parking be assigned by lottery rather than by seniority, several veteran colleagues actually booed the suggestion.[24]

When I presented a new program to the faculty of a large New York City public high school, I too was booed. As a new twenty-three-year-old faculty member, I was asked to train teachers and students in conflict resolution and mediation in order to help prevent and resolve fights and other conflicts in the school. We hoped to decrease suspensions and expulsions and to create a less violent school environment. When I presented the program, I was surprised at the disrespect some of my colleagues showed toward this effort to develop a more peaceful culture there, especially at a school ridden with gangs. Having never been "booed" before, I was initially shocked, yet their confounding behavior came into sharper light as I continued my work there, and it became crystal clear after I had worked in high schools for eleven years. I found that there was low morale among teachers as well as students, that teachers felt downtrodden by sometimes irrational demands from higher-ups, including oppressive state regulations, and that they were often treated poorly by their professional superiors. The result, in my experience, was that these adult professionals treated each other (as well as their students) with the same hostility that they routinely experienced.

Superintendents and others charged with improving schools tend to pile on more zero-tolerance policies and obsessive assessments of schools on teachers and students alike. What most schools need, however, is guidance on how to help students, as well as teachers, to thrive; they need tools to create communities where people are supported in such a way that they can do their best job.

Instead, just as it does among students, school bullying by adults often travels down a pecking order. Over a decade of working in schools, I often heard teachers complain about being bullied by administrators or more veteran colleagues; administrators often feel frustrated by the demands of superintendents who seem out of touch with teacher and student needs; and superintendents can feel as if their hands are tied by larger administrator structures or city or state regulations. Everyone in the field contends with the lack of respect afforded education where teachers are paid less than bankers, lawyers, doctors, or most other professionals. These frustrations can be passed through school faculty and on to students. Bullied adults, then, like many bullied students, often become school bullies themselves.

Teacher Bullies

In a working-class northeastern rural school, one teacher, Ms. Petrey, spoke sadly about how the vice-principal antagonized kids. "He gets in their face and says mean things to them until they snap—like 'I knew you would screw up again. We've given you so many chances and after all we've done for you, you screw up again.' Then the student can't bear it anymore and says, 'Fuck you,' at which point the vice-principal promptly suspends him. It can be for being late or skipping a class, which is not a suspense offense—but mouthing off to a teacher is." Ms. Kahn found the same behavior in her wealthy urban all-boys school. The dean of students would talk to the students "like they were dogs," she said—screaming at the top of his lungs.

Sometimes the bullying behavior is less explicit. At one school where I worked, the dean of students had a gun calendar posted conspicuously on the wall by his desk. As a young counselor in the school, I was concerned. We were trying to reduce violence in the school—a school that had its share of gang warfare, and where weapons were routinely confiscated. The calendar and the dean's attitude conveyed the opposite message. The dean tried to show students that he was tough. The dean's job in this school was to punish transgressing students; the gun calendar conferred on him masculinity status and presumably helped to invoke fear and respect among the students. It also conveyed the message, however, that weapons were not just okay but exciting and even approved of by adults in the school charged with maintaining discipline. The dean modeled bullying behavior in the way he treated students as well as the other adults in the school.

Joanna, a parent from an affluent northeastern suburb who also runs an art program for young people in a less wealthy and more diverse area, has seen teachers bully students in both of these communities. "They make fun of them in front of the whole class," she says. One teacher called Joanna's son "noise pollution," and the rest of the kids laughed. "I don't want him to think he is some sort of pollution," she told me. Her youngest child was called "obscene" by a teacher and threatened with detention because he passed gas. Joanna says the students in her art classes are so used to getting yelled at by teachers that they ask her why she never gets angry at them. "Why would I get mad at them? They are just children."

But Joanna says she doesn't think the teachers are unkind. "They are exhausted and paid very little. If you look at the difference between a stockbroker's salary and a teacher's, *that's* obscene," she said. "Teachers make barely enough to survive, and they are overworked and treated badly. Children who seem to make their lives more difficult or who are less inclined to follow rules sometimes risk the misplaced wrath of a poor teacher who is exhausted, worried, and stressed and who just can't handle it anymore."

Patterson agrees: "Schools and districts that create respectful, supportive environments in which new teachers receive equitable treatment will automatically provide their students with a better education and a chance for a more fulfilling future," she writes.[25] Such efforts are, unfortunately, rare.

When another teacher was bullied by his students, in her northeastern middle to upper-class suburban school, Ms. Willis speculated that he was vulnerable to such abuse because he had never learned to succeed in the high school hierarchy when he was younger. "He didn't have the same experience as I did in high school. I enjoyed high school. When I joined the varsity volleyball team, I knew my place, but I won them over. The authority came from the top down. The older girls hit the balls harder at us, and made us step up to them, and they made us chase after the shagging balls. I don't call that bullying. I call that leadership."

This suggests yet another reason why teachers perpetuate the bully culture: they were taught its harsh rules during their own school years, and they believe, consciously or unconsciously, that these rules still apply. The hierarchy they endured, whether they scrambled to the top or were trampled to the bottom, then gets re-created in their classrooms, and the cycle of bullying continues.

Many students say they are so used to adults yelling at them, that they consider it normal. "I don't know the borderline," Lenny, from a working-class urban school kept insisting as we talked about bullying and sexual harassment, even as he described numerous abusive comments and acts. He clearly sensed that these things were wrong, but years of living in the bully culture, among adults and youth alike, had made him confused. When I talked with Lenny about teachers bullying students, he was unsure where to draw the line. "Teachers yell at kids all the time," he said. "That's what people do. I don't know if that's bullying or a kind of education."

Students Bullying Teachers

In many cases teachers are bullied not just by other teachers, parents, or the administration but by their own students. In Natasha's middle-class suburb, the students in one of her classes badly treated an Asian teacher who spoke with an accent. "They would make fun of her accent; there was no way for her to control the class; no one listened to her and they were disrespectful. She would say a word in a way that was different from the

American version and the class would be hysterical and repeat the word back to her." She ended up resigning soon after she was hired.

Ms. Kahn said she was bullied so much her first year by the boys in her class that "the whole section was ruined. I couldn't get anything done. They would shout me down." One student actually punched the wall beside her and yelled: "Screw you, I'll stab you." He claimed later that he was saying it to another student, "but he was looking in my direction," the teacher recalled. And she noted a lot of sexual harassment of female teachers in this all-boys prep school. "Young women teachers find doodles of penises on work the boys hand in," she shared.

Teachers bully students and students bully their teachers in a culture that values bullying as a means of getting ahead in this economic, political, and socially cutthroat society. In 2008, *New York Magazine* devoted a front-page story to the scandal that had taken place in an upscale private school, Horace Mann in New York City. (The story was considered especially newsworthy because the school was attended by children of famous people, including former New York State governor Eliot Spitzer, Hillary Clinton's pollster Mark Penn, fashion designer Kenneth Cole, and rapper Sean "P. Diddy" Combs.) Students at the school that year used their Facebook pages to attack their teachers. The school discovered racist, sexist, and personally damning rants about some of their teachers on these pages. There was some debate about whether this was a private or public space—whether the children had a right to bully their teachers in this form. Some said the site was private, while others, citing its nine million users, likened it to "posting something in Times Square."[26] Beyond any legal questions, some parents actually defended the behavior of their children: "Students are just blowing off steam," one parent said. "They're very stressed; it's not unusual for them to say racist and sexist things." What could possibly make a parent believe that saying racist or sexist things about anyone is okay? When the gender police tend to valorize domination and power; abuse of others becomes the corollary.

What *New York Magazine* saw as elitism run amok became a nationally publicized scandal questioning whether children of high-status parents should be permitted to defame their teachers. There was a class element here as well, because most teachers at elite private schools have far lower incomes and social standing than the parents of the children they teach. The wealthier children bully their less wealthy teachers in a disturbing class war that is also replayed among students over more minor class differences.

Teachers also get bullied in Rick's working-class rural school. He described one incident where a teacher tried to stop the bullying that was happening in the hallway. The teacher said, "Hey guys, cut it out," and the bullies mocked the teacher: "'Hey guys, cut it out.' What are you going to do, Mr. Morris?" they taunted. "The teacher walked away because he felt bullied, too," Rick said sadly. "It makes the kids who bully feel invincible." Students who were on successful sports teams rarely got in trouble in this school, one of the teachers, Ms. Petrey explained. It becomes frustrating for teachers to report students when they know that nothing will happen if the students play baseball or football for the school. The gender police consistently allow sports athletes a free pass, as they tend to have the highest masculinity status in a given community, and when they win games, everyone gets a patriarchal dividend, á la Connell.

Even as teachers get bullied by both students and other teachers, they are often blamed for not helping students who are bullied. Individual teachers clearly can't change a whole school culture by themselves, though, especially when they are tormented too. Moreover, these behaviors and attitudes are institutionalized in larger social structures, both inside and outside our educational system.

Cruel Schools

Local and national education policies in the United States are more and more based on one-dimensional standards of success, and the impact of these assessment models contributes to more competition and stress and less connection and support among students and between students and teachers. The 2001 federal No Child Left Behind Act (NCLB) added fuel to an already growing movement toward high-stakes testing—tests that can determine a child's ability to progress to the next grade or to graduate regardless of the work he did prior to the exam. U.S. schools have consequently been distracted with these mandates and unable to focus on critical education and community building. A peer-reviewed study conducted at Arizona State University showed that in eighteen states with high-stakes tests, student learning remained at the same level or actually went down when the tests were implemented. This kind of testing is also associated with a significant increase in dropout rates, teachers' and schools' cheating on exams, and teachers' defecting from the profession.[27] Sharon L. Nichols and David C. Berliner, in their 2007 book *Collateral Damage:*

How High-Stakes Testing Corrupts America's Schools, corroborated those findings. In an article summarizing their book's conclusions, they wrote:

> We found reports and research about individuals and groups of individuals from across the nation whose lives have been tragically and often permanently affected by high-stakes testing. We found hundreds of instances of *adults* who were cheating, including many instances of administrators who "pushed" children out of school, costing thousands of students the opportunity to receive a high school diploma. We also found administrators and school boards that had drastically narrowed the curriculum, and who forced test-preparation programs on teachers and students, taking scarce time away from genuine instruction. We found teacher morale plummeting, causing many to leave the profession.[28]

Studies show that the added retention resulting from high-stakes tests where students are held back leads to poor academic performance, high dropout rates, increased behavioral problems, low self-esteem, and high rates of criminal activity and suicide. High school dropouts, in turn, are more likely to be unemployed or to hold dead-end positions, earn low wages, or be on public assistance.[29]

Richard Ryan, an internationally recognized psychology and psychiatry professor at the University of Rochester, writes about the dangers of high-stakes testing; his numerous scholarly articles conclude that these exams limit teacher flexibility, diminish meaningful learning, and increase dropout rates. In a 2008 interview, he said that teachers begin to teach to the test; the tests narrow the curriculum and undermine the potential enjoyment in school for both teachers and students. "It disrupts the student-teacher relationship," he said, and "leads students to be more disengaged." Instead of working together to explore new knowledge, teachers and students both are pressured to help the other look good for external others. "The American Psychological Association considers the practice unethical. Graduation or advancement to a grade should not be based on a single indicator," Ryan shared. Yet these kinds of exit exams are practiced in twenty-five states—exams that will make or break whether the student graduates. Additionally, students tend to develop somatic symptoms, become extremely stressed, and sometimes drop out of school as a result of the grades they get on high-stakes tests. Statistically, in a district with high-stakes testing, the risk of dropping out goes way up, Ryan says.

The curriculum is often so uninspiring that students leave school even if they aren't doing that badly. Teachers, already under pressure from the administration, also have to contend with students who are less curious and less interested. "It's a morale killer across the board," Ryan says.[30]

Historically, high-stakes tests have also been associated with discrimination. The authors of an article titled "High-Stakes Testing, Uncertainty, and Student Learning" point out that in the early 1900s immigrants could be barred from entering the United States as a result of recently invented standardized tests; in public schools such tests were used as evidence of deficiencies that placed students in vocational tracks or even "homes for the mentally inferior." Standardized tests were also used to confirm the "superiority or inferiority of various races, ethnic groups, and social classes." They ensured the perpetuation of an effective caste system in the United States along racial, ethnic, and class lines.[31]

Today, research shows that standardized tests continue to discriminate against students of color and lower economic groups. In some states, the American Civil Liberties Union (ACLU) has protested high-stakes tests. The ACLU of Massachusetts, for instance, argued that standardized testing is unfair because it is "rigid, inappropriate, and inadequate as the sole determinant of a quality education," especially for students who are bilingual or disabled. They argue that it "punishes poor, ethnic-minority students the most."[32] In other words, the testing system further penalizes the same students who already tend to suffer from low status in their schools and in the wider society. Policies such as NCLB can have devastating long-term effects on schools. There is a big difference between measuring output in a competitive framework and developing a school environment where students are most able to learn and grow. City policies must largely follow the state mandates, which in turn are shaped by national guidelines. School administrative organizations try to meet the requirements set out by these dictates, and principals put pressure on other school faculty, who sometimes lash out at students—who then bully one another. The rules often mean that vulnerable students who need help are instead "counseled out" to protect the school's image or even survival.

This was my experience working in New York City public schools. There were demands that students attend school—to decrease truancy—and get passing and high grades on the all-important state Regents exams. One school where I worked, which was actually dedicated to helping truant students or students who were failing or who were "acting out," was threatened by the then board of education that if it didn't improve its statistics it would be closed. Instead of being supported to help the students, the administration began to feel pressure to push needy students out. Students who were not performing at high levels in this "high-risk" school were encouraged to get a General Equivalency Diploma (GED) or find another "second-chance" school, even though we were clearly making progress with them. The school risked its own survival if the students kept our truancy statistics too low, even if the students as individuals were significantly improving over time.

The small community-oriented school Humanities Preparatory Academy, for at-risk students, was responsible for the journey of the now famous Liz Murray, who was the subject of the Lifetime TV film *From Homeless to Harvard*. She had been homeless and truant for two years before coming to our school. Her father was dying of AIDS in a homeless shelter, her mother had already died of AIDS, and she was struggling to graduate from high school in the midst of working to get welfare and related survival services. While the media frenzy characterized her as an "up by her bootstraps" success, the real story, which she documents herself in her 2010 memoir, *Breaking Night*, was that she completed four years of high school in two years only with the help of the whole school.[33] Teachers and students worked in various ways to help her complete her applications and get her the *New York Times* full scholarship that brought her fame and success. She missed a lot of school because she had to stand in long lines time and again to apply for the social services she needed to be able to attend school. Without the understanding of the school faculty (we had more than a few meetings about her situation) and the tireless work on her behalf from so many of us, she probably would not have graduated from the high school. With this powerful community behind her, she was able to get into Harvard University, graduated in 2009, and became a world renowned inspirational speaker.

Many schools and many programs for young people have different ideas regarding how to foster success, and some of these do quite the opposite. Maia Szalavitz, in her 2006 book *Help at Any Cost: How the Troubled-Teen Industry Cons Parents and Hurts Kids*, documents the torture and degradation young people endure in most substance abuse intervention and other behavior-problem school programs set up like tough boot camps.[34] Those programs effectively institutionalize the practice of adults bullying kids, Szalavitz says. "They find emotional weak spots and attack it. They teach other children that to be nice, kind and supportive is enabling. Instead you're supposed to be honest. And their idea of honesty is to say the meanest possible things." Szalavitz recovered from her own heroin addiction (and went on to publish six successful books) with kind support. "It's an outrage that these programs believe that bullying will cure troubled teens—if we're just mean enough to them that will fix them." Instead, she says, "Being kind, empathic, and supportive is what helps people with addiction; the other stuff is just cruelty." Most children who go through these programs relapse or are unable to give up the addiction in the first place. Clearly, mean "rehabilitation" is not the answer to symptoms that often develop from hurtful school and/or abusive family social environments.[35]

Questionable strategies are used in institutions for other kinds of children with difficulties too. In her 2007 article "School of Shock," Jennifer Gonnerman cited electric shocks, withholding food, and social isolation as some of the "methods" used in institutions for autistic, mentally retarded, and emotionally troubled children. She wondered why they were being "treated like enemy combatants."[36]

As we have seen, even students who are not slated for "specialized schools" contend with rough school cultures and callous institutional practices. Rather than a compassionate environment that supports students and helps them grow and develop at their own rate with the resources they need, "rehabilitation" programs and academic schools alike too often become factories where students internalize the need to "produce" and "perform" along narrow academic parameters, just as they must conform socially.

Michel Foucault writes in *Discipline and Punish: The Birth of the Prison*, "By comparing one individual with another, by a continuous assessment of each individual, discipline exercises a normalizing judgment. . . . The turning of real lives into writing . . . functions as a procedure for objectification and subjection."[37] This can take place when students are perceived by the sum total of their grades: one is an "A student," while another is a "C student" or an "F student." Yet in my experience, such grades do not actually reflect what students have learned, as Howard Gardner famously suggests in his typology of spatial, linguistic, logical-mathematical, kinesthetic, musical, interpersonal, intrapersonal, and naturalist intelligences.[38]

Such disparate ways of learning are often utilized in the adult work world but are underappreciated and under-recognized in secondary education. In most schools, students who exhibit intelligences other than linguistic or logical-mathematical tend to be diagnosed with learning disabilities; then they are branded as having special needs and needing special education, instead of being honored and engaged in their different abilities and learning styles.

Assessment-obsessed school environments are not so different from the social cliques that develop there. Students objectify one another in the same way that they are objectified in the grade-oriented models practiced in most schools: those perceived as popular get a figurative A on worthiness, whereas those who are deemed too different or who possess talents less recognized in a given school are saddled with Cs and Ds. Targets are perceived as Fs and treated as such.

Often when students are assessed poorly in either respect, there is little anyone is willing to do to help them. Students are encouraged to deal with their troubles on their own. Then, when things get bad, students flailing academically are often asked to leave the school and find somewhere else to go; students struggling socially are given the same message by other students and sometimes even by an administration concerned about its reputation; and when targeted students retaliate, the school may ask them to leave as well. School shooters responded to this lack of compassion with what they thought then was their only option.

School Shootings and Adults' Responses to Bullying

In the extreme cases represented by the school shootings, the culture of the school and the way adults responded sometimes made the difference between life and death. Many of the school shooting perpetrators claimed that the adults in their communities knew they were being ostracized and harassed by more powerful students. They believed, however, that these adults were single-minded in their focus on athletic success or other forms of judgment and assessment. What was perceived to be a lack of compassion and concern registered also as collusion with the perpetrators' marginalization, if only by turning a blind eye.

Evan Ramsey, the sixteen-year-old who killed a student and the school principal in Bethel, Alaska, in 1997, said that he had spoken to school officials about the constant bullying he was enduring. In an interview with the Secret Service, he described their response: "For a while they would go and talk to the person and tell them to leave me alone. But after a while, they just started telling me to ignore them. I figured since the principal and the dean weren't doing anything that was making any impression, that I was gonna have to do something, or else I was gonna keep on getting picked on."[39]

Evan talked for weeks with friends about what he was planning to do. At least two boys encouraged him. One said it wasn't enough to just scare the bullies by bringing a gun to school. Evan chose three targets, and a friend suggested others; another friend urged him to put the principal on the list. By the time the shooting took place, word had gotten around, and there were perhaps two dozen students gathered in the library to witness it. Yet no adult seems to have known about the plan or responded to the bullying that occurred in this small school in a remote community. The Secret Service asked Evan, "If the principal had called you in and said, 'This is what I'm hearing,' what would you have said?" Evan replied, "I would have told him the truth."[40]

That same year, Luke Woodham, in Pearl, Mississippi, felt similarly ignored. In a prison interview, he was asked: "Where were the grown-ups?" He responded, "Most of them didn't care. I just felt like nobody cared. I just wanted to hurt them or kill them."[41]

Barry Loukaitis talked for a year with eight friends about his desire to kill people, asking some of them how he could get ammunition. Then he got his mother involved. Together they shopped for a long coat, which he wanted so that he could hide the gun; unknowing, she took him to seven stores to shop for the right one. Barry's mother was reportedly in no condition to detect her son's anguish: she was depressed herself after her husband left her for another woman, and she even talked to Barry about the idea of killing her husband, his new girlfriend, and herself.[42] Barry's own poems were filled with references to death—but no one seemed to notice.[43] Alice Fritz, mother of one of the boys Barry killed, was reportedly "haunted by questions about Loukaitis. . . . Why was he teased unmercifully and why did his cries for help go unanswered? 'No one could have saved Arnie,' she says, 'without saving Barry first.'"[44]

One after another, the school shooters expressed despair at being left to fend for themselves in an environment where bullying and hazing were perceived as normal and adults were otherwise preoccupied and did little to intervene—an experience with which, once again, students across the nation contend. In several school shootings, perpetrators killed their teachers or parents—in some cases because they blamed adults for allowing the abuse to continue. After the Columbine massacre, the columnist Dan Savage wrote about the adult neglect and denial that played a role in allowing it to happen. He noted that the media also turns a blind eye to the daily torment taking place in our nation's schools.

The tenth or eleventh time DanCBS/PeterABC/TomNBC told me the massacre in Littleton, Colorado was especially horrific because it happened in a high school, "somewhere children feel safe," I started screaming at the television. What high school were they talking about? I went to three, and in none of my high schools did I for a moment feel safe. High school was terrifying, and it was the casual cruelty of the popular kids—the jocks and the princesses—that made it hell.

"Once upon a time," *People* wrote in a manipulative and dishonest cover story, "the most that kids had to worry about at school was a looming test or a deadline for a paper." What fairy-tale time was that, exactly? In high school, I had much more to worry about than tests and papers. Like most students, I lived in fear of the small slights and public humiliations used to reinforce the rigid high school caste system: poor girls were sluts, soft boys were fags. And at each of my schools, there were students who lived in daily fear of physical violence.[45]

Many of the school shooters blamed adults for their failure to intervene and protect them from daily torment. Some shooters also held adults more directly responsible for their suffering. In these cases, the shooters also lashed out against principals and administrators who suspended or otherwise punished them and teachers who were perceived as failing them.

Retaliating against School Discipline and Harsh Assessments

In at least twenty-four of the school shootings between 1979 and 2009, perpetrators said they were responding to what they saw as academic or disciplinary injustices inflicted against them. In 1978, Robin Robinson, thirteen years old, in Lanett, Alabama, retaliated after his principal paddled him because of a conflict he had had with another student. Threatened with another paddling, Robin came back with a gun and shot the principal. In 1986 in Lewiston, Montana, Kristofer Hans, age fourteen, tried to kill his French teacher after he failed the class; he killed a substitute instead and wounded a vice-principal and two students. In 1992 in Olivehurst, California, Eric Houston, twenty, killed the social studies teacher who had given him a failing grade, along with three students; he also injured thirteen others. Eric was a former student, upset that he had lost a job because he had not graduated from high school. In October 1994 in Greensboro, North Carolina, Nicholas Atkinson, sixteen, wounded the assistant principal and killed himself after he was suspended. In Blackville, South Carolina, in 1995, Tony Sincino, sixteen, was suspended after he made an obscene gesture in response to bullying. He came back to school with a gun, wounded one math teacher, killed another, and then committed suicide. In Lynnville, Tennessee, also in 1995, Jamie Rouse, seventeen, was upset over a failing grade and fired at teachers, killing one teacher and one student and wounding another teacher.[46]

After being suspended, Asa H. Coon wounded two teachers and two students in Cleveland, Ohio, in 2007.[47] And with the most casualties of teachers to date, Robert Steinhäuser killed sixteen people in Erfurt, Germany (thirteen teachers, a police officer, and two female students) in 2002; he was enraged that he had been expelled from school in his final year for failing a final high-stakes exam that he believed effectively doomed his future.

It can be particularly devastating to male adolescents when they fail exams or classes or are humiliated through punishment, since it may affect their sense of themselves as maturing men. Failed grades, suspension, and expulsion are perceived as cutting off the path to money, power, and success, primary male status markers in contemporary society. As masculinity theory reveals in almost every situation from underground drug trades to white-collar crime to school shootings, hypermasculinity pressures (to achieve domination and power in order to win status as men), coupled with overwhelming obstacles toward achieving these goals, becomes a recipe for violence. The extreme reactions of the shooters expose the damage that is done to many students, even though most students respond in less visible ways. Students become depressed, highly anxious, or truant, abuse substances, turn to petty crime, and engage in a host of other destructive behaviors in response to the fiercely competitive and punitive disciplinary school models that label them with bad grades or refer to them as bad kids.

Adults today, inadvertently or directly, help to create school cultures among boys and girls alike that evolve into hurtful and sometimes violent relationships. Adults perpetuate and model these dynamics and often ignore them among children—either because the dynamics don't register as abusive or because the adults also lack the resources or support they need to intervene. Such limitations among adults reflect the powerful social, economic, and political bully society that shapes destructive attitudes and behaviors.

8

The Bully Economy

Schools are microcosms of American society where students are told that financial wealth and superficial gender markers are compulsory for social acceptance. They learn these lessons from each other but also from grown-ups—parents, teachers, and the wider culture they inhabit. As they prepare to enter the adult workforce and social life, children come to understand that being perceived as the richest or prettiest, or the most powerful or confident, could dramatically enhance their futures—and that without these marks of American success they may become lifelong outcasts. They also learn to see life as a zero-sum game, where they can win only if someone else loses, rise only by ensuring that someone else falls. These values are at the core of bullying behavior, and they are also the foundation upon which much of the economic, political, and social life of our nation is built.

Not all cultures are so obsessively focused on winning. In the Southwest, for instance, coaches say that teams of Hopi Indians want to win but that they often try not to win because they don't want to embarrass their opponents. In some traditional cultures, the game isn't over until the two sides are tied. They work hard to make sure no one loses.[1] Even in Europe, as T. R. Reid writes in "The European Social Model," some core human needs are seen as everyone's birthright rather than as something to be "won" through competition with one's compatriots. "To Americans," Reid writes, "it is simply a matter of common sense that rich families get better medical care and education than the poor; the rich can afford the doctors at the fancy clinics and the tutors to get their kids into Harvard. But this piece of common sense does not apply in most of Europe. The corporate executive in the back seat of the limo, her chauffeur up front, and the guy who pumps the gas for them all go to the same doctor and the same hospitals and send their children to the same (largely free) universities."[2]

In the United States, however, hard-core competition and striving to be the best are generally considered vital to keeping people motivated and functioning at optimal levels. Harsh inequalities are considered, at best, an unfortunate consequence. Yet gender pressures—and especially the expectation to embrace hypermasculine values and behaviors—are seldom examined in the context of the larger socioeconomic forces that shape them. In one of my criminal justice classes, I asked students to tell me what words they associated with capitalism. What qualities do you need to be successful in our society? The board filled up quickly: *competitive, aggressive,* and *powerful* were some of the first suggestions. At that point, we were discussing white-collar crime and the unprincipled behavior that had produced both the Enron scandal and the economic meltdown of recent years. Later in the course we discussed school shootings and their relationship to gender, and I asked my students to list some words they associated with masculinity. The same list emerged—*competitive, aggressive,* and *powerful*. Without intending to, my students had highlighted the link between the values of masculinity and capitalism.

The school shooters, for the most part, grew up in the 1980s or later. The rise in school shootings roughly coincides with the Reagan administration's restructuring of the American economic, political, and cultural landscape—a period that glorified unrestrained capitalism and reemphasized an "up by your own bootstraps" ethos. Following a landslide reelection in 1984, Reagan promised an America rich with freedom, individualism, and financial reward for those who skillfully met the standard, coupled with a lower degree of support for those who did not. Increasingly, success was defined in terms of power, economic attainment, and social status—the same barometers increasingly used, at the high school level, to assess masculinity.

Capitalism is hardly new to the United States, nor is the system's relationship to core American values. But as former labor secretary Robert Reich observed in his book *Supercapitalism,* in recent decades the power of unregulated, unrestrained capital has increased to such an extent that it has outstripped democracy as a primary foundation of our society. According to Reich, Americans became identified more as investors and consumers and less as citizens and members of a community.[3]

Further, in this same period, a slew of books documenting America's increasing social problems hit the shelves. The titles alone explain why Americans are more stressed, broke, unhappy, and doing whatever they can to survive: *The Overworked American* (1993), *The Overspent American* (1998), *The Cheating Culture* (2000), and *The Lonely American* (2009). Another set of recent titles document the new plagues with which our children are grappling—increased anxiety, depression, materialism, and even narcissistic personality diagnosis: *Branded: The Buying and Selling of Teenagers* (2004); *The Road to Whatever: Middle-Class Culture and The Crisis of Adolescence* (2004); *The Price of Privilege: How Parental Pressure and Material Advantage Are Creating a Generation of Disconnected and Unhappy Kids* (2006); and *Generation Me: Why Today's Young Americans Are More Confident, Assertive, Entitled—and More Miserable Than Ever Before* (2007).[4] Couple these telling titles with the alarming statistics depicting the United States as scoring highest on almost all of the worst social problems in the industrialized world (including murder, rape, and infant mortality), and it becomes less surprising that school bullying is so common here, or that its vicious and fatal retaliations in the form of shootings are more prevalent in the United States than in the rest of the world combined.[5]

What is a Compassionate Economy?

Competitive and punishment-oriented schools mirror the combative workforce. In the larger world, adults are given little support if they meet hard times and are unable at some point to work at their best, or work at all. Similarly, as adolescents struggle to find their identities and their place in the world, the emotional ups and downs of their journey can undermine academic performance. Even students who tend to do well risk failure, and their confrontations with widespread cliques and bullying only add to the stress. Children's understanding of this antagonistic culture feeds their fury and fear as they find that their every move in school so profoundly affects their future prospects.

In his book *Going Postal: Rage, Murder, and Rebellion: From Reagan's Workplaces to Clinton's Columbine and Beyond*, Mark Ames writes: "The kids are stressed out not only by their own pressure at school, but by the stress their parents endure in order to earn enough money to live in [a prestigious] school district. . . . Everyone is terrified of not 'making it' in a country where the safety net has been torn to shreds."[6] Children who might otherwise look forward to a life after high school see, in the model of their parents and the larger society around them, a similarly brutal environment.

While their safety nets are weakening as well, in most European countries the government still takes some responsibility for ensuring that everyone has basic health care, education, housing, food, child care, elder care, and even indefinite unemployment if necessary. There are real limits on work hours (in Finland, for instance, a six-hour workday), and mandatory paid vacation and holiday time is often four to six weeks.

In contrast, even before the start of the latest recession, workers in twentieth-century America were losing some of the gains they had fought for in the earlier part of that century. The eight-hour day (forty-hour week) that Americans finally won in 1938, under President Roosevelt's New Deal Fair Labor Standards Act, is a dim memory for most Americans today, who tend to toil more often at fifty to seventy or more hours per week.[7] Americans once hoped to achieve the demands made by the Welsh social reformer Robert Owen for eight hours of work, eight hours of leisure, and eight hours of sleep, but most now have little if any leisure and much less sleep. We are working much longer hours than our counterparts in other industrialized countries. John P. Walsh and Anne Zacharias-Walsh write in "Working Longer, Living Less" that the average American works seventy more hours per year than his or her Japanese counterpart and 350 hours or nine more weeks per year than Europeans.[8] Americans tend to work more hours and then spend money paying others to do the services they don't have time to do because of they are working.

Because we Americans work so much, it becomes more difficult to take care of our children and our homes. In many European countries, the government pays mothers as well as fathers to stay home with their young children so they can return to work when the children are older. In the United States, middle- and upper-class adults make money and often pay other people to do these tasks; many small children in the United States are under the care of nannies or some other form of child care worker. Rather than a system designed to meet human needs, our economy prioritizes profit. Instead of opportunities to nurture ourselves, and our friends and family, and larger community, our time is managed by someone else's drive to make money. Walsh and Zacharias-Walsh write that "to argue that an expensive factory should be left idle because workers are tired or that production should be organized using a less efficient but more comfortable process—is considered absurd."[9] Yet the "overworked American," to use Juliet Schor's term, does not necessarily generate more profit. As Anders Hayden notes, "Several shorter-hours innovators in Europe—Belgium, France, the Netherlands, and Norway—are actually more productive *per hour* of labor than is the United States. Higher hourly productivity in these countries is almost certainly due, in part, to shorter work-time's beneficial effects on employee morale, less fatigue and burnout, lower absenteeism, higher quality of work, and better health."[10]

European economies tend to prioritize family and community as a primary value. The notion of "time affluence," not just "material affluence," is important—a concept that is less common in the United States.[11] Instead, Americans work longer and live with their family less. Walsh and Zacharias-Walsh write about one mother of two young children who summed up this collective quandary: "This is the only job I could get that paid enough for me to take care of them, but it never lets me be home when they need me. I can either feed them or be with them, never both."[12] The increased workday also prevents participation in community life—political organizations, social clubs, sports leagues, religious institutions—as well as family life, leading to what Robert Putnam called the "Bowling Alone" phenomenon; other research also notes a related plummeting of social connections and increased loneliness and isolation among Americans.[13]

In recent decades, the U.S. government has taken less responsibility for people's basic human needs. Life has become a struggle for many working parents, especially single working parents. In addition to lacking the government-supported universal health care that is available to citizens in virtually all European countries, the United States does less than any other industrialized country to support parents, who receive no legally mandated paid leave when a child is born or adopted. Among the 168 nations surveyed in a 2004 Harvard University study, 163 have paid maternity leave, while the United States stands in a category with Lesotho, Papua New Guinea, and Swaziland.[14]

The lack of economic support for American citizens means adults are under more pressure and stress to keep their jobs and succeed in them in order to support themselves and their families. Driven to succeed, with dwindling access to community, adults end up forming similar social cliques to those that fester in children's schools. Workplace massacres, then, tend to have causes that parallel those found in school shootings.

Workplace Shootings

Some workplace killers were persistently harassed, intimidated, and ostracized by co-workers, while others felt unfairly treated by their bosses. Some sought revenge when they were fired or found their position or salary considerably reduced. Still others felt rejected by women at home or at work. Just as in the school shootings, many seemed to be seeking to recover a lost sense of manhood.

"Real" men, we are told, must achieve power and wealth, yet at many turns men (and women) are undermined and humiliated at their jobs instead; for all kinds of reasons, men (and women) are let go or not well compensated for their labor. Thus perpetrators in workplace shootings sought instead to acquire masculine power through brutal means, proving their manhood by expressing what has been socially defined as "manly" rage.

In some cases, workplace shooters' difficulty with work mixed with a history of being bullied as a child. Nineteen-year-old James William Wilson, who killed an eight-year old girl, eight other students, and two teachers in an elementary school in Greenwood, South Carolina, in September of 1988, didn't have a job—but he was also ruminating about the ridicule he had endured during his own school years for being overweight and "dressing funny."

Workplace homicides increased significantly since the 1970s when they were virtually unheard of—and now average over 500 per year.[15] Some other statistics are also familiar: in one study, 91.6 percent of workplace shooters were male; at least 13.4 percent of the incidents reviewed involved some type of domestic violence as the motive; and 31.7 percent of workplace shootings occurred in a white-collar job setting.[16] Recall that in school shootings, which also took place in mostly white and wealthy suburban schools, masculinity pressures—including the presence of dating violence—were similarly frequent factors.

In Signal Hill, California, in 2007, three employees at a menu-printing company were injured when a gunman fired on the premises. The gunman was an employee of the company, and his hours at the plant had recently been reduced to zero. Before the SWAT team reached him inside the building, the shooter killed himself with a semiautomatic pistol.[17] In Indianapolis, Indiana, also in 2007, an employee brought a semiautomatic handgun into Crossroads Industrial Services, a company employing mostly people with disabilities, and shot three people in the cafeteria and one in an office. The gunman, who was on medication for bipolar disorder, said that his shooting of the three production workers and an office manager was "over respect."[18] In Pine Bluff, Arkansas, in 2006, two weeks after Tyson Foods suspended him from his job, Julian English returned to Tyson's poultry processing plant with two pistols and shot and seriously wounded a co-worker.

The list goes on and on, and the same themes recur. In a broader sense, workplaces reflect the imperatives of our supercapitalist society, which is driving both adults and youth to extreme lengths as they struggle to compete. In *The Cheating Culture: Why More Americans Are Doing Wrong to Get Ahead*, David Callahan writes that winner-take-all values and harsh economic conditions have increased the pressure to succeed so much that Americans are cutting corners and cheating to get ahead. This contemporary phenomenon is represented by high-profile cases in sports, finances, newspapers, and corporate law firms, as well as in everyday life, from students cheating on exams to music piracy, cable theft, and income tax fraud.

Callahan argues that "economic inequality has led to striking changes in our society."[19] As a result, people feel driven to survive and be successful by any means necessary. Then as they struggle to fend for themselves, American ideals and values are undermined. "Individualism and self-reliance have morphed into selfishness and self-absorption; competitiveness has become Social Darwinism; desire for the good life has turned into materialism; aspiration has become envy."[20]

Callahan documents how a cheating culture then pervades every kind of work environment. Sears auto workers, for example, were once paid a steady salary regardless of how many cars they fixed; today they are paid for each car they fix. Thus mechanics feel forced to make up new problems for their customers' cars so that they can meet their quotas and support their families.[21]

Callahan also observes that in some corporate law firms lawyers know that they place their bonuses at risk and are likely to be downsized in hard times if they don't meet their billing requirements. "Everyone knows who's billing the most," said Lisa Lerman, one of the nation's leading experts on corruption in law according to Callahan, "and it is not always the one who's working the most. The ones who are willing to play with the numbers are most likely to achieve their goals."[22]

Henry Blodget, the Wall Street star who worked for Prudential and then Merrill Lynch and was later accused of securities fraud, urged people to hold on to stock that privately he confessed was "a piece of junk," causing investors to lose billions in the tech stock crash. "The system was sordid," one analyst at Prudential said. "But because everyone knew it was sordid, it no longer seemed sordid anymore."[23]

These values figured prominently in the subprime mortgage crisis and subsequent financial meltdown and recession. Regulators like Alan

Greenspan, who for decades cavalierly insisted that the financial firms would "police themselves," then expressed "shock" that short-term profit motives proved a more powerful motive on Wall Street than long-term sustainability.[24] Such motivations were the bedrock of the cutthroat culture on Wall Street, and anyone who failed to embrace them was unlikely to succeed. Workplaces, like schools, are in desperate need of structural change. These environments often make young and old alike feel invisible, alone, and insignificant, pressured to succeed at great costs to their own psyche and well-being. Collapsed with related strangulating gender pressures, competitive and alienating schools and workplaces do much to trigger the anger and self-hate that has motivated so many rampage shootings by children and adults alike.

Adult Status Wars

Economic, political, and social pressures work together to produce harmful values, which in turn fuel destructive gender identities and incite conflicts and violence. The pressure to conform to these distorted ways of being starts early.

Children and adults alike need to be accepted, respected, and loved and will go to great lengths "to be seen." While the status wars that go on in schools are often particularly blatant, the extreme competition and social exclusion found among adults, as well as the similarly ruthless dynamics modeled on TV, are the images students reflect in their schools.

More than ever before, Americans buy cars, clothes, homes, wine, and other commodities merely to create a particular image. Traditional gender norms still drive these purchases—cars that appear manly and fast; clothes that seem feminine and sexy, or masculine and tough; homes that reflect success and power. Even since the women's rights movement and feminism became part of the public discourse, many men feel pressured to acquire "trophy wives" as evidence of both their monetary success and their sexual potency (which are often equated with one another), while many women—once again in a double bind—are expected to measure their own worth by some combination of their own achievements and their husband's. Women are encouraged to believe that love—and their own worth as women—can be measured by the size of their diamond engagement rings, and men in turn are told that these same rings reflect their own success and power as a man.

By many accounts, the drive to acquire possessions as a means to achieve status and recognition has gotten much worse. "Seventies consumerism was manageable," writes Schor in *The Overspent American*. "The real problems started in the 1980s as an economic shift sent seismic shocks through the nation's consumer mentality. Competitive spending intensified."[25] The size of houses has doubled in less than fifty years, and the "right" home, neighborhood, and furniture are seen as the most important expressions of status in a given community; these possessions are used primarily by those on the higher rungs of the ladder to devalue those below. Such pressures, in fact, helped to create the housing bubble that has now burst, plunging the nation into recession. Those suffering most are the less affluent Americans who—longing to feel successful according to the external markers demanded of them, and lured by lenders who saw profits to be made, often through deceptive measures—took out mortgages and loans they could not afford and have now lost everything.

Just as status markers determine the treatment students receive from their peers in school, Schor notes that for adults "what you wear and drive affects how people treat you. In the past, researchers have found that if you delay at a green light, you are less likely to be honked at if you are in a prestige automobile. . . . In experiments, subjects characterize more favorably people pictured in front of upper-middle-class homes than those in front of lower-class homes. And studies have demonstrated what most people know already: the way you dress affects how salespeople treat you, even the price you are asked to pay in some contexts."[26]

Of course, status markers can also have a more profound effect on adults' lives, just as they do among teenagers. They help determine who will get a desirable job, who will be admitted to an elite club that in turn offers access to more wealth and influence, and who will be stopped by police while walking or driving down the street. Just as it does in school, lack of status in adult life can be emotionally devastating. Schor notes that lacking money to buy symbols of status results often in "feelings of deprivation, personal failure and deep psychic pain."[27]

I heard plenty of stories related to adult status wars in the United States when I talked to parents. Anna, a mother of three children aged seventeen, thirteen, and eleven, in a northeastern wealthy suburb, said that in her experiences she found that "all bullying comes from parents." The children who bully usually have bullies for parents. "You can hear the moms talking badly about other people with their girlfriends— 'She's weird,' or 'She's divorced.' Then they make fun of other drivers in road rage. Kids will exhibit this same behavior when they see their parents talking badly about others," Anna explained. "It's so apparent at the football and soccer games. The parents are critical, envious, and gossipy, tightly run, high-strung, and intolerant; the kids take it on and become bullies."

Anna explained that there is tremendous pressure to fit in and conform in their town. The rules are palpable: "Just like the children get teased if they don't fit in: 'It makes me cooler by pointing out you are different,'" said Anna. The same culture is evident among the adults. "Everyone talks about the same news on television. You have to wear pastel when you go to a PTA meeting. If you're against the war, don't talk about it when new people are around. Try to blend in. Don't swear. Criticize people who don't look right. Don't take a stand against or for anything." In fact, Anna exclaimed, often the parents make fun of kids, too, in the same way kids do. "I heard a group of mothers at a luncheon talking about a fourth-grade boy. 'That kid is gay,' they said. I had a fit. I said: 'How could we know, he's a little baby. Don't label him,' and finally, 'So what if he's gay, or different.' We're supposed to be a good influence on our kids—at minimum we shouldn't pick on them."

In a less affluent but also wealthy suburban community, I heard people feeling sorry for a neighbor because of his car—a twenty-year-old Volvo. Anna, in the wealthier suburb, pointed out that people distinguish themselves from others through class comparisons. "Affluence is a big deal here. They talk about the poor families who can't buy the Ugg pink boots or go on vacation on the holidays. We're Stepford wives. Like Dante's Inferno, compare and contrast—the social and financial status of each family permeates the lives of our children." When adults feel they have to conform to be accepted in social groups, children are likely to feel the same way.

Veronica, also from an affluent suburb, talked about how insecure her mother was about the amount of money they had. She was always encouraging Veronica to feel sorry for kids who had less money than they did and went on seemingly less wonderful vacations. The attitude seeped into Veronica's peer group, where fierce competitions were waged about who went on the best vacations and had the coolest "stuff." "You should feel bad for Tina," Veronica's mother would say: "They envy you. Their home is a mess; they don't have as nice a home as we do." Veronica's mother's concerns defined the way Veronica related to people at school in terms of status and hierarchies. A common concern among the girls in her school became who was wealthier—and therefore "better"—than whom.

Tommy came from a wealthy suburb too. "It's a tough town if you're middle class," he explained. Tommy said his family wasn't able to go to many of the village activities because they were less wealthy and therefore outcasts. When the village had a seventy-fifth anniversary party, Tommy's parents and some of his other more middle- and working-class friends' families signed up to come. They were dismayed when they got there and found that an extra table had been created for them "in the back corner by the kitchen door. It was noticeable that we were excluded from certain activities." Even in church functions, Tommy said, "the pastor would schmooze with the upper class; unless you donate a significant amount to the church, he acts like he doesn't know who you are. The wealthy people give a lot to the church and then they are very picky about who they allow to be their friends."

Beverly, from another wealthy community, concurred. She and her husband, who raised their children in the area, used to be board members for a number of charities; they often went to their gala fund-raising events. Now gala tickets can run $1,200 a person, says Beverly. "We can't afford it anymore; the establishment is being forced out."

Appearance is another factor that can either contribute to or lower status. Parents of girls are often as obsessed with their daughters' appearance and popularity as the girls themselves are, and children of both sexes learn from their parents and from the larger society to value looks above deeper qualities. A 1998 study by economists Daniel Hamermesh and Jeff Biddle used survey data to examine the impact of appearance on a person's earnings. In each survey, the interviewer who asked the questions also rated the respondent's physical appearance. Respondents were classified into one of the following groups: below average, average, or above average. Hamermesh and Biddle found that the "plainness penalty" was 9 percent and that the "beauty premium" was 5 percent after controlling for other variables, such as education and experience. In other words, a person perceived to look below average tended to earn 9 percent less per hour, and a person perceived to look above average tended to earn 5 percent more per hour than a person perceived to look "average." Hamermesh and Biddle found that the "plainness penalty" and the "beauty premium" existed across all occupations.[28] Such prejudice, or lookism, as Chancer describes it, could well be ameliorated if adults and children alike were encouraged to be more accepting and appreciative of themselves and one another independent of their looks.[29]

Instead, our competitive, status-focused culture pressures adults to become part of the gender police for both boys and girls. "Parents as well as kids refer to girls as slutty," Anna said. "But where is the parenting? Who is buying them the clothes?" Anna despaired about eight-year-old girls who had words like *juicy, precious,* and *princess* "plastered on their butts . . . They come from affluent, seemingly cultured homes. Aren't they concerned about the message they are giving their children? We're not just instilling in the girls a sense that they should see themselves as a sexual object, we actually spell it out in plain old English."

Parents are not only compelled to encourage status seeking in their children but they are also made to feel a need to acquire status on behalf of their children. The *New York Times* reports that competition for private preschools has "propelled to such a frenzy . . . it could be mistaken for a kiddie version of *The Apprentice*."[30] Parents are told that if their four-year-olds don't make it into a top preschool, their chances of getting into an excellent college are seriously diminished—which in turn means less chance for success, economic and otherwise, in a society where winning feels like the only option. A child's admittance to a prestigious school, a sought-after dance program, or a varsity team confers status on the parents as well.

Parents often tell me about the bully environments in some of these schools. One of my neighbors told me that there were parents at her child's school who had parties for their three-year-olds that excluded certain children, even though there was a policy that all children in the class must be invited to all parties. "I felt hurt," my neighbor confided. "Who made the decision not to invite Russell, and why weren't we invited?" Another neighbor told me about a girl who was hitting other children at a party she went to with her four-year-old child. "The parent is a bully," my neighbor said. "I can see where she learned this behavior."

These social cultures contrast significantly with the environments in Denmark's schools, according to Richard Morrill. Morrill writes about the community focus of schools there, where the same children, teachers, and parents are with each other through sixth grade. Then

each child has a ready-made group to rely on and interact with during his or her developing years. Traditionally in Denmark, birthday parties, class parties, trips, and so on are arranged at the level of the school class. A child may well have good friends outside the class, but many of a child's social activities will be focused on the class. It is considered extremely bad form not to invite a classmate to a social event. Consequently, no child has to worry about being excluded or being a social outcast. There is a peer group that will include him or her as a matter of course.[31]

Just as children need more supportive communities, adults are recognizing that they may need more welcoming programs too. In wealthy areas in Connecticut, so many new families said they felt excluded from the social life of their towns that dozens of "newcomer clubs" were created by those who felt shunned and isolated.[32] When adults feel belittled, disrespected, alienated, and disconnected, it is also harder for them to get children the help they need. No wonder, then, that bullying becomes accepted as a normal aspect of both adults' and children's lives.

Further, parents are at the mercy of the now ubiquitous advertisements their children are bombarded by at every turn. We are often quick to say that children's problems are their parents' fault, but parents are up against multi-billion-dollar industries that are putting all their stock into getting children hooked on their status-conferring commodities. Parents sometimes can't imagine why their daughters, for instance, are obsessed with princesses and the related clothes and other purchases their girls now demand. Disney, on the other hand, has worked hard to make sure it is Disney values these girls aspire toward, rather than any individual family's particular preferences.

Advertisements that equate particular purchases with social survival increasingly target boys too. One colleague described his childhood aptly: "As boys we felt pressured to look cool in a particular way, and we were terribly self-conscious about our shortcomings in a society focused on looks and presentation of self." Now that he is an adult, he says, it's much the same, only "now it's more expensive, because there is the illusion that you can buy the clothes or other products you need to perfect that image and thus become acceptable."

Cradle to Grave

The messages adults receive as they battle through the status wars are transmitted wholesale to children and teens. As part of their strategy to boost sales and profits, corporations have increasingly directed their efforts toward the "youth market." In her book *No Logo*, Naomi Klein discusses the rise of "branding," in which companies seek to "sell" not just products but also the illusion of a status, identity, and lifestyle that go along with them. Although the power of the brand now extends to all age groups, it is most prevalent among teenagers—no accident, according to Klein and Alissa Quart in her book *Branded*, who documents a concerted shift toward marketing to teens and even younger children, beginning in the 1980s.[33] The companies believed—rightly, as it turned out—that youth, with their fragile identities and susceptibility to peer pressure, would do anything to possess the "right" brands. It is worth noting that Klein chose to subtitle her book *Taking Aim at the Brand Bullies*.

In 1998, Western International Media Century City and Lieberman Research Worldwide conducted a study on nagging to help companies figure out how to get children to nag their parents most effectively so that parents would yield to their wishes. The study was created to help companies increase their profit margins rather than to help parents cope with nagging or to improve family dynamics, says Susan Linn, professor of psychiatry at Harvard's Baker Children's Center. Lucy Hughs, vice president of Initiative Media and Co-Creator of this study, "The Nag Factor," explained that children "are tomorrow's adult consumers, so start talking with them now, build that relationship when they're younger . . . and you've got them as an adult." Hughs continued: "Somebody asked me, 'Lucy, is that ethical? You're essentially manipulating these children.' Well, yeah, is it ethical? I don't know. But our role at Initiative is to move products. And if we know you move products with a certain creative execution, placed in a certain type of media vehicle, then we've done our job."[34]

Given this new trend to spend billions marketing to children, parents are up against powerful campaigns intent on getting children and teens to think they "need" expensive products. Parents are expected to provide these products and are told to handle the bullying that often takes place if children don't have the "right" status items in school. Parents are also often blamed for capitulating to children's demands either too much or not enough. They may want their children to have less brand-oriented values, but they also feel pressured by the need to buy certain things so that their children will be treated well in school. Even if they are inclined to resist the consumer culture, parents must battle these industries that profit from promoting brand-oriented values among children and teens. The fact that advertising is now allowed in schools, museums, and other previously off-limit children's spaces makes it even more likely that children will be manipulated by these larger forces. Dr. Linn says: "One family cannot combat an industry that spends 12 billion dollars a year trying to get their children. They can't do it."[35]

Marketing firms try to hook children on products from "cradle to grave." This is a distinctly different use of the term from Sweden's use—a country that provides for numerous and generous "cradle-to-grave" public support programs for the entire population in the interests of increasing economic equality.

The U.S. cradle-to-grave marketing trend epitomizes the bully society. Companies push us to buy particular items with direct or more subtle advertisements cautioning that *not* purchasing will contribute to one's social or economic demise. People often feel they must have all sorts of consumer items that have contributed to the increased debt among Americans. In *The Overspent American,* Schor writes that Americans have more debt and save less than any industrialized country in the world.[36]

Cradle-to-grave marketing strategies then tend to try to micromanage the minutiae of social life to maximize profits. George Ritzer shows in his article "The 'New' Means of Consumption" that consumers have become a primary object of twenty-first century exploitation. Instead of exploiting only workers, companies devise ways to make profits by manipulating consumers.[37]

Companies still make money by ensuring that workers are paid as little as possible, and they still expect them to work long hours, but the new emphasis is on getting consumers to work so that fewer workers are needed in the first place. In fast-food restaurants, for instance, consumers are expected to bus their own food so that waiters are unnecessary, and to throw away their own debris so that sanitation workers become dispensible. Consumers now even scan their own products for price checks at superstores and do their own checkouts at self-service counters in markets and gas stations.

In addition to getting consumers to work, companies try to control communication between salespeople and customers in order to maximize profits; they manufacture scripted conversations to replace what could otherwise be a more spontaneous moment between these individuals. Such simulated conversations replace authentic self-expression and interactions. In earlier days, people were more likely to ask about each other's day and care about the answer to someone's "How are you?" Instead we have "Can I get you anything else? Did you find everything you need?" Consumers respond in kind, "Yes, thank you," and move quickly out of the store. Sales conversations are meant to increase the amount of money a given customer will spend and to move each customer through the doors quickly so as to make way for the next potential sale. People who work at registers are often penalized (i.e., docked in pay) if they spend too much time between rings—an indication that they may be having a conversation, rather than moving things along toward increasing sales. Then our conversations and interactions become merely copies, or simulations, as Ritzer explains—using the notion of "simulacra," a theoretical contribution from postmodern French sociologist Jean Baudrillard—of what could otherwise be authentic connections.[38] These scripted conversations bear little resemblance to the human interaction that might otherwise develop if people were allowed to freely interact in the given moment.

The profit-oriented conversations we are expected to engage in while shopping pervade our other social relationships as well. Corporate focus groups work to create a "buzz" so that their products are the main topic of conversation among potential customers: "What is that? Where did you get that?" are examples of the consumer conversations that replace more meaningful discourses with one another as a result of carefully planned advertisements and other marketing strategies. Many of our social interactions focus on our looks and consumer purchases—using up opportunities in which people might otherwise speak about their experiences and the feelings and community concerns that matter to them.

In the absence of meaningful exchanges and honest and intimate sharing, people focus on buying accoutrements that they believe will win friends, popularity, status, and the envy of others. Human relationships are reduced to instruments for maximizing profit and status. In schools (and among adults), some popular discussions are "I like (or don't like) what you're wearing," "This is how to lose weight (or gain muscle)," "How much did you have to pay for that bag (or car)?" "Is it real?" and "Are you invited to this or that exclusive party (where you will wear such and such)?"

The thoughts and actions of consumers are manipulated when companies get people to consume a greater variety of things that they don't necessarily need and that may even cause them harm, writes Ritzer. Businesses tend to get consumers to buy in ways that help the sellers rather than the consumer. Ritzer includes a short list of such disadvantageous effects, which have escalated since supercapitalism took off in the eighties. For instance, fast-food restaurants lead people to eat foods that are harmful to their health because they are high in cholesterol, sugar, and salt. The rise of the fast-food industry parallels the rise in obesity rates, diabetes, and related heart troubles. Businesses work to get people to pay all the money they have on hand and all the money they might get in the future, since credit cards have become a financial staple in American families. Credit card companies encourage "debt purchases" by offering new credit cards to pay off older ones. This keeps the money coming while crippling American families' savings and security. Elaborate shopping malls entice people to buy things they do not need, rest and eat at a restaurant, or participate in some other mall activity and then buy some more. TV shopping networks and cybermalls permit people to shop twenty-four hours a day, seven days a week, making it more likely that people will make impulsive and unnecessary purchases.[39] Where historically imperialism was more focused on colonizing and controlling other countries, Jurgen Habermas writes that "colonization of the lifeworld" is a feature of advanced capitalism.[40] People become unable, not just unwilling, to question the status quo. We are seduced into purchasing products and persuaded that these items or services will boost our confidence and social standing. Then we ended up viewing these commodities as essential to our identities.

Convinced, then, that we are too fat or that we need to drive a sexier car, or that we embody any related social dificiency, we become anxious and unfulfilled on a daily basis. Buying expensive products rarely relieves the stress, as new insecurities created by advertisements promoting other products that promise to relieve even more inadequacies. Anxiety levels in the United States are extremely high and have increased markedly since the 1970s.[41]

We have become easy prey to new forms of entertainment—the preoccupying sounds and sights of video games, 3-D films, and other hyper-lit and fast-moving virtual realities, amusement parks, superstores, and advertisements. These promise to distract us from the loneliness and anxiety that have become so common in the United States and allow us to withstand our distraught feelings longer. We develop a higher tolerance for our discontent—and look forward instead to the next "high." At the same time young and old alike are increasingly receiving diagnoses like attention deficit disorders.

Further, Americans suffer not just from typical addictions to alcohol and related substances but also from dependence on overspending, debting, shopping, sex, and food, as well as sexting and other Internet activities. Many people are unaware that they are engaged in compulsive behaviors in their own desperate efforts to find some sense of comfort in a social, economic, and political environment that prospers (in both its legitimate and its underground forms) from people's anxiety and stress. Consumed by unease and malaise, and distanced from the deeper happiness that comes from having meaningful relationships with oneself and others, people often look for momentary joy in various forms of obsessive behaviors and inadvertently treat themselves, as well as others, badly.

Neil Postman's *Amusing Ourselves to Death* (1985) articulates this phenomenon, as does Aldous Huxley's *Brave New World* (1932).[42] Huxley predicted in his classic dystopia that Americans would be hooked on "soma" or happy pills and desperate for entertainment as a distraction from their banal lives. Postman argues effectively that this time has come, writing that Americans are intent on "amusing themselves to death." We are addicted to all sorts of entertainment, and the proportion of people on antidepressant and antianxiety medications increases exponentially every year. One in ten American women takes antidepressants, and the use of such drugs by all adults has nearly tripled between 1994 and 2004; between 1994 and 2002, the number of children taking antidepressants also tripled.[43] Americans convey in many different ways that they are desperately trying to manage their increased depression, anxiety, and isolation. But rather than change the social conditions that breeds this discontent, more of us are taking different forms of "soma" to just get by.

Yet these distraught feelings are directly connected to an economy that thrives on anxiety. Without the gender pressures and status wars that incite relentless consumption, capitalism as it is today could well implode. People would no longer be vulnerable to feeling not man or woman enough— or need to purchase everything and anything that might prove they had achieved related status. Americans spend more on beauty products each year than they do on education and social services combined.[44] Industries that profit from persuading people that they are unattractive and need to be somehow "fixed" would surely crumble if people appreciated themselves and others more independent of anyone's ability to replicate Barbie and GI Joe faces and figures. We would then be unmoved by products that promise to improve the self, attract a partner, or otherwise elevate our social positions.

The pressure to look right, rather than develop internally strong and centered selves and relationships, drives young and old alike to work to purchase more, and converse less. A century ago, labor activists sacrificed their lives to protest excessive child labor, and in 1938 President Franklin D. Roosevelt passed the Fair Labor Standards Act, which placed limits on many forms of such work so that youth could instead pursue their education. Nonetheless, young people are now demanding to work long hours during the school year so they can buy the stuff they need to be accepted at school. One study showed that 150,000 minors were illegally employed each week; the result is not just decreased time to do homework but also increased depression and substance abuse.[45] Far from demonstrating an important work ethic, many youth are forsaking their education on behalf of menial jobs to buy themselves superficial brand markers.

Barbara says that in her rural town they work at McDonalds, Hannaford, and the local ice cream parlor. "Kids do whatever they can to get the 'new cool thing,'" she says. "They work for it so they can buy it themselves or their parents buy it for them." This occurs even though many in her area live in or on the verge of poverty. Allison Pugh writes about the "symbolic indulgence" some parents engage in—buying children status objects even when they can't afford them, to make sure their children have the right artillery for school.[46]

Lola, from a middle- to upper-class suburban school, talked about how she started working to keep up with the other kids, most of whom came from families wealthier than hers. "There was a difference between those who had money and those who didn't. I felt bad about it. My mother had two jobs and couldn't always give me money for lunch. I started working. The things I wanted I had to buy myself." Children are getting on the treadmill early, working in order to consume. They are also running up debt: according to a 2006 report, almost a third of high school seniors had their own credit card or one signed by a parent, and the average credit card debt for college freshmen was over $1,500.[47]

Marketers exploit youths' desperate desire for status and social capital, but also their deep wish for connections with others, by equating those connections with the purchase of the right clothing or cell phone. "Kids want things they never wanted before," writes Quart, in *Branded*, "because non-saleable objects like friendship are routinely juxtaposed with goods for sale."[48] This creates a mood of anxiety that can be dispelled only by buying. Brand marketers have a lock on teens' insecurity and their desperation to buy what they think they need to acquire human connection and support. Rebecca recalled working madly to keep up with the rich students at her school—making sure to brand herself as a popular girl with the right clothes. She couldn't afford most of the products the other girls had, but she struggled to fit in by devising ways to look as if she fit the bill. She managed to survive by joining the bullying of others girls and by acting as if she were wealthy too. But nowhere did she get the support she needed and the friendship she craved. At home she had to deal with her schizophrenic mother and absentee father, and she was teased mercilessly in her neighborhood for these perceived deficiencies. Rebecca told me she was grateful that she got teased only about her weight at school and that no one there knew about her mother. She was able to buy some brand-name clothes to minimize her social difficulties—something from Louis Vuitton or Prada as was expected in her school. But Prada in the end was a poor substitute for the compassion and love she craved.

Wendy admits that even as an adult she still feels a desperate need to acquire the prestigious objects that will win her acceptance. "I shop a lot now. I spend all my money on bags, clothing, jewelry, and makeup because I almost feel like me all by myself isn't good enough, and this is reinforced when I show someone my car and they want to be my best friend." Wendy told me that she longed for a particular Louis Vuitton bag:

> I'm obsessed with this bag. Two or three years ago it was $500, now it is $700. I've been so close to getting that bag. I figure if I own this bag, people will know I'm well off and it is crucial that people know that I'm well off, but I'm not, but I try. But as long as people think that, I'm happy. I work for all my money. I'm a waitress. I've been a waitress for too long. Everyone has that bag. I'm taunted by it. The scary thing is that everyone has it. Is a bag this size worth $700?

Wendy drew the bag for me on my notepad and continued: "I think I need it to fit in. But there's no way I would fit in." She sighed. "In elementary school, it was the Tiffany bracelet; in middle school it was the Kate Spade backpack; in high school it was the couture sunglasses. But this bag is the prettiest thing on the planet. I'm still stuck in high school. I need that item to be cool."

Wendy's lack of self-acceptance is in part created and encouraged by the status-seeking culture around her, and thus she is convinced that purchasing the right status markers will at least marginally improve her sense of self as well as her social position. Yet it is a vicious, expensive, and lonely cycle.

Looking for Authentic Connections

In 2008, the consequences of such values became clearer as an economy of overconsumption, fueled by debt, collapsed. Less obvious are the huge social and emotional costs. We suffer from what Richard Ryan calls "time poverty."

Ryan said in a 2008 interview: "People work more because they want more stuff, but it costs psychologically and it doesn't make them happy. It costs people a lot of happiness in the time it takes to acquire these things." Ryan explained that material goods are promoted as capable of fulfilling needs but they instead amplify insecurities. The drive to acquire things, he said, "crowds out love and community and things that do matter. These values get pushed to the periphery while we chase things that end up hurting us." Ryan suggests that chasing material goods also contributes to more fragmented families. "People go where their jobs take them and they don't have built-in supports as much with people we are biologically related to. And as we become more fragmented socially, marketers exploit those insecurities."[49]

We are not just disconnected from one another, as Ryan and Ritzer suggest; in many ways we are distanced from our more classic relationships to reality too. Baudrillard's concept of simulacra—simulated worlds—applies to the extent to which we live our lives alone in front of computers rather than in active relationships with other people. Online is where we shop and socialize, where many adults do most of their work, and where many children play. Meanwhile we are alone and becoming increasingly lonely.[50]

Psychiatrists, therapists, social workers, life coaches, and other such paid professionals have replaced old-fashioned friendships. One of my college students explained: "Why would you confide in someone who could easily be competing for something you want? You don't want to give them any inside information on you or anything you want to achieve." It is safer to pay someone who is not involved in your daily struggles for status and achievement.

Further, as the psychiatrists Jacqueline Olds and Richard Schwartz lament: "Our culture currently views isolating behaviors as marks of high status."[51] They continue: "There is the rising status of being too busy to chat or even to answer the telephone; it is so much more efficient to have the machine take a message and then respond in one's own good time, or resort to the silence of email." Ironically, they add: "People sometimes answer their cell phones no matter what else they might be doing, sacrificing the connections of the moment to prove that they have even more important connections in their lives."[52]

Olds and Schwartz blame the "overscheduled, hyper-networked intensity of modern life" in the United States as well as the "American pantheon of self-reliant heroes who stand apart from the crowd. As a culture, we all romanticize standing apart and long to have destiny in our own hands. But as individuals, each of us hates feeling left out."[53] Barbara Ehrenreich refers to the "cult of busyness," with "its vicious cycle of staying busy to avoid seeming lonely and feeling lonely because there seems to be no time to cultivate relationships."[54] Men especially are seduced into living an isolating, unhappy life or risk being tormented and teased for expressing emotion or depending too much on others—a mark against their masculinity even though it might nourish their psyches.

While intimate relationships have decreased, "friends" have increased. On Facebook a person may sport thousands of "friends," but this number has little resemblance to the intimate connections on decline. Facebook friends tend to confer popularity status or demerits similar to the more superficial indicators seen in so many schools. We become objects with exchange value: certain friends are sought after because they might increase one's social capital or lead to more professional or economic capital, or because they have gossip or other forms of information capital that might increase someone's status; others are shunned because they might be seen as threatening a person's social position; still others are bullied in order to demonstrate how superior the abuser is to the abused. Isolating one another is commonplace, even as such exclusion—exile—is acknowledged to be the greatest punishment we can mete out to our cruelest criminals.

School shooters, derided for their lack of masculinity and bullied relentlessly, yearned for human connection; they repeatedly raged against the lack of support in their lives, their social isolation, and the expectation that they handle so much on their own. Adrian Stone's novel *Intertwined* (2005), about a school shooting, reflects his more than ten years of experience as a physical education teacher and football coach at Bucksport High School in Maine. The character who commits the shooting and then kills himself leaves behind a video to explain his actions, which contains these words:

> For the rest of the world, I can't really say I'm going to miss you. You did this to me. You know, a simple kind word or even a smile and hello on my walk home last night would have kept me from doing this, but I realized last night that there is no hope. Even one of my favorite teachers, who I thought understood and maybe even cared for me, blew me off when I just needed someone to talk to. If I can't even get a smile from someone I pass on the street or a kind word from a classmate what use is there?[55]

The fictional note in some ways echoes the writings left behind by real-life shooter Luke Woodham: "I did this to show society, push us and we will push back. . . . All throughout my life, I was ridiculed, always beaten, always hated. Can you, society, truly blame me for what I do?. . . It was not a cry for attention, it was not a cry for help. It was a scream in sheer agony saying that if you can't pry your eyes open, if I can't do it through pacifism, if I can't show you through the displaying of intelligence, then I will do it with a bullet."[56]

As heinous as school shootings are, they expose some of the most devastating social ills of our time—cruel schools reflect our less compassionate, less empathic larger society, as documented further in Bruce Perry and Maia Szalavitz's book *Born for Love: Why Empathy Is Essential—and Endangered.*[57] People see each other less, confide in each other less, and even smile at each other less. Our fast-paced twenty-first century is characterized by bottom-line social relations—a form of a "How can you help me succeed or I'm not interested" kind of attitude toward one another—or worse, the pervasive "Perhaps putting you down will make me look better." People's relationships, even friendships, are largely instrumental—"How can I get something" rather than "How can we connect and appreciate one another."

Ritzer argues that to combat the related alienation, isolation, loneliness, and mechanized communication that supercapitalism breeds we need to value and prioritize authentic communication with one another. There is an opportunity for political, social, and economic change in every opportunity for conversation. As part of a social movement, following Baudrillard, Ritzer suggests, for instance, that instead of merely discussing money and goods in stores and fast-food restaurants (and with one another generally), we should exchange "emotions, feelings, experiences, knowledge, insight, and so on."[58] Insist on treating clerks in stores like real people, and refuse to participate in the script. Instead of "Yes, I have everything I need," make the effort to share something meaningful with this person. Such seemingly little efforts could topple the whole system, Ritzer writes.[59] Many people don't want to have a meaningful connection with the random store clerk—we've bought into the rushing, fast-paced lifestyle that characterizes our economic and social realities. Conversation with others just slows us down. But not slowing and stopping leaves an increasing void, and most of us are harried by all the rushing—and we are ultimately unsatisfied when we ignore the people next to us, spending "quality time" instead with our technological devices.

Resistance to the mechanization of human communication and the objectification of human relationships entails authentic and meaningful appreciation of one another. Today, connecting with other human beings and ourselves, valuing other people as priorities in one's life, caring for others, and living with compassion and empathy are unusual; in fact, true friendship based on love, trust, and support of one another is literally revolutionary.

To address these debilitating social ills, which contribute to so much despair in (and out of) schools, we can begin by working to transform schools into safe spaces, rather than harsh social environments. Ideally, schools can spearhead powerful social change. Young people need a reprieve from the cutthroat competition in the larger society. To combat school bullying and related violence, we can start with policies that focus on helping schools create the kinds of communities that support caring relationships. Current U.S. education policies tend instead to emphasize punishment, policing, and more security. The difference in these methods is, to borrow from John Gray's 1992 bestseller, as huge as the distance between Venus and Mars.[60]

9

America Is from Mars, Europe Is from Venus

On November 7, 2007, Pekka-Eric Auvinen took a pistol to Jokela High School in Tuusula, Finland, a quiet lakeside town thirty miles north of Helsinki. Pekka-Eric, an eighteen-year-old student at the school, shot its principal, the school nurse, and six students and injured twelve others before shooting himself. As with the U.S. school shootings, there was a scramble to "explain" the teenager's violent actions and to find the motives behind the rampage. Police reported that Pekka-Eric shouted, "Revolution!" while he ran through the school firing his pistol. The media quoted from his Internet posts. In one, he wrote: "I am prepared to fight and die for my cause. I, as a natural selector, will eliminate all who I see unfit, disgraces of human race and failures of natural selection."[1]

Pekka-Eric apparently shot some seventy rounds at random, in a rage against the entire school, which he also tried to set on fire. Like most of the American shooters, he was described as a "bullied social outcast" who dressed strangely and seemed depressed and isolated at school.[2] The only other school shooting in Finnish history, in 1989, was carried out by a fourteen-year-old boy who targeted two other students who bullied him.[3]

To those in the United States, the story was all too familiar. School shootings are most prevalent in the United States, but over the last three decades they have occurred in smaller numbers all around the world. The motivations for the shootings elsewhere have much in common with U.S. shootings. What are most striking are the different types of responses such shootings tend to garner within and outside the United States.

The dichotomy set up in John Gray's book *Men Are from Mars, Women Are from Venus* serves as effective shorthand for the differences between the U.S. and European approaches to school violence. In Gray's book, men and women are perceived to be on opposite extremes of a continuum of behavior—indeed, as distant from each other as different planets.

Where men tend toward "masculine" ways of dealing with stress—more self-reliance and self-protection—women, Gray writes, tend towards more "feminine" approaches—expressing emotions and wanting to connect in their relationships.[4]

These are socially constructed images associated with masculinity and femininity, though in Gray's approach these differences are treated as "natural" essentialist categories. Contrary to Gray's thesis, masculine-associated responses are often made by women as well as men, and men do indeed demonstrate feminine-associated behaviors, even if they are tormented by others when they do.

Men and women should be allowed and encouraged to express the full continuum of their personalities—that which is associated with being masculine as well as that which is associated with being feminine. Problems occur when people are pigeonholed—expected to exhibit only narrow responses related to one end of the continuum or the other. Likewise, in response to social problems, countries can and should implement polices associated with masculinity as well as those more associated with femininity.

When it comes to school violence responses, though, European and American policies tend to align in the same way that Gray defines female and male polarities. America bends more toward increasing protection through security and punishment; European countries, on the other hand, have done more to enhance relationships by building peaceful school communities. Do we need to keep our political, social, and economic responses at such distant ends? Is there, perhaps, a more mixed approach to school violence that would be more effective than the two extremes represented by the United States and Europe—Mars and Venus—a response that might be more effective here on Earth?

Like the United States, European nations deal not only with school shootings but also with the problem of lower-level, everyday violence in schools, including violence related to bullying. Between 1998 and 1999, for example, France had more than six thousand serious incidents of secondary school violence.[5] European nations have responded in ways that are distinct from the predominant American responses, however, which some European officials complain "transform schools into high-security zones."[6]

These variations take place in different societal contexts, differing particularly in the overall rate of violence. For instance, in 2002, Europe's annual murder rate was ten per million population, but in the United

States it was ten times higher—over one hundred per million.[7] In fact, the United States ranks worst among its peers on a number of disturbing indicators: in addition to the murder rate, the United States ranks first in its reported rapes, robbery, incarceration rate, drunk driving fatalities, cocaine use, greenhouse gas emissions, contributions of acid rain, forest depletion, hazardous waste per capita, garbage per capita, the number of children and elderly in poverty, homelessness, inequality of wealth distribution, bank failures, divorce, single-parent families, reported cases of AIDS, infant mortality, the death of children younger than five, and teenage pregnancy. Whereas 20 percent of adults in the United States live in poverty, the average in European countries is 6 to 7 percent.[8]

European countries also have significantly different policy responses to their social problems. The U.S. approach largely tries to motivate citizens to work for the supports they need. If citizens find they are lacking essential resources, the thinking goes, they will be inspired to work that much harder to earn what is necessary to get their needs met. Taxes are kept low so that citizens can pocket their earnings and spend their money as they see fit. European countries tend to have much higher taxes and thus more generous social support programs.

Not surprisingly, research shows that European countries and the United States consistently vary on their responses not only to school violence but also to crime in general. By reviewing the non-U.S. school shootings, as well as the social, political, and policy responses among the different nations, we can develop more insights into what can be done to prevent school violence and to create more peaceful school communities.

Strict Father versus Nurturant Parent

George Lakoff's model of political metaphors provides a relevant framework for looking at social factors behind responses to school shootings in Europe and the United States. In his 1996 book *Moral Politics*, Lakoff, a linguist, laid out a groundbreaking theory of the differences between conservative and liberal thought in the United States. Characterizing the state as a figurative "parent" and citizens as "children," Lakoff argued that ideologies of the Right and Left are founded on different models of morality as applied to raising families. He calls these approaches the "strict father" and the "nurturant parent."[9]

For conservatives, the operative model is the strict-father family, based on the view that life is difficult and that the world is fundamentally dangerous.[10] Lakoff describes this model as centered on the idea of "a traditional nuclear family, with the father having primary responsibility for supporting and protecting the family as well as the authority to set overall family policy. He teaches children right from wrong by setting strict rules for their behavior and enforcing them through punishment."[11]

This model, in which survival depends on competition, is based on typically "masculine" values, which emphasize self-interest and authority. For Lakoff, these values are exemplified by a laissez-faire economic ideology in which competition has no limits and those who fail are not protected by "coddling" social services. In this universe, moral strength means finding the courage to overcome fear and hardship.[12]

By contrast, the nurturant-parent model is founded on cooperation and interdependence. Its inherent values of caring and interaction are associated with women, rather than with the "masculine" traits of competition and authority. In keeping with a liberal framework, Lakoff adopted the gender-neutral term *nurturant parent* for the model he describes as follows: "The primal experience behind this model is one of being cared for and cared about, having one's desires for loving interactions met, living as happily as possible, and deriving meaning from mutual interaction and care. . . . The obedience of children comes from their love and respect for their parents, not out of the fear of punishment."[13] In the state corollary, people are supported through social services and become concerned citizens who help one another. The nurturant-parent model is based, not on a system of rewards and punishments, but instead on the idea that children learn through loving and secure attachments with their parents.

In the United States and Europe, the predominant approaches to most aspects of civil society fall clearly along the lines of the conservative strict-father model and the liberal nurturant-parent model, respectively. This dichotomy accounts for the vast divergence in responses to crime in general and to bullying, youth violence, and school shootings in particular.

Historically, the central debate in U.S. social policy has been whether we should create policies that protect citizens from poverty, unemployment, and high health care costs or whether the market should determine who gets wealthy and healthy as well as who will languish at the bottom of social and economic life here. Since the 1980s, proponents of market based solutions have dominated our political landscape. With the partial exception represented by President Barack Obama's efforts at health care reform, politicians have tended toward dismantling whatever social services we had in place.

This historical trend over the last three decades reflects the "survival of the fittest" notion associated with both hypermasculinity and super-capitalism. This period since the 1980s has also seen school shootings and workplace massacres become staples of U.S. society.

At the same time, academic problems among U.S. youth have also become more visible. Compared to other industrialized countries, we have a higher proportion of students who graduate from high school barely literate. Our students also fare badly in comparison regarding math and science aptitudes; we fall short regarding high school graduation rates; and the gap between the highest- and lowest-performing students is larger than across the Atlantic. Because colleges and universities are so expensive, they are also increasingly less available to children of middle-class parents as well as to children of the working class, working poor, and poor.[14] In contrast to European countries working to level the playing field, U.S. education reinforces a division between the "haves" and "have nots."

Historically, it was European countries that maintained these tiers. In *Solutions to Social Problems*, D. Stanley Eitzen writes that in the 1920s wealth inequality was much lower in the United States than in the United Kingdom. "America appeared to be the land of opportunity, whereas Europe was a place where an entrenched upper class controlled the bulk of the wealth. By the late 1980s, the situation appears to have completely reversed, with much higher concentrations of wealth in the United States than in Europe. Now Europe appears to be the land of equality."[15] Europe also has a much lower rate of violence and much fewer school shootings. This leads to the obvious question regarding what causes these disparate statistics representing European and U.S. social and economic life.

School Shootings Elsewhere

As discussed, American boys are taught to fight to protest accusations that they are gay or effeminate, to dominate girls, and to consistently demonstrate masculine-associated prowess. This is consistent with the strict-father perspective, which emphasizes that youth are responsible for demonstrating independent agency. Societal demands for self-reliance discourage U.S. schools from providing support that might alleviate the pressures that lead young men to violence—violence that too often is itself rooted in expectations for young men to embody power and dominance.

European boys face a somewhat different set of expectations. They benefit from the more compassionate effects of Europe's nurturant-parent political orientation. European policies make empathy and support essential components of most of their public policy; they guarantee economic supports from cradle to grave, including a structured system of free, high-quality education. They suffer, though, as a result of policies related to academic access where students can be denied education as a result of failure on a few designated markers.

Thus, in addition to pressures to repair damaged masculinity through demonstrations of strength, the European shooters visibly responded to a sense of futility at poor academic prospects, which in the rigid European education and career track system could severely impair a young person's future economic prospects and in fact determine the course of his or her entire life—the equivalent of the United States' growing trend toward high-stakes testing.

Robert Steinhäuser, who killed sixteen people in Erfurt, Germany (thirteen teachers, a police officer, and two female students) in 2002, had been expelled from school in his final year, prompting him to plot the shootings that took place six months later. He had failed the final high-stakes exam called the Abitur and therefore had no opportunity to get a high school completion certificate or attend a university. Robert believed that failing this exam had doomed his future. In rage and despair, he waged a war against the school and then killed himself. Even after the massacre, surprisingly, German students came out in droves to protest the grueling Abitur, which wielded so much power over their futures.[16]

In a significant number of the European school shootings, such assessments on a student's future became the trigger of an attack. The seventeen-year-old who shot a deputy principal in The Hague in 2004 faced a lengthy suspension, and some students said he had already been expelled.[17] The sixteen-year-old who held four students and a teacher hostage before freeing them and shooting himself at a school in Waiblingen, Germany, in 2002 had been expelled from four schools and had "chosen to vent his anger on the last," police said.[18] The sixteen-year-old who killed the headmaster of a school in Branneberg, Germany, in 2000 had been expelled by his victim. After being fired at a factory in Eching, Germany, in 2002, a young man killed two at the factory and then traveled to Freising to kill the principal of the technical school he had once attended.[19] While the boys in the United States by and large targeted their peers, sometimes along with teachers and parents, the boys in Europe killed a proportionally large number of school faculty, who were often their primary targets.

Many of the European shooters had received negative school reports or punishments. Many of the U.S. shooters, on the other hand, were particularly talented academically and were in fact teased for being smart and doing well in school. When U.S. boys have targeted teachers and school administrators, though, it has been increasingly because of academic failure or punishment too: twenty-four of the U.S. cases were directly related to perceived academic or disciplinary injustices inflicted against the perpetrator at school. U.S. students also have targeted adults because they believed these people failed to protect them from the harassment they experienced at school, even after repeated requests.

Many European cases involved masculinity issues similar to those present in the U.S. shootings. The Erfurt perpetrator was thought to be gay by his parents, and his teacher noted that he "wasn't very brave in sports."[20] Mirroring many of the U.S. shooters, he bought violent computer games and devoted himself to Satan and the occult and heavy metal.[21]

In Veghel, Netherlands, a seventeen-year-old boy, whom classmates said was upset about a failed relationship with a girl, opened fire, injuring three students and a teacher.[22] In 2006, nineteen-year-old Sebastian Bosse shot and wounded a teacher and several students in his former high school in Emsdetten, Germany, because of the bullying he had endured there. In his suicide note, he wrote: "The only thing I was properly taught at [school] was that I'm a loser. . . . I hate people. . . . I'm outta here."[23]

Other countries in the Americas also fit similar causal patterns. In a 1999 case in Taber, Alberta, in Canada, the fourteen-year-old boy who killed one student and wounded one other had dropped out of school after being severely ostracized by his classmates. According to his peers, he was the object of teasing, name-calling, and incessant bullying. They considered the "slight" boy "neither a jock nor a brain," and one student said that "even the nerds picked on him." In first grade he was doused with lighter fluid and his classmates threatened to set him on fire. On a Boy Scout trip, he was left stranded on a ledge screaming for help; no one came to his aid. Depressed and lonely, he posted a web page with personal information "to show people he was not such a bad guy."[24]

The fifteen-year-old boy who killed three students and wounded six in Carmen de Patagones, Argentina, in 2004 was described by a local education official as "a timid boy, who was having difficulty integrating," though "he never displayed any violent attitudes."[25] Kimveer Gill, the shooter at Dawson College in Montreal in 2006, had been rejected by the military—an institution known for "making men feel like men." Gill had briefly received military training from the Canadian Forces Leadership and Recruit School in Saint-Jean, Quebec, but had been deemed unsuitable for military service and had agreed to leave.[26] Many of the U.S. shooters (for instance, Eric Harris at Columbine High School) committed their crime just after being rejected by the military too, which may have felt like a final condemnation of their masculinity. Boys across the world are forced to grapple with expectations relating to being "appropriately masculine"—which often translates into "You are not acceptable the way you are" and "You must prove some association with violence and aggression to be accepted as such."

Despite some differences among these shootings, boys tended, in all of them, to feel weak and unsuccessful and to believe that the school had failed them. The similarities suggest that there are ways to transfer successful programs and prevention strategies from one environment to the other.

U.S. Responses to School Shootings

The most dramatic contrast between school shootings in the United States and Europe comes not in their causes but in their effects. (Tables 1 and 2 provide a snapshot of the extreme differences in school shooting policy responses by the United States and European nations.) Each school shooting in the United States brought calls for tighter security, including metal detectors, surveillance cameras, police officers, limitations on speech, and more expansive use of the death penalty. Each also led to individual lawsuits by the families and victims of the killers against the parents of the perpetrators, as well as against gun manufacturers and the entertainment industry.

The surviving perpetrators have been sentenced for the most part to multiple life sentences unless they were significantly underage—as in the 1998 Jonesboro, Arkansas, shooting, where the eleven-year-old and thirteen-year-old perpetrators were kept in juvenile court, and in Michigan in 2000, where the child who wielded a gun was only six years old. A local blogger in Moses Lake, Washington, commented that "Barry Loukaitis has become a poster child for the tough-on-crime crowd that want

TABLE 1. Sample of U.S. School Shooting Responses, 1996–2004

Date	Name/Age	Killed/Wounded	Policies Advocated and/or Adopted
Oct 1, 1997 Pearl, Mississippi High School	Luke Woodham, 16	Killed: 2 female students, mother Wounded: 7 students	Christy's Law: made it a capital crime to kill on school property
December 1, 1997 West Paducah, Kentucky High School	Michael Carneal, 14	Killed: 3 female students Wounded: 5 students	Bookbags and backpacks forbidden in schools; security became so tight, and omnipresent, students started calling their school "Heathcatraz," after the famous Prison Alcatraz
March 24, 1998 Jonesboro, Arkansas Middle School	Mitchell Johnson, 13, and Andrew Golden, 11	Killed: 4 female students, 1 female teacher (pregnant) Wounded: 9 female students, 1 male student, 1 male teacher	Demands that youth as young as 10 should get the death penalty; new fences were built around the high school, as part of the zero tolerance, high security plan; students complained that the fences actually locked people in, and in the event of another attack from inside the school, they would actually prevent people from fleeing. Due to the new zero tolerance program students were expelled or sent to the Sheriff's office for increasingly smaller infractions
April 20, 1999 Littleton, Colorado High School	Eric Harris, 18, and Dylan Klebold, 17	Killed: 8 female students, 4 male students, 1 coach, selves Wounded: 23 students	President Clinton asked Hollywood to address violence in films; NRA temporarily and slightly receded; i.e. cut back its conference in Colorado from three days to one day; Marilyn Manson was asked to cancel his concert tour; he obliged. Many schools banned trench coats, "Goth" style clothing, and clothing related to Marilyn Manson
January 15, 2002 New York, NY High School	Vincent Rodriguez, 17	Wounded: 2 male students	School was closed after the incident; MLK JR. High School was dismantled and divided into smaller schools

TABLE 2. Sample of European School Shooting Responses, 1996–2004

Date	Name/Age	Killed/Wounded	Policies Advocated and/or Adopted
March 13, 1996 Dunblane, Scotland Primary School	Thomas Hamilton, 43	Killed: 16 (5- and 6-year olds), teacher, self Wounded: 15	Even stricter gun laws across Europe; for example, Great Britain outlawed pistols
April 26, 2002 Erfurt, Germany High School	Robert Steinhäuser, 19	Killed: 13 school faculty, 1 police officer, 2 female students, self Wounded: 1	Two hours later, even stricter gun control laws were passed; National Anti-bullying and violence and prevention programs launched including the hire of school social workers for multiple new projects
October 29, 2002 Vlasenica, near Sarajevo, Bosnia-Herzegovina High School	Identified as Dragoslav Petkovic, 17	Killed: 1 teacher, self Wounded: 1 teacher	Government offered amnesty from prosecution if citizens would hand over their weapons and ammunition voluntarily; weapon possession is illegal there, but available since the war
January 13, 2004 The Hague, Netherlands College	Murat Demir, 17	Killed: 1 Headmaster	In addition to hiring counselors, the "5-track method" for dealing with bullying was developed, with a focus on supporting (nurturing) the students, including help for the victim, help for the bully, help for the silent majority (bystanders), help for the teacher, and help for the parents. Officials in the Netherlands took this program so seriously that it was launched in the most important international press conference, a center in The Hague, where the Dutch vice-Minister for Education, and other high officials were invited to sign the first National Protocol against Bullying. On the same day, the Protocol was sent to 10,000 schools for implementation. The program was also translated into other languages. Parents' organizations in Italy, Austria, Belgium, Denmark and Norway said "yes" to the project

to lock up juvenile psychopaths and throw away the key. And that's how Barry's case was handled. The community came together, not for justice, but for revenge."[27] After Luke Woodham's 1997 rampage, the state of Mississippi passed a new law making it a capital crime to kill on school property, called Christy's Law, after Luke's ex-girlfriend, whom he had killed.[28]

In addition to punishment and revenge, U.S. responses focused on security and control. At Heath High School in Kentucky, security after the 1997 shooting was so tight that students started to call it "Heathcatraz," after the famous prison Alcatraz.[29] Other responses included bans on book bags and backpacks; photo-identification tags and computerized access devices; calls for the death penalty for children as young as ten years old; and calls for bans on Goth clothing accessories as well as the trench coats that were often worn by the shooters.[30]

The Safe and Drug-Free Schools Program of the U.S. Department of Education was passed in 1994, partly in response to high-profile reports of guns in schools. The high-security, "zero-tolerance" approach taken by this and other antiviolence initiatives was influenced by the "Just Say No" drug programs of the 1980s War on Drugs, especially DARE (Drug Abuse Resistance Education). A 2002 study by the National Research Council, though, found that students who had been exposed to the DARE program used drugs at the same rate as students who had not. A 2003 report by the Government Accountability Office gave DARE a failing grade, concluding that the program, which was receiving $600 to $750 million annually in federal funding, had "no statistically significant long-term effect on preventing youth illicit drug use." By 2007, many school districts began abandoning DARE after having followed the program for twenty years or more.[31]

Nonetheless, the Safe and Drug-Free Schools Program was reauthorized in the 2002 No Child Left Behind Act; it is responsible for the allocation of hundreds of millions of dollars to states each year in the form of grants for school security, including safety technology, crisis management, consultants, and software.[32] Yet in violence prevention, as in drug abuse prevention, the approach falls short on success indicators. From the mid-1990s through 2000, levels of violent crimes in schools did decline, but at rates consistent with the decline in the overall U.S. crime rate, and since then most have stayed the same or gone up slightly.[33] Statistics on school bullying, however, continue to increase, especially in the middle-school years.[34]

The ubiquitous zero-tolerance programs in the United States have been studied in depth and come up wanting, as demonstrated in a 2000 report from the Indiana Education Policy Center, "Zero Tolerance, Zero Evidence: An Analysis of School Disciplinary Practice." The report's author, Russell Skiba, argues that "zero tolerance is a political response, not an educational sound solution." It sounds impressive to say that we're taking a tough stand against misbehavior, but the data suggests it hasn't been effective in improving student behavior.[35]

The report found that zero-tolerance policies are not only ineffective but also unjust and damaging, in that they mete out harsh punishments that can destroy students' educations—and even their lives—often in response to minor infractions:

> Zero tolerance discipline attempts to send a message by punishing both major and minor incidents severely. Analysis of a representative range of zero tolerance suspensions and expulsions suggests that controversial applications of the policy are not idiosyncratic, but may be inherent in zero tolerance philosophy. There is as yet little evidence that the strategies typically associated with zero tolerance contribute to improved student behavior or overall school safety. Research on the effectiveness of school security measures is extremely sparse, while data on suspensions and expulsions raise serious concerns about both the equity and effectiveness of school exclusion as an educational intervention.[36]

The American Bar Association's Juvenile Justice Committee, in a 2001 report on zero-tolerance policies, concluded:

> Public policy towards children has moved towards treating them more like adults and in ways that increasingly mimic the adult criminal justice system. The most recent version of this movement is so-called "zero tolerance" in schools, where theories of punishment that were once directed to adult criminals are now applied to first graders. . . . Zero tolerance means that a school will automatically and severely punish a student for a variety of infractions including "threats" in student fiction or giving aspirin to a classmate. Zero tolerance has become a one-size-fits-all solution to all the problems that schools confront. It has redefined students as criminals, with unfortunate consequences.[37]

Some of these "unfortunate consequences" were catalogued in a 2000 report from the Justice Policy Institute and the Children's Law Center. The cases described included a hyperactive twelve-year-old charged with making "terroristic threats" and jailed for two weeks after warning students in the lunchroom line not to eat the potatoes or "I'm going to get you"; two ten-year-olds suspended and then charged with a felony for putting soapy water in a teacher's drink; and a fourteen-year-old disabled student charged with armed robbery and held for six weeks in an adult jail for allegedly stealing $2 from another student. In this last case, the local prosecutor responded to criticisms by saying that "depicting this forcible felony, this strong-arm robbery, in terms as though it were no more than a $2 shoplifting fosters and promotes violence in our schools"—and dropped the charges only after *60 Minutes* showed up at the child's hearing.[38]

The ineffectiveness of these types of measures is borne out by facts from the U.S. school shootings. Security measures were already in place in some schools before the shootings occurred—as in Georgia, for example—and obviously did not prevent the violence. After the shootings, new fences were built around schools in Arkansas and Kentucky; students complained that the fences locked people in and would prevent people from fleeing another attack from inside the school.[39] In Pennsylvania, new metal detector wands created long queues, forced school to start late, increased tension and crowding among people, and ironically made the school community even more vulnerable to an attack.[40]

Before the 2002 shooting in New York City's Martin Luther King Jr. High School, the school had not only metal detectors but a heavy police presence; at the urging of Mayor Rudolph Giuliani, the New York Police Department had taken over school safety in 1998. A 2007 report from the New York Civil Liberties Union concluded that "the environment created by the massive deployment of inadequately trained police personnel in schools . . . is often hostile and dysfunctional." These "school-assigned police personnel are not directly subject to the supervisory authority of school administrators," the report said, "and because they often have not been adequately trained to work in educational settings, [they] often arrogate to themselves authority that extends well beyond the narrow mission of securing the safety of the students and teachers." Some teachers who questioned the NYPD's treatment of students were subject to "retaliatory arrests," while students were routinely subjected to "inappropriate treatment," including "derogatory, abusive and discriminatory comments and conduct; intrusive searches; unauthorized confiscation of students' personal items . . . ; inappropriate sexual attention; physical abuse; and arrest for minor non-criminal violations of school rules."[41]

In one of the New York City public high schools where I used to work, metal detectors were placed in the school on a rotating basis with other "at-risk" high schools. Ms. Jameson, a teacher there, said: "They treat the students terribly. They create long lines so we can't start our classes, and they make teachers and students angry." That's a difficult way to start the day. "If a student leaves the metal detector line, even to buy a bagel before class starts, the New York City police run and tackle them," Ms. Jameson shared. "Even if they were going to cut school, the police don't have a right to attack them." These issues are, of course, more likely to fuel frustration and rage among students, especially those who already feel abused by their peers or the adults in their schools and larger communities.

When asked by the police whether metal detectors would have stopped him, Luke Woodham said: "I wouldn't have cared. What's it going to do? I ran in there holding the gun out. I mean, people saw it. It wasn't like I was hiding it. I guess it could stop some things. But by the time somebody's already gotten into the school with a gun, it's usually gonna be just about too late."[42] Getting weapons was easy for the perpetrators, according to a study of school shootings conducted by the U.S. Secret Service. Most of the attackers were able to take guns from their homes or friends, buy them (legally or illegally), or steal them. Some received them as gifts from parents. Many of them went to school specifically to show off their guns.[43] Metal detectors were not a deterrent for them when the potential to finally reverse their status as victims and prove their manhood was at stake.

States across the country are finally mandating that schools develop comprehensive antibullying programs and policies; unfortunately, this mostly means that schools are using suspension and expulsion, more often, as a way to broadcast the strong message that they are "tough on bullying." Schools have new complicated chains of command for reporting bullying behavior; teachers are held responsible if they neglect to make an appropriate report; and every incident must be recorded and filed appropriately. Some schools have character education programs or after-school workshops; while well-meaning, none of these measures do much to build peaceful communities by helping people build relationships with one another and themselves.

Thus the emphasis on security is harmful in yet another way: it overrides and obfuscates the need for other kinds of interventions and solutions to school violence. After the school shooting in Jonesboro some counseling was offered, but few people used the service because of the social stigma it carried. Many teachers who did see the need for help felt there was not enough counseling or compensation for people who needed time off to recover; they were expected to return to work the next day or their pay would be docked.[44] Thus, in a climate already hostile to counseling and social work, long-term psychological needs were left to individuals and families to manage on their own—an expected but regrettable outcome in a strict-father culture.

Doriane L. Coleman, the American author of *Fixing Columbine: The Challenge to American Liberalism*, explains: "The reason we turn to metal detectors and student profiling is because we can't get at the deeper stuff, but the Europeans can. Europeans may look at metal detectors, but it's so clearly a Band-Aid. They just do a much better job taking care of their children."[45]

European Responses to School Shootings

Typifying the European attitude, Germany's interior minister, Otto Schily, argued: "We can't turn our schools into fortresses."[46] In the 1998-99 academic year, the French government hired thousands of school counselors, doctors, nurses, and staff aides to address violence in their schools.[47]

When school shootings took place in Europe, counseling became even more specialized. There are now psychiatrists in France who specialize in post-traumatic stress syndrome for teachers who have been victims of school violence.[48] In the Netherlands, in addition to hiring counselors, one successful program, the "five-track method," dealt with bullying through a complete focus on supporting the school community members: help for the victim, help for the bully, help for the silent majority (bystanders), help for the teacher, and help for the parents. The program was translated into multiple languages and adopted in Italy, Austria, Belgium, Denmark, and Norway.[49] A significant decline in bullying in Europe is attributed to such antibullying campaigns and other counseling services and programs.[50]

The Norwegian Bullying Prevention Program was found to reduce bullying by as much as 50 percent.[51] In 2002, Norway's prime minister initiated a central edict against bullying, inviting all schools to participate in antibullying programs.[52] The most successful initiative in Norway is the anti-bullying program Zero, developed by researchers at the Center for Behavioural Research at the University of Stavanger. This systemic program is aimed both at individuals and at the larger society. The program was implemented in 146 primary Norwegian schools, and in 2001 and 2004 evaluation studies found that it significantly reduced bullying.[53]

In parts of Germany, school counselors started working in sixty-four projects at seventy schools, in cooperation with the school and juvenile welfare service.[54] Spain focused on creating *convivencia,* or "living together in harmony." Discipline is educational and rehabilitative and should "guarantee that each student respect the rights of the rest of the students and bring about improvement in the relationships of all the members of the educational community."[55] This is a stark contrast to the U.S. tendencies toward zero-tolerance, suspension, and expulsion models in which students are routinely excluded from the community to improve the school climate.

In a keynote address on creating initiatives to combat bullying in European schools, a speaker from the United Kingdom advocated training so that students could support victims of bullies instead of becoming complicit bystanders. Peer supporters then received ongoing help from the school.[56] Italy used a "befriending" model aimed at enhancing students' sense of responsibility for confronting bullies.[57] In Finland, a new policy states that "the provider of education must make sure that students will not experience acts of violence or bullying during school hours or in any other school related activity."[58]

After the school shooting by a sixteen-year-old in Waiblingen, Germany, there were calls for more "self-examination and national debate."[59] There were also demands for more school reforms, stiffer gun-control laws, and crackdowns on violence in the media, but the emphasis was consistently on improving relationships among adults and children. Toward this end a host of programs for teachers build peer support, for instance using the "empowerment" approach in Norway.[60] Indeed, a focus in Europe on fighting deeper social ills to combat school violence has been credited as instrumental in efforts to decrease violence in schools.

One area where the United States and European countries both struggle is in addressing racism. Racism is still a major problem in the United States, but in European countries immigrants in particular also experience severe prejudice and discrimination. School shooting perpetrators across the Atlantic and beyond retaliated against others who harassed them and called them names related to their race or ethnicity. Much more needs to be done to help students make real connections with those who may seem different from them. This is one of the most essential ingredients of a successful antibullying program.

Recognizing the prejudice that persists toward their growing minorities, particularly immigrants, many European countries have begun actively working to improve their racial and ethnic relationships. Reflecting a sense of public responsibility for solving social problems, their programs tend to receive considerable government support. Extensive race and ethnic sensitivity work involving videos, conferences, and petitions against racism occurs, for instance, in Luxembourg's schools; Greece has multicultural education programs, special TV shows, after-school activities, and the promotion of antiracist attitudes in schools.[61] Other types of race awareness efforts are being implemented in Germany, Spain, Norway, and Sweden; there are also human rights and gender equality programs in Finland.[62]

European countries do implement security measures in their schools, but not to the extent seen in the United States. They have added school guards in Portugal; in Finland, pupils have been given "alarm bracelets" to call for help if they are threatened or attacked.[63] Yet in a school violence report on seventeen countries in the European Union, there was no mention of metal detectors and only one mention of surveillance equipment.[64] Even when extra security measures are implemented, the focus is still primarily on "pedagogical principles and encouraging pupil self-esteem and responsibility."[65]

One reason for the lower level of security concerns in European schools, of course, is that controls on firearms are far more stringent than in the United States.[66] Further, despite already having strict gun control laws, European nations made those laws stricter following school shootings.[67] In Germany, for instance, where the most horrific of all the European attacks took place, gun control laws were tightened immediately after the attack. While each U.S. school shooting revived attention to this issue, the political climate in the United States became more emphatically against gun control.[68] Today presidential candidates believe that if they openly support gun control laws they have no chance.[69] The National Rifle Association rallied repeatedly on the sites of school shootings following the massacres to protest any efforts to limit guns as a result of these incidents. Such different attitudes toward gun control are emblematic of differences between the strict father and the nurturant parent—guns needed for prioritizing self-defense and retaliatory responses versus guns limited in the interests of focusing on prevention.

In any case, gun control policies, while important, cannot address the deep rage, loneliness, and lack of support that drove so many of the perpetrators to act. Even if guns were completely inaccessible and school shootings became therefore impossible to commit, the gender-based and related bully culture in our schools would persist—and with it, the high levels of suicide, truancy, depression, anxiety, eating disorders, self-cutting, and other despairing responses. Depression and anxiety in particular are at all-time highs; one in eight adolescents is depressed; and even among adults, levels of well-being have declined over the last three decades.[70]

While stricter gun control laws cannot affect these grim realities, they could prevent the escalating numbers of fatalities and injuries made possible by easy access to powerful weapons and ammunition, and they might stem the tide of reactive massacres triggered by despairing youth. They might also signal a shift toward a society where conflicts are resolved by more constructive means, rather than primarily through revenge and violence.

Mars and Venus Meet on Earth

Creating more compassionate communities in U.S. schools is a necessary but not sufficient step for ameliorating violence here. We need to examine our larger strict-father-oriented culture and become more critical of the bully society it creates.

Even our political talk shows tend to glamorize those who seek to dominate by trying to harass, denigrate, and verbally batter one another. Politicians often infuse their campaigns and speeches with masculine language. They've declared a war on crime and drugs; and profess to be tough on immigration; and they deride their opponents as weak and feminine. Shortly after being elected governor of California, Republican Arnold Schwarzenegger called his Democratic legislators "girlie men."

Without changing some of this language and related values, even U.S. efforts to create more positive dynamics in schools will tend toward more of the strict-father family model (Mars) rather than the nurturant-parent model (Venus) more characteristic of European countries. Even when U.S. schools focus on resources other than punishment, the emphasis tends to be more on building character and personal power than on self-acceptance and compassion for others. This is an unwise emphasis, as recent research shows that young Americans already show significantly less empathy and increased narcissism.[71]

Thus in the midst of this crisis students are told that they need to be completely focused on themselves, missing opportunities otherwise ripe for teaching creative conflict resolution skills. For instance, in *Scientific American Mind*, Cindi Seddon writes that it is the responsibility of the victim to stop the bully: "By not showing weakness, a child, suggestively, can lessen chances that a bully will target him or her." Some of the suggested tactics include "to stand straight and tall; to look the bully straight in the eye; to be polite but firm and tell the bully, 'Stop it,' or 'Leave me alone;' to walk away if one cannot hide his or her fear, or to report events to a trusted adult."[72] These kinds of directives put the onus on the victim and implicitly absolve not only the bully but the other students, teachers, and school as a whole of any responsibility for creating a more compassionate community. Such expectations also reflect the strict-father environment that itself often leads to school violence. Students are pushed to feel that they need to handle everything on their own, develop a hyper sense of self-reliance, and not expect anyone else to support them in the process.

Many U.S. instructional media also teach girls and boys that they need to develop personal skills so that they can handle conflicts by themselves. In the culminating scene of the HBO film of Rachel Simmons's book on girl bullies *Odd Girl Out*, the protagonist insists that she has to "handle things on her own" and triumphantly tells off her bully by herself as her peers look on.[73] A *Dragon Tales* DVD for young children called *Considering the Feelings of Others* sends a similar message in the chapter "Teasing Is Not Pleasing." The female protagonist, Emmie, is teased by female dragons on the opposing basketball team. Emmie's friends are indirectly supportive, but no one is willing to help Emmie directly in her interactions with the young dragons who are calling her names. The lesson the cartoon conveys is that Emmie should tell the teasers her feelings and say she doesn't want to be called names; that she should not let their words affect her; and finally that she can outsmart them and win by her wits— effectively, that all by herself she can and should handle the bullies.

In fact, in these situations, friends can help one another create a more compassionate culture rather than look on passively. Even in these instructional lessons meant to help children deal effectively with bullying, the assumption is that bullying will necessarily take place and that no one can do anything to stop it other than the victim. This belief is neither true nor effective. The goal should instead be to build a culture where bullying is not tolerated and where everyone in the community is expected to take responsibility for supporting one another. The empathic values endemic in such an environment will both prevent bullying and be more effective in dealing with incidents should they arise.

The approach taken by many U.S. social workers reflects these empathic values and could have a powerful impact on creating more peaceful schools if more widely implemented. Ann Weick defines social work as a profession dedicated to "comforting, healing, and strengthening those who are most injured by social inequities, and least able to muster the wherewithal to envision a better life."[74] As Weick observes, though, social work is "hidden" by its association with women's work, nurturing and family caretaking. By extension, social work is not a particularly respected profession in the United States. Weick notes the "parallels between the status of women in society and the status of social work as a women's profession"—a good metaphor for the strict-father model's disdain for the nurturant parent as a primary guiding principle.[75]

This might help explain why in Europe professional social workers are held in much higher esteem than in the United States.[76] Indeed, many U.S. policy makers insist that emotional issues should not be addressed in school and scoff at the idea of anything resembling "sensitivity training"—that is, the more typically European, "feminine" approach.[77] One of the biggest challenges for U.S. social workers who hope to expand more supportive approaches in U.S. schools, then, is to overcome the societal strict-father mentality that encourages some of the root causes of school violence. Bullying as a means of control and domination, revenge against other bullies, punishments in the form of suspensions and expulsions, hyper-self-reliance as a primary response—all stem from a strict-father approach and play a role in school shootings as well as the "lower-level" everyday violence that triggers them.

How, then, can U.S. school social workers or others in helping professions apply the more nurturant-parent approach—or minimally, integrate a more nurturant approach with the more strict-father approach that is most prevalent in the United States? Above all, it is important to move away from the strict-father model's requirement that students resolve social problems on their own. Instead, students could be encouraged to access school- and community-based support structures, designed to provide early intervention in the violence cycle. These supports could give students the learning tools they need to resolve social problems together without resorting to violence. Successful antibullying strategies also must include a diversity component to prevent the targeting of minorities and to help students appreciate the differences among them. Finally, every antibullying program should address issues related to gender that lead to gay and slut bashing in almost every school across the United States. School counselors with whom I've spoken often balk at the challenge ahead. They say that their administrations do not seem open to prevention interventions that involve restructuring the school in ways that focus on creating community. If this is the case, counselors can create smaller communities in their schools. Group counseling, for instance, can become an important community for students where they feel cared about, supported, and appreciated by their peers as well as by adult facilitators. Since so many students are stuck in relationships with themselves and others that are unfulfilling and undermined by values related to purchasing brands and obtaining status, any opportunity to connect authentically with themselves and others will provide some degree of comfort and peace and consequently reduce school bullying.

Another challenge is the opposition from some groups that believe that antibullying programs "promote homosexuality to kids." In Michigan, in November 2, 2011, the state senate passed an anti-bullying bill that protects school bullies rather than their targets. Students, teachers, and others in the school community are allowed to bully on behalf of "a sincerely held religious belief or moral conviction." Whether the bill passes in this form, an effective pro-bully lobby remains an obstacle to eradicating cruel behavior in schools. One Long Island principal blocked a Gay-Straight Alliance in his school because she said that gay slurs weren't such a "big deal"[78]—this while nine out of ten lesbian, gay, bisexual, and transgender youth report being harassed at school, and while heterosexual students, such as many of the school shooters, who are perceived as not meeting the expectations of their school's gender police are similarly targeted for gay bashing. Creating communities where students can appreciate one another as well as their differences are vital to preventing the bully society that otherwise becomes the status quo. Such communities are a prerequisite to living in a civil society and need to be developed in spite of the challenges to creating them.

In Europe, successful programs have included two components: a nationwide priority on preventing bullying and individualized approaches tailored to specific communities and schools. In the United States, with its culture of self-reliance and individualism, perhaps the best approach is for school faculty to begin at the local level, establishing programs in individual schools that can eventually spearhead a national effort. At the same time, members of the helping professions could continue to bring the need for building compassionate school communities into the national consciousness. One article in a social work journal declared the need for more social workers to assume the roles of activist and community organizer: "School social workers who learn about the values of the community and build from the strengths of the existing community will be most successful in organizing and facilitating change."[79] Helping students and faculty build sincere and supportive friendships is also critical for creating peaceful schools.

Finally the United States also needs to broaden its definition of violence, so that what adults may view as small slights do not escalate into fatal shootings when students find such "slights" hurtful. Part of the problem in the United States is the widespread acceptance of bullying in school communities as a normal part of life. In a study comparing teaching interventions to bullying in the United States and in other countries, the U.S. teachers intervened 35 percent of the time, while the teachers in other countries intervened in 85 percent of the cases.[80] Certainly, some of this lack of intervention can be explained directly by the self-reliance aspect of the strict-father framework. Indirectly, the strict-father approach also inhibits intervention by minimizing the perception that a problem even exists, because bullying is consistent with the competitive, stereotypically masculine social model. According to one report, the public tends to identify violence as the number one problem facing schools, yet even when high levels of violence are reported in an individual school, school personnel do not perceive their school as having a "big violence problem."[81] Indeed, a high level of tolerance is evident in what Peter Smith, editor of the book *Violence in Schools: The Response in Europe*, identifies as the American definition of violence: "aggressive behavior where the actor or perpetrator uses his or her own body or an object (including a weapon) to inflict (relatively serious) injury or discomfort upon another individual."[82] In some European countries, the much broader definition of violence includes "any interpersonal activity or situation in which a member of the education community is being physically, psychologically, or morally damaged."[83] A few European countries include school climate, insecurity, and any stress that creates feelings of disorder.[84] American social workers are beginning to recognize the problem of underattributing violence and are advocating for a definition more akin to that of the Europeans.[85] It is important that counselors empower themselves and one another to work toward these goals, and help others contribute to creating a more compassionate community in their school—if not smaller and more numerous microcommunities within the larger institution.

In a broader sense, violence prevention must recognize the culture of masculinity and its ties to the strict-father social structure. Schools need to expand the definition of masculinity to alleviate both perceived and real peer pressure that may motivate young men (and women) to engage in physical and sexual aggression to affirm their masculinity.

To have a significant effect in schools, we need to create more peaceful environments in other institutions too. Because U.S. law barely recognizes bullying as anything but a normal part of economic and social competition, there is little legal recourse for victims. Some laws and corporate policies offer workers a measure of protection from sexual and racial harassment—in other words, from bullying directed at a person's particular gender or race. U.S. institutions rarely, if ever, protect anyone else, and those that have gender and race antiharassment policies are often ineffective at either preventing this behavior or handling it effectively when it occurs.

In workplaces, as well as schools, the onus continues to be on the victims to prove that the harassment they experience is bias based; if not, the abuse is allowed, despite an increasing body of research that shows how emotionally and physically damaging bullying can be.[86]

In the workplace, the United States also continues to resist policies that would protect people from non-bias-related bullying. In contrast, many European countries, as well as Australia, have implemented national policies aimed at protecting employees in these situations. In 2000, Gary and Ruth Namie, in their book *The Bully at Work,* noted that the United States is at least twenty years behind Sweden, ten years behind England, and four years behind Australia in implementing workplace bullying policy.[87] They wrote: "Thanks to the American media obsession with the mantras—'globalization,' 'competitiveness,' and 'productivity'—our attention gets diverted from the mistreatment of colleagues at work."[88] Not much has changed since that writing. Thirty-seven percent of Americans are bullied at work, and there are still no laws to protect targets of workplace bullying.[89] While European countries and in particular Scandinavian countries recognize bullying as a work environment health and safety issue and have implemented needed measures to prevent it, the United States remains conflicted about whether bullying is, in fact, all that bad.[90] In a 1998 Supreme Court decision, Justice Antonia Scalia wrote for the unanimous court that the law "does not prohibit all verbal or physical harassment in the workplace. . . . Common sense and an appropriate sensitivity to social context will enable courts and juries to distinguish between simple teasing or roughhousing . . . and conduct which a reasonable person in the plaintiff's position would find severely hostile or abusive."[91]

The Supreme Court effectively ruled that some harassment in the workplace is acceptable and that workers should be left on their own to fend off these attacks. Namie and Namie argue that the United States needs new laws and policies if it is to make headway toward eradicating workplace harassment.[92] They cite a 1998 *Washington Post* editorial that calls for Congress to "write specific anti-harassment laws that do not require sex, race, or national origin protections, but instead require only that a work environment be sufficiently abusive." The editorial notes that "what bothers people about abusive workplace conduct, after all, is not the fact that it may be discriminatory but that it is abusive in the first place."[93] Yet to date the United States has limited, if any, protections for workers who are abused at work unless they can prove that the harassment is based on gender or race discrimination.

European countries have had success with their community programs in both schools and workplaces. Clearly, the U.S. strict-father approach could benefit from incorporating nurturing and empathy, which has the potential to influence cultural norms so that bullying is less acceptable, revengeful punishment is less widespread, supportive counseling programs are more widely implemented rather than disabled, and school social workers are seen as alternatives to—or at least vital additions to—high-security systems. Acknowledging the benefits associated with Venus as well as those that reference Mars will help policy makers, teachers, and school social workers develop increasingly effective responses to everyday school violence and may reduce or even eradicate its extreme expression in the form of school shootings.

A few model initiatives indicate that there is some constructive movement within the United States, but successful programs are too often challenged by funding needs—less an issue in European countries where governments more often pay the bills. The Vera Institute of Social Justice with the New York City Department of Education created a program where they trained school police officers to "catch students doing something good." Instead of looking only for infractions and perceived deviance, the school security official would say: "Thank you for holding the door for this student. That was great," or "You responded to that conflict with a lot of maturity. I like how you handled it." The goal was to create an environment where students felt they were being rewarded for good behavior rather than just punished when they were perceived as "acting out"—in hopes that the positive culture would help reduce violence. The program was unfortunately discontinued, but it remains a prime example of an effective meeting of Mars and Venus approaches. Sadly, many such related efforts in the New York Police Department that have tried to mix security with proactive efforts to create more supportive and positive communities are prematurely defunded.

Officer Ortiz, a policeman on patrol in the South Bronx in New York City, told me that a similar program in community policing had met the same fate. "It was great," Ortiz said. "If a store owner was concerned about something, they would call us, and we'd help resolve it. It is one of the most critical roles the police can play in a community, but there aren't enough people to do it anymore." Ortiz said that when he had been a community police officer he was able to see what people on the street needed before situations escalated to violence. "You become part of the community, and it takes away the feeling to people like 'Here comes the Man to harass us.' Instead they remember you were the person that helped their son when he was being bullied. You are a cop with a name and not just a badge. And we rode bikes, so people liked seeing us and talked to us and felt like we were there with them. They'd see us when they waited for the bus and we're walking around instead of being in a luxurious car." Now that the program is no longer around, he said, cops have once again become part of the problem. "New sergeants in charge of patrol just become triggers. They have macho ways—like 'I'm the sergeant and what I say goes.' In the majority of situations, it doesn't help and often it causes the situation to become more volatile, more violent." Community policing is another excellent model of an effective meeting of Mars and Venus in efforts to ameliorate violence.

Unfortunately though, many excellent programs in the United States continue to lose funding at the same time that more money is poured into high-security and safety systems. Without training of the kind Officer Ortiz recommends, however, more police do not necessarily mean more protection.

U.S. legislation tends to focus on punishment and also mandates that school personnel report suspicious behavior. Penalties for fighting as well as for not reporting a fight are increasing. These kinds of laws hope to make students scared to hurt one another and to pressure teachers and other school faculty to report disturbing behavior. Yet people will treat each other with greater kindness and trust one another enough to report potential crimes when schools work to create more compassionate communities. Our Mars approaches must be minimally supported by Venus efforts. Ideally, schools need to implement programs that will help them transform their school cultures—merging Mars and Venus for more effective mixed approaches on Earth. Some excellent existing programs do just that, manifesting in their schools a powerful "collective courage"—necessary in school buildings as well as cyberspace.

⅛ 10 ⅛

Creating Kinder Schools
and Cyberspaces

A transformation of the larger bully society, as well as the microcosms that exist in schools, would require systemic social and economic change, accompanied by sweeping changes in perspectives, attitudes, and behaviors. Our educational system alone cannot bring about such change. Nevertheless, our schools can make a significant contribution by becoming safe havens where real learning takes place. Schools can also inspire students to become leaders who help to create more peaceful futures— a welcome alternative to the otherwise more likely scenario, where our future leaders merely recreate the same bully cultures they have always known.

Some distinctive programs that have already made a significant difference can be replicated. Particularly successful initiatives tend to help schools build close-knit communities where students and faculty feel valued and appreciated—and where some of the damaging socialization discussed in this book can be transformed. Indeed, small schools are often heralded as the answer to school violence, but they are not particularly effective without focused efforts on changing the community culture.

In New York State, for example, there are thirty-nine consortium schools that have gotten waivers for high-stakes tests and replaced them with portfolio assessments. These alternatives allow students to delve deeply into an area of interest, pursue that passion, and work closely with mentor teachers who guide them in the process of research and discovery. As Vincent Brevetti, former principal of Humanities Preparatory Academy in New York City and currently Senior director for Program Development at the Institute for Student Achievement, said in an interview, students in these schools are both challenged and supported. "Some of them have difficulty coming up with a topic, and some have difficulty following through, and others have difficulty with the critical thinking. Wherever their challenges lie, teachers support and encourage them. Students always express tremendous pride in their accomplishments."[1] This is a stark contrast to the disdain many students feel toward high-stakes tests. When I was a student at a highly competitive New York City high school, for instance, students carried out a ritual of destroying their study guides after the all-important state Regents exams were completed.

Every state in the United States has some version of successful alternative models. "They survive on the margins," says Richard Ryan.[2] In addition to building self-esteem and a passion for learning, these schools tend to create more close-knit communities because students bond with other students as well as adults as they work collaboratively on challenging academic and community projects. These schools are also more likely to combat the extreme gender socialization that develops in the absence of alternative values.

Assessment-heavy schools often breed judgmental and hierarchal cultures, whereas a focus on critical and innovative thinking is more likely to encourage acceptance as a more prevalent social feature. Schools that allow young people to express the full continuum of who they are help make it possible for both students and adults to appreciate themselves and each other and to develop the meaningful relationships that all people crave. Further, programs that focus on transforming school cultures—rather than merely providing after-school curricula or one- or two-day workshops—are most effective at creating both peaceful and academically excellent schools.

U.S. Programs Addressing Masculinity

Paul Grafer, introduced earlier, was the program director and a trainer at the Sports Leadership Institute, started at Adelphi University. He worked hard to try to get adults and students to take more responsibility around issues of destructive gender socialization and its relationship to institutionalized bullying and hazing. In one of their programs, Athletes Helping Athletes, the Student Athlete Leadership Team program trained high school student athletes to be motivational speakers, peer mentors, and leaders for elementary school students. The high school leaders discussed issues like sportsmanship and substance abuse prevention, and they helped raise awareness about the harmful connection between masculinity pressures and bullying. The underlying premise of the programs was that sports are a venue for learning, that athletes can be constructive rather than destructive role models, and that athletes can help one another, as well as younger students, address important social concerns.

Most of the program's trainers were, like Grafer, former athletes themselves, so they knew intimately the culture that breeds daily violence. "I'm ashamed to say that I took part in hazing when I was a soccer player. Now I know how destructive that was," said Grafer, who once played soccer professionally and later became the U17 Men's National Team assistant coach at the U.S. Soccer Federation in Sarasota, Florida. With this inside experience, Grafer was respected by the high school athletes he trained, and he used that to help them become different and more productive kinds of leaders. "We tell them that they are school leaders," Grafer told me in an interview. "Other students look up to them and they can be a leading force in decreasing violence and improving the school climate. They get excited about that."[3]

The founder and executive director of the Sports Leadership Institute, Don McPherson, was a professional football celebrity who used his status to reach out to teens to "make a better society." While sports can be a vehicle that promotes altruism, teamwork, and dedication, today, McPherson says, it is also "a cancer in our society." McPherson continues: "I'm often asked about the connection between sexual violence and sports. My response is simple. Early in life most boys hear the 'insult' 'You throw like a girl' or something of this nature. I call it the language of sport as it attacks one's masculinity in an effort to inspire or degrade. The reality is that it teaches and perpetuates sexist and misogynistic attitudes, and until it is addressed, sports will continue to be a breeding ground for narrow masculinity and misogyny."[4]

Grafer described one coach's particularly disturbing intervention made when he found fault with two of his players. The coach made the boys hug each other throughout the entire practice as a way of demeaning them. The message was clear: being caring and affectionate should be associated with scorn and humiliation. Beyond its homophobic and heterosexist implications, this kind of lesson teaches boys that being empathic and warm is inappropriate. Little wonder, then, that boys feel so pressured to appear tough, to hide their emotions, and to resist the intimate relationships and supportive friendships they want so badly as sentient social beings. Grafer says we need to "try to create a caring, more empathic coach rather than an authoritative coach."

Over six hundred thousand children in four states and Canada were served by the Adelphi University programs, which addressed masculinity challenges, including gay bashing and violence against girls. Grafer says that parents could be even more influential than the programs are but that often it is the parents who teach their children to be bullies in the first place. Ultimately, "parents don't want their child to be the bully, but they think it is much worse if their child is the victim." They treat their children's being bullied as a rite of passage and respond by teaching them to fight back. Fathers especially have been known to reward their children for fighting a bully and winning. Grafer says parents he worked with often talked about their children needing to be tough. Their concern was about their boy's manliness, not his basic decency or emotional well-being.

The Sports Leadership Institute not only trained young people but also worked closely with high school coaches because these harmful attitudes are reinforced by many coaches who follow "a traditional male model," says Grafer. Generations of men are taught to be insensitive—"Spit on it, wipe it off, be tough, there is danger out there." These are the messages coaches send, and boys learn that to be men they need to lose their caring, empathic selves and focus on winning and preventing shame.

Grafer says most coaches are open to hearing new ways of approaching their teams, especially when they hear the research that alternative approaches can be more effective in winning games. Some coaches, however, are stuck in the traditional model. "They see us as male bashers," Grafer explains. "'Why is it wrong to be a man?' they ask. "They don't see the limiting nature of who we can be as men today. They ask about chivalry toward women. 'Is it promoting a male-dominating society when men hold the door for girls?'" To prevent violence and bullying, though, students need to learn to be respectful to all people, Grafer says.

This idea is, unfortunately, not common in most high schools, where pressure to achieve manliness is the trigger for countless acts of violence. The Sports Leadership Institute raised awareness about the limitations of masculine expectations and showed students how liberating and rewarding it is to be kind and compassionate regardless of whether such behavior is associated with being masculine or feminine. With their new attitudes and values, influential athletes and coaches can have a profound effect on the climate of the school with which they work as a whole.

While programs like the Sports Leadership Institute are an exciting phenomenon, they are also rare—and, sadly, getting rarer still. Even as bullying and hazing continue to rise, programs available to address the hardest issues related to gender continue to be undermined. California started a statewide program in 1998 that ended in 2001 as a result of limited funding and the state's financial crisis. Adelphi University's Sports Leadership Institute met a similarly disappointing fate in 2008, when it was discontinued for budgetary reasons. Athletes Helping Athletes does continue under the director and original founder of the program, Warren Breining, but it is not clear that it continues to emphasize the work on masculinity that was integral to the program when it was under the Sports Leadership auspices.

U.S. Programs Addressing Girl Bullying

Rosalind Wiseman, who wrote the influential book *Queen Bees and Wannabes*, in 1992 founded a violence prevention project called the Empower Program. More recently, Wiseman launched the "Owning Up" curriculum, which "is based on the premise that social cruelty, degradation, and violence can be deconstructed and understood by examining how our culture teaches boys to be men and girls to be women." Further, the curriculum "teaches children the skills to speak out against injustice and recognize that they have a responsibility to treat themselves and others with dignity."[5]

The Ophelia Project—which takes its name from Mary Pipher's 2002 book *Reviving Ophelia*—is another program that emphasizes the problems with "relational and other non-physical forms of aggression," especially as they play out among adolescent girls. While bullying of girls by girls is often dismissed because it is thought to be less likely to include physical violence, the Ophelia Project "recognizes the urgency of targeting low levels of aggression."[6] While the Ophelia Project's "Creating a Safe School" program targets all members of the school community, as well as parents, a main component is a peer mentoring program that "empowers older students as trained mentors to their younger classmates, and models positive social interaction and courageous intervention."[7] In this way, it parallels the Sports Leadership Institute's approach, using mentoring and modeling to undermine the bullying behaviors produced by gender pressures. Instead of encouraging children to "stay out of it," they show

how such silence gives aggressors power. Everyone is given tools, tactics, and language to try to end the emotional warfare among children. Teachers talk about the need to view bullying as a "public health issue." Others testify to their pride in becoming part of a "counter-culture that is working to prevent relational aggression."[8]

The "Smart Girl" curriculum is another successful program that uses teen mentors from nearby high schools or universities to teach intensive seminars to middle school girls.[9] The program is based in Colorado and works to help students become more sensitive to differences and to develop emotional as well as other intelligences so that girls can more deeply appreciate themselves and other people. The program is growing and working to incorporate a curriculum related to gay bashing as well, so prevalent among both boys and girls.

Collective Courage Programs

There are many techniques and programs dedicated to creating and building positive relationships among community members, as well as programs that help students support one another when they are in tough situations. Collective courage programs encourage people to support one another so much and so often that students can start to feel assured that if they reach out to someone they are bound to get help from other people in the vicinity who will also stand up for their values, such as mutual kindness and consideration. In the absence of this culture, the bully society prevails and students are left woefully alone.

Laurie Mandel, the founder and director of the Get a Voice Project, is an art teacher at Murphy Junior High School in the Three Village School District in suburban Stony Brook, Long Island—a school of about a thousand students, 92 percent Caucasian and generally middle class. Her program operates in seventeen schools on Long Island. The program mission is to create a "youth empowerment project designed to raise awareness about the power of language and words. It seeks to help students to use their voice in a proactive, productive, responsible, and respectful way"—in a way "that empowers and connects rather than degrades, puts down and incites others toward violence," says Mandel.[10]

Through professional development for a core team of adults in the school, Mandel and her small team of collaborators try to get adults in the community to "create and/or shift a culture from one that is often disrespectful to one that is more positive—where students and adults feel safe, valued, connected, and empowered." The program has reduced the number of incidents that get reported to the principal's office, and the students' benefactors have significant and inspiring transformations as a result of the program: "I spoke up and that person listened. I made a difference," the students often say with some surprise. "It is very exciting and empowering."

Mandel said in a 2007 interview with me that she tries to help support students to develop what she calls a "collective courage." "On their own they won't stand up and say something," she explains, so the program tries to enable them to "use voices of courage and leadership"—and to work together, so that if they see something happening and speak up, "someone else will say something too. When they do it together, it works really well." Mandel repeated a story one of her students told her about an incident on the school bus, a notorious site of bullying: "These sixth graders told some third graders not to sit somewhere on the bus, and the student said, 'You can't say that. Why can't they sit there?' And then someone else said, 'Just 'cause he's in third grade doesn't mean he can't sit there.'" Mandel said: "Older kids who defended the third graders felt good about protecting the younger ones—and the younger kids were so happy they were being protected."

"We do a lot of modeling as we work with core teams of teachers, administrators, and people from the PTA," continued Mandel. "There's a lot of authenticity about how they bring it to their school. This is not a boxed program. They do it in their own way and we give a lot of ideas on how to do it." For example, a fourth-grade class was asked to write letters to adults in the school community—bus drivers, teachers, administrators, school nurses, parents. They were asked to persuade each person to become a part of the Get a Voice Project. They wrote about why the person's participation could make a difference, and then they mailed out the letters. Twenty-four students wrote letters, and eighteen adults accepted the invitation. The students felt empowered because they were able to use their voices to gain adult attention and participation in something that mattered to them.

The Get a Voice Project collaborated with the Sports Leadership Institute for a conference called the "Language of Leadership" for middle school students, where I also served as a facilitator. Mandel described our process: we talked to them about "who they code as 'inside the box,' who is popular and who is not, who is voiceless and who has the voice. Sometimes the voice they are listening to is not the most respectful voice; it is just the most popular voice."

In other trainings, Mandel has heard boys share things they haven't said anywhere else. They talk about the pressures they feel to prove their manhood. "You have to be a certain way, even if that's not who you are," said one. "You have to be tough, you can't show it if you're not." Mandel said, "It was a new concept to them that there was an option to be any other way. The message they get and that they tend to relay to one another and to themselves is that you're tough and macho, or you are gay. If you're a skater or an athlete that makes you cool, but you need to show signs of heterosexuality. If you're short, you better be a good athlete. If you have any qualities that are considered less masculine, you must have other qualities that prove you're a man." Some boys have shared intimately how painful the pressures to demonstrate masculinity can be. In one of Mandel's workshops, one boy said: "When my grandfather died, I was really upset and I wanted to cry and how do you do that—'cause you are considered a wuss and your friends don't know what to do with you if you cry." Another boy said: "Wow, I didn't know you felt that way. It should be okay. I lost my dog and I was so upset too." Another boy said: "What are you supposed to do with all that emotion?" These conversations had far-reaching effects, Mandel explains. "Some girls articulated that they felt bad that the boys couldn't cry and vocalized that empathically to the boys. It gave permission for other boys to vocalize their concerns."

The Get a Voice Project is notable for how it addresses the pressures on boys to achieve masculinity. "An important part of our work is the homophobia piece. Nationally and internationally, it's the last acceptable bastion of prejudice going on," Mandel says. "Heterosexism is ubiquitous in middle school. It's not about whether a kid is gay, it's about kids coding what it means to be a real man; when they see another male outside that coded perception, someone who they believe isn't tough and macho, not an athlete, or not arrogant or confident, or obsessed with girls, they code them as gay. Their belief system is that they must be gay, even though they know they aren't. By and large when they say 'It's so gay,' they really mean 'You're not masculine enough.'"

Mandel recognizes that too few programs address issues relating to masculinity. "Most of the projects that get funded are initiatives with girls," she says. "But we can't have this conversation with girls if we don't have this conversation with boys. We've expanded what it means to be female, but we haven't expanded what it means to be male." Mandel's small program is powerful and effective, yet it can only do so much. It's effectively a one-woman program, and she still works as a full-time art teacher. She has six people who help her do workshops, and they receive small honorariums for their work—but it is largely a labor of love. Don McPherson and Paul Grafer's Sports Leadership Institute had three staff members before it closed because of financial issues. These programs tend to be strapped for funding. "If it was a priority in our society, it would be easier [and we] would still be there," Paul Grafer explained.

I know, from my own experiences as well as from my study of some innovative programs, how much difference some interventions can make, especially if they encourage boys to reconsider the codes of masculinity they are pressured to obey. Jameel and James were referred to me by the dean in a large New York City public school where I worked. They had a rough fight outside school, and other students quickly got involved. Each brought friends to back him up, and finally eight kids were suspended from school and nursing serious bruises. A handful of the boys involved were part of a well-known gang.

When I asked Jameel and James how all this started, neither of them wanted to speak. Jameel finally volunteered that James had bumped into him in the staircase on the way to class. "Yeah, I said, 'Sorry,'" James responded. "Oh, well, I didn't hear that," said Jameel, looking a bit surprised. It was another case of perceived lack of respect leading to violence. Both boys looked chagrined. They agreed that their conflict was "squashed," and they promised to tell their friends to lay off one another too. They were committed again to treating each other with respect.

Both boys seemed a little embarrassed that things had gotten so out of hand as a result of a misunderstanding. The code of respect and honor is so strong among their peers that it can be difficult to resist or overcome. They both seemed to appreciate this safe space away from that world— a chance to talk and to be treated and to treat each other with a much deeper kind of respect and honor.

Jameel became a leader in the mediation program I coordinated, and recruited many more student mediators—students whom he might otherwise have recruited into a gang. He talked about that mediation session as a turning point for him, a moment when he significantly changed how he understood what it meant to "be a man."

In this case, a personal intervention helped change the boys' perspective as well as their behavior. On a larger scale, what is needed is a transformation of cultural consciousness, one that makes violence and revenge unacceptable responses. We need to replace the idea that masculinity and femininity are diametrically opposed gender identities with a more continuous experience of attitudes and behaviors in which anyone can participate. School programs need to address and transform our deeply embedded social beliefs and help boys feel powerful and confident without relying on violence and domination.

A number of other programs are making inroads against bullying, although few adequately address the gender issues that are so endemic to the problem, and many have other problems as well. Challenge Day is recognized as one successful model that has been used in 450 cities in thirty-nine states in the United States, as well as Canada, Japan, Germany, and Australia. The central intervention is a daylong program that, according to its website, was "created to build connection and empathy, and to fulfill our vision that every child lives in a world where they feel safe, loved, and celebrated."[11]

One of my students brought in a video of one school's Challenge Day from YouTube; the students were coming up to a microphone and apologizing directly to students to whom they knew they had been hurtful. At this particular school, there seemed to be one student in particular who had endured most of the abuse. The students were crying as they confessed their hurtful deeds and apologized profusely. My class was awed and inspired by what they saw.

When I interviewed Daniella, though, a student from a northeastern working-class rural area who had experienced Challenge Day firsthand, she was less optimistic. "I honestly don't think that bullying behavior will ever completely stop," she said. "But there was one thing that we did this year as sophomores that stopped it for a few weeks at least." She described the Challenge Day experience as "amazing": "We learned about what was really going on in each other's lives and why we acted the way we did." However, she said, "It helped for a while, but soon wore off."

Ideally, however, the program is supposed to jump-start a new culture in the school. Before Challenge Day occurs, the school is supposed to build their own "Be the Change" school team composed of both students and teachers. Then they are charged with planning events, service and mentoring programs, and other activities in the name of Gandhi's slogan "Be the change you wish to see in the world." The program boasts a 67 percent drop in disciplinary incidents when done correctly. It depends, though, on the school to support such ongoing activities.

Barbara, who attends the same school as Daniella, explained sadly: "We won't do [Challenge Day] next year because of our principal. I think it helped a lot even if it was just for one to two weeks afterwards. We were a lot different to each other during that time. I think the principal thought it was too emotional and too personal, but I don't agree with the idea of not doing it. It was a really good program." I was struck by Daniella's feeling that even two weeks of less violent school dynamics would be worth the major intervention Challenge Day offered. Imagine what could happen if there were ongoing efforts to increase community in school.

The Challenge Day program was not only abandoned after a single day but extended to only a portion of the students at Barbara's school. My students at Adelphi University also speak sadly about their experiences with Challenge Day in that it was only offered to a select group of students. The program's help is limited if the students who are inspired to be more compassionate toward one another are still being belittled and harassed by students who didn't participate in the program.

"When we were there," Barbara said, "people thought it would last a long time, and then we went back and the other three grades were still how they were. If the whole school went to it, it would be really good." Barbara fantasized about a monthly assembly where teachers and students would talk about the effects of bullying and inspire discussions similar to those that occurred on Challenge Day. Instead, she said, "bullying has gotten a lot worse in high school."

Daniella had a less positive vision for the future. Discouraged after the loss of Challenge Day at her school, she said: "The only thing that could really stop bullying is if everyone saw what it did to hurt people, and I don't think that will happen anytime soon. So, for now, punishments are what should happen: detention, suspension, expulsion, stuff like that. Sorry if I sound pessimistic or anything! I really don't mean to. It's just what I think."

There are other problems with Challenge Day, however. Maia Szalavitz, author of multiple books including *Help at Any Cost*, says the emotional intensity of Challenge Day is similar to the encounter-style seminars popularized by organizations popularly considered "brainwashing cults." In Seattle, Washington, parents were encouraged to send their children to expensive workshops at Resource Realizations (the company that runs Challenge Day) following Challenge Day. Szalavitz says that Challenge Day is a toned-down version of the World Wide Association of Specialty Programs (WWASP), programs for troubled teens that she has described as abusive.

Some of the most successful programs are those that schools develop internally to deal specifically with the issues that have developed in their particular environment. For instance, Raquel had a more positive experience with an antibullying program at her northeastern lower-to-middle-class urban school, and she felt more hopeful. Her school's symposium was focused on race. People of all different ethnicities stood up and told the school how hurt they were when they heard the stereotypes and ridicule about their cultures. "One girl said, 'It really hurts me when people say Hispanics are lazy. My parents work very hard, and I can't believe they have that stereotype that they are lazy.' I didn't realize how badly it affected people," admitted Raquel.

Teaching—and Learning—Nonviolent Communication

Another essential skill for moving beyond a bully society is embodied in Marshall Rosenberg's concept of nonviolent communication, sometimes referred to as "compassionate communication." It's a type of conversing that moves away from passive, passive-aggressive, and aggressive forms of speaking and works to "get everyone's needs met through compassionate giving." As defined by the Center for Nonviolent Communication (CNVC), its four main components are

1. Differentiating observation from evaluation, being able to carefully observe what is happening free of evaluation, and to specify behaviors and conditions that are affecting us;
2. Differentiating feeling from thinking, being able to identify and express internal feeling states in a way that does not imply judgment, criticism, or blame/punishment;
3. Connecting with the universal human needs/values (e.g., sustenance, trust, understanding) in us that are being met or not met in relation to what is happening and how we are feeling; and
4. Requesting what we would like in a way that clearly and specifically states what we do want (rather than what we don't want), and that is truly a request and not a demand (i.e., attempting to motivate, however subtly, out of fear, guilt, shame, obligation, etc., rather than out of willingness and compassionate giving).[12]

Nonviolent communication is a way of communicating that is "cooperative, conscious, and compassionate"—precisely what is missing in most of our schools and largely lacking in communication used by many youth (as well as many adults). The most common passive-aggressive behaviors, such as talking behind someone's back, often take place because someone did not feel comfortable enough to speak directly to a particular person about his or her concern(s); bullying is of course aggressive, where the bully thinks only of his own needs and not of anyone else; and passive behavior occurs when the person thinks only of the other person's needs and not his or her own. Nonviolent communication, on the other hand, helps people to honor their own feelings and needs as well as those of others, to create respect and empathy in their interactions, and to get what they need without hurting one another. Rosenberg wrote a book for schools so that students could learn these essential techniques early and respond to one another compassionately if there are conflicts: *Life-Enriching Education: Nonviolent Communication Helps Schools Improve Performance, Reduce Conflict, and Enhance Relationships.*[13]

I'm certified to teach nonviolent communication and I have participated in a few practice classes. During these sessions, no one looks at his or her phone for other messages; everyone is present and engaged. Sharing empathy creates remarkable emotional and cognitive shifts. When people are compassionate toward one another, their anger and sadness tend to dissipate and understanding remains. Nonviolent communication is known for creating more peace within individuals, in their personal relationships, and in schools and families—and has even been used internationally in global conflicts.

It is rare to experience such a deep sense of connection, especially in our contemporary culture, where so many friendships have been relegated to Facebook virtual connections. There is a crucial need in our society, I believe, for less Facebook and more "face." The Pew Research Center study showing that young people are texting and communicating more online then in real time with real people raises concerns about whether young people still have the skills important for face-to-face relationships.[14]

Teaching nonviolent communication is one way both to decrease bullying and related hurtful communication and to teach skills related to conversing constructively with other individuals face to face. Nonviolent communication has been effective in many schools. For instance, the Manhattan Country School in New York City, an economically and racially diverse independent school, is one of many schools that uses nonviolent communication as a primary method for building community and preventing or intervening in potential bullying situations. There students start learning how to communicate compassionately when they are four years old.

Nonviolent communication has been successful in all sorts of environments, even the New York City Police. Officer Ortiz, introduced in the previous chapter, uses nonviolent communication in his foot patrol in the South Bronx and tells many stories about how he averted violence when he was able to guess people's needs and feelings. "We helped a couple in a domestic dispute, prevented a man from jumping to his death, and helped an 'emotionally disturbed person' go willingly to the hospital for his medication rather than under duress with handcuffs. It is powerful work," Ortiz told me. "People just need to know that someone understands how they feel and what they need."

Many New York City parents of preschool-age children participate in a weekly course at the Weekday School at the Riverside Church, which teaches nonviolent communication-related skills designed to maximize effective and compassionate parenting. The courses are taught by Shelly MacDonald and are based on works by Adele Faber and Elaine Mazlish, including *How to Talk So Kids Will Listen and Listen So Kids Will Talk, Siblings without Rivalry: How to Help Your Children Live Together So You Can Live Too,* and *Liberated Parents, Liberated Children: Your Guide to a Happier Family.*[15] The skills parents learn and practice focus on validating children's and parents' feelings and on problem solving without hurtful judgments. These techniques create more harmonious relationships in the family, which then generate more positive feelings among siblings as well as between parents and their children. Parents often are floored by how powerful such compassionate communication can be at home; of course, when these techniques are practiced in families, it is more likely that the youth involved will use constructive communication in school too and less likely that they will lash out as punitive members of their schools' gender police.

Much of this important communication is also evident in classes at this preschool, where teachers with similar commitments related to compassionate communication work tirelessly to build respectful, kind, and loving community not only among the children but among their parents too. Children often come out with strong values against yelling and hitting—as well as a sophisticated ability to include others in their play and speak clearly about their feelings and needs, and an increased disposition toward kindness and empathy. Students who have these skills will surely be in a better a position to lead and support efforts to create more compassionate school communities and are also likely to be effective communicators and leaders as future professionals.

Among older children, in a New York City public high school where I worked as a school social worker, I helped organize a community meeting where students could openly share their feelings and concerns about gay bashing and sexual harassment. Students there had learned how to communicate in large groups and were expected and schooled in respectful communication methods. We asked a few students who had said they were upset about the "teasing" they heard in the school to speak up about their concerns. These students were also willing to publicly support other students who spoke up about how hurt they felt by this behavior. Students opened up about being teased and shared stories about how upset it made them to see other students get hurt. Once the first students took the initiative, others started sharing too. Faculty members also made a point of publicly supporting the students who spoke about the pain they experienced.

Supportive discussions like these create a social climate among students and a collective courage—as Mandel calls it—that no longer tolerates name-calling and other forms of harassment. They introduce ways for students and teachers to help others affirm and care about one another, and they help the school take more responsibility for protecting its community members. Regular discussions of this nature can significantly reduce the debilitating abuse that is considered normal in many schools. Students become more articulate when they are given forums to talk openly and candidly about matters they care about—working together to create a more peaceful community also helps their personal development. Students from this diverse school (25 percent African American, 35 percent Latino, 25 percent white; 10 percent Asian/other, ranging from abjectly poor and homeless to upper class) consistently reference these opportunities as the preparation that helped them become confident speakers and active participators in college classes.

We can even glean lessons about building community from the school shootings. In the stories told by surviving shooters, you can hear how alienated they felt from their school communities and how little hope they had that adults would or could intervene to end the bullying they endured. They chose to make themselves heard by making themselves notorious instead.

In its study of school shooters, the U.S. Secret Service found that attackers often told their friends, directly or obliquely, what they were planning. Rarely though, do those friends, or the shooters themselves, tell an adult.

The Secret Service asked Luke Woodham (the Mississippi shooter) why he didn't talk to an adult about his feelings.

> Q: Did any grown-up know how much hate you had in you?
> A: No.
> Q: What would it have taken for a grown-up to know?
> A: Pay attention. Just sit down and talk with me.
> Q: What advice do you have for adults?
> A: I think they should try to bond more with their students. . . . Talk to them. . . . It doesn't have to be about anything. Just have some kind of relationship with them.
> Q: And how would you have responded?
> A: Well, it would have took some time before I'd opened up. If we kept talking . . . I would have . . . said everything that was going on.[16]

Luke shares that an adult might have prevented his attack. He craved connection and support—but felt alone and isolated. We need to create environments where students and adults feel comfortable talking to one another, where adults are prepared and willing to reach out to children who need help, where students and adults are courageous in their support of one another, and where the whole school supports these relationships.

Whole-School Approaches

How do schools begin to create compassionate communities integral to dismantling bully cultures in our schools? Policies are necessary, though not sufficient; and policies focused on punishment are likely to be less effective than policies that push schools to make community and awareness of hurtful gender issues integral to their curriculum and mission. Students have the right to learn in a safe and compassionate space; they should not be forced to learn in a hostile school environment.

Whole-school efforts will have more lasting impact than after-school programs or one-day workshops. An inspiring example is Manhattan Country School (MCS), which started in 1966 as an independent school dedicated to democracy, social justice, community, and diversity. Martin Luther King Jr.'s beliefs and writings continue to be an inspiration for the school's philosophy and mission. Its director, Michèle Solá, said in an interview with me in June 2010 that starting in 1990, "our goal became to make gender equity as much a part of the bloodstream as race equity."[17]

Working with the program Seeking Educational Equity and Diversity (SEED) out of Wellesley College, as well as "Quit It!", a program for K-3 students, MCS teachers have been trained in a variety of techniques, including nonviolent communication. MCS was attracted to working with SEED because the program is also committed to addressing issues of social justice more generally. Solá said: "We want our children to make the program their own. We encourage them to enter a creative space where they no longer believe they have to accept bullying and other forms of injustices." Her comments are especially pertinent, as so many young people I speak with can't imagine—literally can't imagine—a bully-free school because they are so resigned to daily school violence.

Change often starts with a director or principal who recognizes there is a problem. Solá stated, "Homophobia is all over the world, so it is going to be in the schools too. How we talk with teachers and students about it is important. We don't look the other way when we hear people call each other 'faggot' or 'ho,' we notice it and bring it up. We also make it a part of the curriculum, and teachers appropriate the material in their own ways."

Solá admitted that building such a respectful community might be easier for MCS than for other schools: "We wove this inquiry into the fabric of our school from its inception," she explained. "It is harder in some other schools to unbuild the walls of exclusion and bias than it is to keep building our work that is already founded on being inclusive. We've always been striving to make democracy as perfect as we can make it and to help our kids be part of a hopeful project." The inclusive work at MCS starts by having children visit each other's homes from all parts of New York City: "Everyone's home is worth visiting, and every neighborhood has equal value."

This year, the MCS seventh and eighth graders titled their annual activism project "Safe Schools for Everyone"—and devoted their work to recognizing how "LGBTQI (lesbian, gay, bisexual, transgender/transsexual, questioning, intersex) young people, as well as straight kids" are bullied when they are perceived as not fitting gender norms. They are building partnerships with other New York City schools to create more safe spaces for youth.

Such work might be more difficult in schools that have to start from scratch, but given the extent of despair in our schools, such efforts are imperative. Solá says her school's motto is "by any means necessary." "I never feel disappointed by an effort to introduce this kind of language. I would never say it is not worth it to try."

Other Approaches

The whole-school work endemic to MCS takes different forms in other schools. Some public schools in Manhattan, for instance, have their own versions of a more progressive structure and attitude. Manhattan School for Children (MSC) involves parents directly in many aspects of its curriculum, focuses on group work over teacher-centered education, and educates a significant portion of students with physical disabilities. Every day MSC students are made aware of the efforts necessary to include youth with physical challenges in their educational experiences; this awareness induces a more inclusive environment among all the students, and bullying behavior is considered rare there.

Such efforts are necessary for creating bully-free environments. Schools may find it difficult to support and help a so-called bully in their midst, yet without such widespread compassion, bully cultures fester. Schools need to find ways to help targets of bullies, bystanders who live in fear that they will be next, and the bullies themselves. Michelle K. Demaray and Christine K. Malecki write that bullies tend to get less support in the classroom because they are often perceived as more frustrating to teachers.[18] It is not clear whether parent and teacher support decreases as a result of bullying behavior or whether lack of support helps trigger bullying behavior. The authors recommend that teachers support and help students perceived as bullies as well as the other students.

Demaray and Malecki also found that while bullies may get less teacher support, victims tend to feel they have less peer support, because bullies are not necessarily punished or excluded by their peers when they exhibit bullying behavior. In fact, most research, as noted, shows that aggressive boys and girls are perceived as more popular when they present themselves as tough and powerful.[19] Students who took turns playing the bully and victim (bully-victims) perceived that they had the lowest levels of support from parents, classmates, and the school, according to Demaray and Malecki. Schools need to be more proactive in creating social supports where all students feel supported and included in the school community.

In Denmark, for instance, where principals say they are hard pressed to remember a fight in their schools, nationally recognized pedagogies tend to create bonds among teachers and students—rendering bullying virtually nonexistent. Typical classrooms consist of a heterogeneous mix of social classes and interests; there is no tracking or other form of ability grouping; and tests and quizzes are not used through grade 6. Furthermore, the use of threats and punishments to discipline and motivate children is relatively absent.[20]

Morrill writes that Denmark prioritizes social harmony and works to avoid gaps in wealth between social and occupational groups, starting with their educational system. The vast differences in social wealth that are typical of the United States in recent decades, he writes, are regarded by the Danes as a primary cause of social pathologies. Socially, Denmark is primarily concerned with creating unity and harmony in their schools—a significant difference from the more competitively oriented models found in the United States.

There are no tests or quizzes through grade 6 because the Danes do not "want to sort students into groups of winners and losers," they "don't want to label anyone as a failure, which is what tests are seen as doing," and "there is skepticism about the utility of tests and quizzes as motivating factors," writes Morrill. "Making a competition out of learning may be compatible with the American culture, but it poses something of a threat to the value that the Danish culture places on cooperation and social unity," he continues. "It also detracts from the pleasure of learning for the sake of learning." Furthermore, testing is not perceived as "necessary for purposes of accountability because of the excellent involvement of parents with the 'class teacher.'" Finally, the idea of teaching extensively to the test, as frequently happens in the United States, is foreign to Danish teachers and parents.[21]

Morrill writes that this cooperative and gentle attitude transfers to the larger cultural relationships among children and parents: "While it is common to hear parents in the U.S. say mean things to their children or scream at them in such places as Wal-Mart, I have never experienced anything similar in 10 years of shopping in the Danish cooperative grocery stores."[22]

Regarding discipline, "Students are not sent to stand in the hall; or sent to the principal's office; or suspended; nor are students scolded harshly as they often are in American schools." Morrill writes that the U.S. model "assumes that children are better motivated by fear than by praise and encouragement" and that it erroneously "teaches the child that problems and conflicts are to be resolved by the use of power rather than the use of reason and persuasion. The idea of using authoritarian measures to prepare children for life and work in a democratic society" is not acceptable in Denmark.[23]

To create the kind of community that is effective in preventing bullying cultures from developing in the first place, classrooms in Denmark feature "a high degree of group work" and the use of "cooperative projects." Their schools focus on cooperation instead of competition. Danish youth tend to feel safe in their learning environments, and they outscore American students in international math and science competitions.[24] Denmark has also been a leader in the antibullying models acclaimed internationally. They have also never had a school shooting.

Further, since Danish schools tend to keep their students in the same class with the same teacher for years at a time, students are helped to make lasting and deep connections with one another, as well as with faculty, members. Such relationships are vital for creating peaceful communities. In the United States, class compositions are more often changed every year, so that burgeoning friendships are repeatedly interrupted and undermined, contributing instead to the disjointed and disconnected character prevalent in so many American schools.

In the United States, there is some concern that a more cooperative school model would inadequately prepare students for the "real world." Yet even in business schools there is a trend toward emphasizing teamwork and improved interpersonal relationships. Many successful and forward-thinking businesses and nonprofit organizations teach their employees to use appreciative inquiry as a model that maximizes creativity, growth, and productivity. Appreciative inquiry involves the "unconditional positive question"; employees are encouraged to ask questions about what is working and to develop creative and innovative ideas, rather than to focus on what is wrong and needs fixing. According to Appreciative Inquiry (AI) Commons, an online site hosted by Case Western Reserve University's Weatherhead School of Management, "Instead of negation, criticism, and spiraling diagnosis, there is discovery, dream, and design."[25]

This kind of approach is a move away from the bully society more traditionally found in large firms. Top business schools from Harvard to Columbia University also now teach students to work in groups and strive to work together for common goals. Books such as David Faulkner and Mark de Rond's edited collection *Cooperative Strategy: Economic, Business, and Organizational Issues* articulate the benefits of cooperation over competition even in America's cutthroat economic culture;[26] "working with" rather than "against" others is more likely to produce the best results in myriad circumstances. Many U.S. schools are out of step with this new direction even as American businesses are catching on.

Because the evidence is so strong that a cooperative, compassionate school environment can help prevent and combat a school bully society and help students succeed academically, we need to work harder to make this kind of school a national trend, as many European countries have done. Further, a whole-school effort must reach beyond the classroom into the home and into cyberspace too.

Creating a Supportive Cyberspace

Even schools that work to create compassionate school communities face another, perhaps even more difficult problem when it comes to cyber-bullying, which is an increasing menace for school-age children. Cyberspace is an uncharted and ever-changing frontier. Online bullying has the same impact as offline bullying. Students end up feeling depressed, anxious, and in the most extreme cases suicidal or full of lethal rage. These conditions are prevalent and increasing in the United States.[27] Schools need to be part of the solution. While schools have legal rights to prohibit certain language or behaviors on school property or at school-related activities, these rights do not tend to extend to the Internet. Thus the U.S. zero-tolerance, one-size-fits-all approach is even less effective in cyberspace, where school jurisdiction is limited.

A compassionate culture at school is more likely to breed kinder communication on the Internet, but questions regarding follow-up and intervention are more complicated. In some cases, online bullying may be addressed efficiently because a log can be found of exchanges. More often, however, users hide behind anonymous names and identities. Given the difficulty of making cyber-bullies answer for their actions, it is that much more important to hold the school community accountable for any bullying a student in their midst experiences.

Schools need to be proactive about helping students commit to being part of a compassionate community, and further, to support targeted students with all the collective courage they can muster. In this way, cyber-bullying will decrease as well as the emotional ramifications targets otherwise are forced to endure alone.

Even when lawyers do find ways to hold offenders directly accountable for online bullying, these efforts are unlikely to reduce the prevalence of cyber-bullying. Instead, in "Cyber-Bullying and Harassment of Teenagers: The Legal Response," Alisdair A. Gillespie writes that education is essential. Cyberspace must be perceived on some level as an extension of school, now that students use technology as a primary means of socializing and communicating with one another. Potential cyber-bullies need to understand the anguish their actions can cause, and potential victims need education on the dangers lurking in cyberspace and how to minimize threats.[28]

Even some of the school shootings could well have been averted by more adult awareness and discussion of what was being posted on personal websites and blogs. In the most notorious case, the Columbine shooting, Eric Harris had his own website that contained direct threats against fellow students, and many of the other shooters' postings also revealed anger, rage, and murderous intentions. While direct, violent threats are not protected by our First Amendment, censorship alone is not the answer; it is a shortcut that misses deeper issues that spawn school shootings. Schools that find evidence of impending violence should of course intervene and directly address the students who made the threats, but they would also do well to discuss these issues immediately with the entire community.

A look at recent legislation involving cyber-bullying reveals some other pitfalls involved in efforts to legislate away such behavior. As mentioned earlier, in January 2006, the U.S. Congress passed a law making it a federal crime to "annoy, abuse, threaten or harass another person over the Internet." Approximately thirty-six states passed similar legislation. However, these laws apply only to people over the age of eighteen, so they don't necessarily help the cyber-bullying problem among children and teens. In addition, rumors about an underage individual are not considered slander or libel. A young person cannot take someone to court for hurting his or her reputation. For example, only an adult whose livelihood or romantic prospects are threatened by rumors can turn to the courts. Many jurisdictions don't want to investigate or prosecute these (underage) cases, says Al Kush of WiredSafety.org, an Internet safety advocacy group based in Seattle, Washington. "They are short-staffed and busy pursuing what they call 'real crime.'"[29] Surely this is not the most effective way to deal with bullying.

Laws are also misused when it comes to some forms of cyber-bullying such as "sexting," the practice of sending or posting sexually suggestive text messages and images, including nude or seminude photographs, via cell phones or over the Internet. When adults engage in this activity with other adults, it is often considered free speech and even encouraged, with instructive suggestions in popular women's magazines. Cyber-harassment is new, though, and few laws directly address sexting when someone underage ends up getting hurt. In some cases when underage youth engage in this practice, it has been considered a felony and the sender has been convicted under federal child pornography legislation.

The bullying effect of sexting arises when suggestive photos are distributed, sometimes internationally, by vindictive ex-lovers or others intent on being hurtful. The current legal trend, though, to prosecute children as adults guilty of distributing child pornography, is considered by many to be an inappropriate response to a serious problem. When young people send photos of themselves to one another in respectful rather than harassing ways, it is questionable whether the law has any place at all. Julia Saldino writes that "statements from the Congressional Record demonstrate that Congress intended to punish criminals who performed heinous crimes and exploited children rather than teenagers engaging in the consensual exchange of suggestive pictures, as is the situation in [current case] *Miller v. Skumanick.*"[30] Educating students about the ramifications of these kinds of behaviors would make a more lasting difference than prosecuting children as adult pornographers.

Schools need policies that support safe and healthy conditions for students, and these need to be far-reaching. Sexuality, for instance, is both encouraged and demonized in contemporary society and within schools. As discussed, children and teens perceived as exhibiting "inappropriate" sexuality are widely attacked by adults and young people alike who function as their schools' gender police. Gay bashing, slut bashing, and other forms of gender attacks are heard daily by American students on and offline. Sex education even in HIV/AIDS prevention lessons in United States public schools, still mostly stress abstinence.[31] Students are given few if any arenas to speak with responsible and compassionate adults about their questions, concerns, fears, and/or anxieties regarding their own and others' sexualities.

Yet in a historical moment, when, as a result of sexual slurs and related attacks, students are being killed, committing suicide, and perpetrating massacres—as well as enduring high levels of depression, anxiety, and other emotional breakdowns—we can no longer afford to keep these issues out of schools. Policies are needed that support discussion and respect among community members, especially around difficult issues related to gender and sexuality. Students don't need more punishment and criminal charges; they need guidance, support, and education.

As it is, though, most efforts to address these kinds of problems remain in the legal realm. At a roundtable discussion to which I was invited, New York State senator Kemp Hannon introduced language that would amend existing laws for public schools to increase penalties for hazing and prohibit bullying and cyber-bullying. The proposal suggests that the Regents ensure that in grades K-12 there will be a "component" of "instruction in civility, citizenship and character education" and that a school employee must report a suspicion of bullying or cyber-bullying to the principal, who must report it to the superintendent, who would report it to local law enforcement for investigation.[32] The policy is well-meaning and effectively makes school faculty "mandated reporters" regarding bullying and cyber-bullying, just as they are "mandated reporters" for child abuse—where a school faculty member must report any suspicion of child abuse to child protective services. In this legislation, a single statewide hotline would be established that all persons would use to make telephone calls alleging instances of bullying and hazing. The hotline would be administered by the commissioner of education, who would report calls to appropriate authorities.

States across the country have implemented similar statutes. New Jersey's 2011 Anti-Bullying Bill of Rights is considered the toughest regulation against bullying in the United States—a response to Tyler Clementi's suicide. While some school faculty are spearheading some important community work, much of the larger focus requires more reporting and police intervention.[33] Another effort, a Missouri bill, makes cyber-bullying a criminal offense. The legislation was passed after the 2006 suicide of Megan Meier, the young teen who hanged herself in her closet after receiving hurtful messages on Myspace from a person she thought was a boy she had met online. A first-time offense could mean up to a year in prison. Adults twenty-one or older who repeatedly bully a minor online could face up to five years in jail.

Many of these edicts remains impotent, however, because young people under age sixteen years still have some legal recourse as juveniles, and most law enforcement agencies are busy doing what they refer to as the "more serious stuff." Legal limitations only make it more necessary that school climate be pursued as a primary intervention and that this work be extended to creating more positive social interactions on the Internet as well. If a school is able to create a environment where students are expected to treat each other with respect, compassion, and warmth, it is more likely that these behaviors and attitudes will extend to Internet relationships among students too. Students who find that their schools support them, help them support others, and recognize and appreciate them have far less reason to lash out indiscriminately at others, in real time, or in cyberspace. In fact, students are more likely to turn to one another in positive and empathic ways if they consistently receive positive rather than punitive reactions.

Furthermore, most new mandates require that students and school faculty report cyber-bullying to authorities; but given the mistrust among students, and between students and teachers, as well as the pervasive belief that it is wrong to "tattle-tale" or "snitch," prevalent social norms are more likely to discourage such reports, just as students are reticent about reporting other forms of bullying. Unless schools create environments where school faculty and students unite to create a supportive school culture, it is unlikely that many people will come forward.

Right now, unless we change tracks, we are most likely to keep implementing draconian laws with more extreme punishment for more defined offenses. I hate to think about where this will leave us in the next thirty years—perhaps with still more people in prison, in a nation that already has the highest incarceration rate in the world, and with more imprisoned people feeling smug about their status as outlaws capable of the most severe revenge. There are more effective alternatives.

Fellow parents, teachers, administrators, and legislators often ask me what they should do if a child is being bullied in school buildings or in cyberspace. The answer is that schools need to create a collective courage among their community members such that students and faculty members are expected to stand up for one another if any student (or faculty member) is treated with a lack of respect. We need to embark on whole-school efforts to hold one another accountable to ethical values relating to respect and compassion toward others. Any student who experiences bullying behavior, whether in cyberspace or face to face, should be supported by the entire school community in homeroom discussions and all-school meetings—whether or not anyone knows who the bully is—since in cyberspace the perpetrators often remain effectively anonymous.

Adults and youth in schools can spearhead a movement toward empathy and compassion where students are recognized and appreciated on a daily basis, to such an extent that no one needs to do something "big" in order to "to be remembered," as so many of the perpetrators set out to do. If a student is insulted on the Internet (or face to face), people in the school can declare their indignation and reaffirm their commitment to creating a school culture where all people are treated with respect. The school can rally behind the hurt individual (without necessarily focusing on the perpetrator, who may or not be known) and make it clear that the target is cared about and that the whole community takes the insult personally.

Adele Faber and Elaine Mazlish offered this sound advice for parents in their best-selling book *Siblings without Rivalry:* punishing the aggressor will tend to pigeonhole him or her as the "bad one." Then he or she is likely to repeat the behavior in order to fulfill the expectations of that role. Parents, instead of giving attention to the aggressor, should "attend to the injured party." The parent can say to the injured party something to the effect of "People are not for hurting. Your sibling needs to learn to ask for what she wants with words, even when she's angry. Let's put some ice on your arm."[34] Similarly, schools can give attention to targets of bullying, discuss the different ways students can learn to express themselves, and offer the victim the support, warmth, and attention that most people who are hurting crave. When the aggressor is no longer rewarded through attention (negative or positive), the behavior is more likely to decrease.

Bullying behavior must be attacked rather than individuals so that bullies no longer receive praise and status for acting hurtfully toward others. Schools can help make compassion more popular than aggression and render bullying behavior impotent as a means for students to gain recognition and popularity. Any person in a community can become a leader in these efforts; and in the current bully climate resulting in so much fear and pain, it is likely that others will quickly join a burgeoning movement.

Granted, it is not easy to change a school culture, but persistence and hard work are hallmarks of any success. As MCS director Solá suggested, "by any means necessary" is a vital motto for creating positive change in a school community. Some efforts will not work, others might feel like steps backwards. Yet most people are concerned about the ramifications of school bullying, and there is going to be something a parent, guardian, student, teacher, school social worker, administrator, coach, or other person can do that *will* work. Creative efforts to build community and oppose violent proclivities will help students (and school faculty and parents) feel safe, supported, and thus able to thrive and learn—and to develop the important relationships they need with themselves and others to become empowered, empowering, and educated individuals.

While a counselor and school social worker in schools for over a decade, I saw students on and offline get gay-bashed (regardless of their sexual identity) and slut-bashed (regardless of their sexual activity). As discussed, I've also seen students leave dangerous gangs and become leaders in their school's mediation programs; and I've seen gang victims find that a new school's caring community helped them get out of such treacherous circumstances, and then into prestigious colleges, all expenses paid. Violence of all kinds can be mitigated by creating communities where people are supported and where they are given guidance and expectations related to treating themselves and others with respect and kindness.

Schools need only dedicate themselves to this goal. More than a "component" in the K-12 curriculum, it must be a sustained effort integral to the school's mission. Getting rid of one bully after another through suspension or expulsion will only perpetuate the problem; in the present climate, bullies will continue to get status from their peers regardless of the punishments they endure. Schools instead need to be more innovative about finding prevention methods that speak to the members of their community. Anyone reading this book could well become the catalyst that helps create a more peaceful school.

Conclusion

From a Bully Society to
Compassionate Communities

On the first day in one of my criminal justice classes, I asked my students to tell me why they thought school shootings occurred. One student said something similar to what many of the Columbine jocks said about Eric and Dylan after Columbine. "They couldn't take the bullying. Why didn't they let it roll off them?" and then, "Something had to be wrong with them." The boy later shared that he had been a victim of bullying for most of his school career and that this was how he coped. "No one was going to help me," he said, "so I just had to try not to let it bother me." Another girl said something similar: "All my girlfriends were called 'sluts' and 'whores.' Get over it." Many other students nodded in agreement: "It has always existed. It's everywhere." They talked about their own bullying experiences in school, in the workplace, and in college. One student declared, "It's a competitive society, survival of the fittest—and that's how it's going to be in schools too."

We had a long discussion about the mental health of the shooters. Why couldn't they withstand the abuse like everyone else? Why couldn't they just suck it up? And then someone suggested that perhaps it was the jocks and other tormentors who had the mental health problem. "Why do they get pleasure from hurting other people? What's wrong with them?"

We discussed these questions: Is it necessarily the shooters who have a mental health problem? Was there something wrong with the "jocks" who were the most common bullies of the shooters? Or is there something wrong with our society so resigned to the school violence revealed by school shootings? Is there something disturbing about the fact that children expect that their schools will have high levels of gay bashing, slut bashing, violence against girls, racism, and violence against those who are less able or otherwise "different"? What does it say about our schools, our workplaces, and our society, that everyone thinks it is so normal to be tormented, abused, harassed, stalked, threatened, and beat up, on a daily basis? This seems like an unhealthy way to live—yet millions of children, as well as adults, feel that they simply have no other choice.

I was startled by the student who matter-of-factly said: "It's a competitive society—'survival of the fittest'—and that's how it's going to be in schools too." I had somehow thought it was more hidden—that our culture had so normalized issues related to competition, domination, and power that they were invisible to anyone raised in its midst. My students confirmed that this was no secret to them. They understand that their world is cutthroat. They know that they have to compete to survive and that they will be judged for nothing short of how powerful they look and how much influence they wield. That's clear. What is more elusive to them is that it doesn't have to be this way.

When we study political theory we study multiple ways of organizing a society and different models for getting our needs met. The sociologist Talcott Parsons famously describes the functions a society needs to address—how a society distributes necessities like food and clothing, *Adaptation;* how we come to have similar *Goals;* how we maintain solidarity among one another *Integration;* and what he calls *Latency,* creating and maintaining similar values among people in a given society (*AGIL*). Any political or economic framework needs to address these functions—but the way we address these concerns can vary significantly across societies and cultures. Yet most of my students cannot even imagine a society, much less a school, founded on principles that prioritize community, compassion, and cooperation rather than individual profit, self-interest, and winning at any cost. I understand why, as they tend to learn these lessons at almost every turn.

Always Alone

Our hyperindividualist, hyper-self-reliant, hypercompetitive culture causes students to often end up alone and lonely. Their attempts to combat the loneliness—to find connection, support, and belonging—often end up feeding the bully society. Students tell each other their secrets with an interest in gaining closeness, a special friend, advice—yet in many schools their special private moments morph into "juicy gossip" and become a form of information capital that other students use to increase their own social standing. Students hope to find friends, people they can trust and rely on, and instead find that with one "wrong" move they are excluded, isolated, and teased. They learn early that it is "immature" to trust others. Girls and boys both start to explore their sexuality, hoping to find intimacy and fulfilling connections—and again they are often met, instead, with cruel slut bashing, gay bashing, ridicule, and ruined reputations.

We all have vulnerabilities and want to connect deeply with others. Adolescents are experiencing these needs acutely as they mature, and instead of receiving a human response they are often hurt and abused. Rather than developing their humanity, they find themselves wounded and undermined. Like so many of the people I interviewed in this book, young people find that as adults they have difficulty trusting friends, developing intimate relationships, asking for support, and developing self-esteem and confidence.

Tatania, who became a teacher in her thirties, came from an inner-city northeastern school and had been bullied and humiliated for years during her adolescence; she describes one traumatic experience that affected her permanently. She went to Burger King by herself because her best friends were absent that day. A guy she liked came up to her and said "really loud: 'Don't you have any friends?'" Tatiana started crying. "Up to two years ago, I wouldn't eat in a public place by myself," she shared. "If I had to, I just wouldn't eat. I lost a lot of weight in college when my friends got really busy and weren't able to eat with me. Then I started listening to music and having my Walkman on so that people wouldn't say anything to me. It helped me feel safe."

In response to the bullying she experienced, Tatiana tried to appear indifferent to others and fiercely independent, warding off any impression that she was lonely or unliked. Embracing expectations to appear hyper-self-sufficient, though, is considered largely self-destructive by many scholars. After conducting extensive research and interviews relating to individualism in American life, the authors of the national bestseller *Habits of the Heart* concluded: "We deeply feel the emptiness of a life without sustaining social commitments. Yet we are hesitant to articulate our sense that we need one another as much as we need to stand alone, for fear that if we did we would lose our independence altogether."[1]

This American expectation to "stand alone"—the perception that needing help and support is a sign of weakness—plays out in the dynamics of bullying. Bullied students are expected to "take it"—an attitude directly connected to hegemonic masculinity expectations. Even girls are increasingly encouraged to "act like a man" and handle things on their own. When Wendy was bullied in middle school, "Teachers never helped and I would come crying to my mom. My mom thought it was normal and I was being a baby about it. She wouldn't call the school. The teachers would say, 'Are you sure this happened?' And they would question me rather than question the bullies." The experience made Wendy feel isolated and abandoned. "No one was helping me. Nobody cared. My mother knew I was miserable, but didn't do anything. All these kids are ganging up on me. Mom doesn't care. Teachers don't care. Father's not around. I blamed myself and I thought it was only happening to me."

Bullying often ends up undermining close family relationships too. Raquel, from a northeastern lower-to-middle-class urban area, described an experience in which she felt forced to abandon her own sibling. She explained: "My brother has been bullied his whole life." Jared was overweight and had glasses; between kindergarten and fifth grade, the boys in the neighborhood excluded him from everything, called him gay, and teased him mercilessly. Raquel said: "He would go inside to calm down and get upset and cry . . . I didn't do anything. I thought it would cause more problems if his older sister was defending him instead of himself. . . . Mom was going to call the police, but they gave my mom a hard time for protecting him too. He was supposed to hold his own. 'You're such a little baby,' they taunted him. I couldn't stick up for him. I didn't want to encourage more teasing."

Children and parents often find that the fear, shame, and isolation that bullying victims feel creates a wall between them. Natasha from a northeastern wealthy suburban area, had a close relationship with her mother, but she believed, as many youths do, that telling her mom about the six years of torment she experienced at school would just make it worse for her. "She would talk to the other parents or tell the school, and they would think I was weak or scared of them, and a tattletale," Natasha said. "I told my mom I wanted to leave school, but I couldn't tell her why, so she wouldn't let me leave." Later Natasha's mother was horrified that she hadn't switched Natasha out of the school when she requested. Natasha understood: "You didn't realize how cruel the children were being." Natasha wishes she had told her mother what was going on, but the values that demanded she "handle things on her own" and show that she was "able to take it" prevented her from seeking help and kept her a captive victim.

Shantique, from a southern poor rural area, also quickly learned that "once you tell, it is over. You'll never get back. They will pick on you forever." Recalling her daily ordeals on the school bus, where she was targeted for relentless bullying, Shantique said: "You had to figure stuff out on your own. I would get off the bus and cry and I knew I had to clean up before my grandma saw. I had to figure out how to do it myself. I couldn't tell anyone. It would be worse. 'You're like a baby,' they would say." Shantique echoed many other students as she described how it felt to be dealing with constant harassment, completely on her own: "Overwhelmed. I remember feeling scared, but also that it is just what you're supposed to do, figure that stuff out by yourself. Some things you just can't tell people."

Like so many others I talked with, Shantique told me that her experiences had affected her permanently. "I'm in therapy now," she says. "I still feel overwhelmed that I have to figure out everything by myself." She tells me that at forty-six, "I don't have a husband and children. I still have to figure it out. I have very good friends, but there are things about me that they don't know. I would never ask them for real help." She continues, "I think this message that I have to do things by myself has cost me. I've been in bad situations where I could have used some help."

The overvaluing of independence in our culture means that often a child's relationship with his or her mother becomes a direct target for bullying. Mothers are the only members of society who are expected to be supportive of others (though not necessarily supported by others). They are likely to be a child's main support and the person with whom he or she has been most vulnerable. The very closeness of this relationship often becomes the focus for hostile attacks. "Mama's boy" is the most typical—but the slurs are innumerable.

Several of the people I interviewed for *The Bully Society* talked about the torment they experienced because their mothers were seen as deficient in some way. Vanessa's mother, Karen, said students at her daughter's northeastern urban school would make fun of her when she came to get Vanessa after track practice; sometimes she saw that girls rolled their eyes at her. Lenny was teased because his mother had a physical disability. Rebecca said she was relieved that the kids in school harassed her only about her weight. "They didn't know my mother was schizophrenic. The abuse I got in my neighborhood was even worse."

Students routinely look for perceived "differences" or weaknesses in other children's parents and exploit them as fodder for teasing. This tendency to undermine even the closest familial relationships shows how deeply our society fuels children's isolation through values regarding hyperindependence. In the twenty-first century, more American families live across the country from one another; careers routinely trump familial ties and connections; and in a society that offers little in the way of economic support for families when they come upon hard times, many families find that, having acquiesced to our hyperindividualist culture and moved far away physically or emotionally, they don't necessarily have one another either.

School as Prison

In the absence of authentic self-expression and relationships, we become accustomed to the irrational foundation on which our lives are structured and accept some unacceptable ideas: that this is as good as it gets; that competition is better than cooperation; that things are more important than people; and that inequality makes more sense for a society than equality. Similarly, while we purport to favor positive school environments that support children's potential, we still consider it normal and inevitable that our children feel terrorized and tormented on a daily basis.

Lenny recognized the function that bullying serves and explained to me that he thought bullying was "normal." "Everyone gets bullied," he said, "or at least gets tested." "This is a capitalist society," continued Lenny, who never finished high school but now runs a successful business. "You have to take out your aggression. If you don't have money, you're not anything. You can't do anything, can't take care of your family, can't handle life the way you want to." Many youth recognize the damage done by bullying and have even experienced it themselves but nonetheless completely accept it as an intrinsic and inevitable reality, just as they accept the value system that spawns it. This acceptance traps them in a prison without walls. The eighteenth-century French jurist and reformer Joseph Servan put it clearly:

> When you have thus formed a chain of ideas in the heads of your citizens, you will then be able to pride yourself on guiding them and being their masters. A stupid despot may constrain his slaves with iron chains; but a true politician binds them even more strongly by the chains of their own ideas; it is at the stable point of reason that he secures the end of the chain; this link is all the stronger in that we

do not know of what it is made and we believe it to be our own work; despair and time eat away the bonds of iron and steel, but they are powerless against the habitual union of ideas, they can only tighten it still more; and on the soft fibres of the brain is founded the unshakeable base of the soundest of Empires.[2]

We are bound not by physical chains but by beliefs that render us docile—obedient to strangulating conventions. Students (and adults) come to believe that being popular, purchasing brands, and dominating others are necessary and all important. No one has to point a gun—so many of us accept these precepts without question.

In *Against Schooling: Towards an Education That Matters*, Stanley Aronowitz argues that schools are social training grounds for these kinds of expectations rather than sites for education. In a related article, Aronowitz wrote: "While acquiring credentials that are conferred by schools remains an important prerequisite for many occupations, the conflation of schooling with education is mistaken. Schooling is surely a source of training both by its disciplinary regime and its credentialing system. But schools transmit not a 'love for the world' or 'for our children' as Arendt suggests and, contrary to their democratic pretensions, teach conformity to the social, cultural, and occupational hierarchy. In our contemporary world they are not constituted to foster independent thought, let alone encourage social agency."[3]

Aronowitz laments the state of schools today and compares them to aging vats where students learn little of importance, other than how to tolerate boredom. Instead students "accumulate social capital—the intricate network of personal relations that articulate with occupational access."[4] In a 2008 interview, Aronowitz, said that schools are essentially places where middle-class students in the right high school and college "meet the people who can advance their career and make their career." The school is like a day prison, with cops prowling the halls, and adults who ask all the wrong questions, says Aronowitz. They ask: "Why isn't this kid in class—but they don't ask the essential question: What is it about this class that doesn't meet the needs of so many kids?"[5] Richard Ryan concurs. For instance, he says, the punitive tendency to suspend and expel students "fails to diagnosis or address the real problem."[6] This discipline-and-punish approach fails to mitigate the violence in our schools and in the worst cases actually nurtures it. Learning and creating community are often forsaken in the interests of control and containment.

Seth Kreisberg, from Harvard University, and one of my graduate education professors before he met an untimely death, detailed with concern the extent to which students' every move is carefully controlled and monitored—to the point that in most schools they have to ask permission to go to the bathroom. They are compelled to speak at certain times and be quiet at other times. Domination and control, two characteristics associated with being masculine, are hallmarks of typical teacher pedagogies and institutionalized school practices.

The challenge, Kreisberg writes, is to move from a position of "power over" to "power with." Rather than imposing "facts and analyses upon their students," he suggests that teachers invite students to become part of "a shared inquiry, a mutual exploration of issues."[7] Kreisberg recommended restructuring schools with these concepts in mind and shows that these "reforms" turn students from "feeling powerless and acting in very destructive ways" to becoming "active, involved, and constructive members of the class."[8] Schools with top-down structures, where teachers have excessive control over their students' futures and are forced into a hyperassessment of their students' work, are often experienced by students as arbitrary and degrading.

Kreisberg's recommendations—similar to practices in more peaceful and academically thriving schools in Denmark—include that teachers bond with their students and help students bond with one another in the classroom. When students feel connected to a community at school, they tend to be more engaged and feel more fulfilled by the experience. Teachers can help students reach across ethnic, economic, social, cultural, and even gender divides to help them get to know people with whom they might not otherwise speak; teachers can also query students about their interests and gear lessons in directions that engage their students' curiosity.

I'm often asked to train school social workers and psychologists on how to help their students build resiliency to bullying behavior, but this question implies, on some level, that students should learn how to take the abuse and develop a thicker skin—just as the bullies themselves expect. Others ask for specialized techniques for counseling targeted students, but this approach also pathologizes the victim. I'm asked to help identify "red flag" students; instead, I think we need to become aware of "red flag" social cultures. When I'm asked to help determine who is most likely to become a "troubled teen," I suggest a new goal—diagnosing disturbing values endemic to a particular school. Schools that transform their school cultures— and work vigilantly to build a compassionate community and dismantle their gender police—will find that they don't need this piecemeal approach; students will rise to the occasion, and bullying will decrease or even disappear. Then individual work with students to improve communication skills and develop more authentic relationships with self and others will be about making life richer, rather than just making it bearable.

Ace went to a northeastern urban public school—where I worked as a social worker—that was dedicated to building such a compassionate community. "It was a different school than my other schools," he recalled. "It was like a mini-college with smaller classes that met for longer times. The teachers were always there for you. It wasn't just about passing tests; the classes were designed to make you think instead of summarizing. I got to think and that helped me in college." With my help and the support of the school community, Ace got a full scholarship to a prestigious school, where he studied psychology and anthropology. "The discussions helped a lot. [The school] was vocal, you had to speak up, and that helped me speak up in college."

Ace was born and raised in the Bronx. His family is from the Dominican Republic, and Ace went back there for a while after his mother died, then moved back and forth a few times as he stayed with one aunt or another. His father was dealing drugs and couldn't help out. Before he began attending our school, he was in a nearby school ridden with gangs; he was once beat up as part of a gang member's initiation rite. Ace, like many students at our school, might have had a very different life if he hadn't gone to our community-focused and self-reflection-oriented school. Ace himself says that he's not sure he would have gone to college if he hadn't gotten my call that he'd been accepted there. He started the same day.

Ace's application to this college got lost in the mail three times. I helped him send it over and over again, and I called repeatedly to let them know about Ace and to advocate on his behalf. Students need faculty members to fight for them, to be aware of the problems that students are facing, and to stick with them to make sure everything works out. Most schools are too big or otherwise focused, so that this help and follow-up do not happen. Instead, school faculty can get overwhelmed and rely on an easier, faster kind of approach. They don't have the resources or the time to give students the attention and support they need. Students need to be helped to dream big, and then they need help to make their dreams happen. We were able to do this for our students, but it meant the faculty worked overtime every day as well as on weekends. Public schools need the funds to make this kind of future accessible to students everywhere in our nation.

Such efforts will be limited as long as our surrounding culture clings to hypermasculine values driven by a supercapitalist economy. Schools can nonetheless help students make their own way and maintain their dignity and integrity in smaller settings. A new cadre of graduates may lead us to a different kind of culture that more pervasively breeds the support and compassion so many of us crave.

Messerschmidt writes, following Connell, that schools should pursue "the explicit goal of social justice because many masculine practices in schools perpetuate injustice—such as peer abuse—and therefore pursuing justice in schools requires addressing the gender patterns that support these practices. Arguably developing programs in schools that challenge division and emphasize empathy are essential."[9] These are wise words, but we have a long way to go: right now, prejudice and bigotry are triggers for most bullying behaviors yet are still largely invisible as such to adults and students alike.

We live in a world where, trying desperately to break free from the schools and social situations they found brutal and oppressive, school shooting perpetrators unleashed rage with a lethal and devastating impact again and again and again. There is no end in sight. The shooters themselves didn't try to replace the old hierarchies with something new. They were as resigned as everyone else that school bullying was an immutable fact of life, and they believed the only thing they could do was destroy their schools and themselves as they became the biggest bullies. School shootings proliferated throughout the period in which I wrote this book. New cases were added regularly as the book evolved. We need to offer our students a different method of resistance and a clear vision for transforming their bully cultures. Too many new antibullying programs are stuck in old mind-sets—teaching children to speak up for themselves but neglecting the importance of community and supporting others.

Aronowitz asks another essential question: "What are the requisite changes that would transform schools from credential mills and institutions of control to a site of education that prepares young people to see themselves as active participants in the world?"[10] Surely when students are connected to their schools, excited about learning, and feeling fulfilled by their classes and engaged by their teachers, they will be far less inclined to turn on one another. Students who love school and feel recognized and empowered in their classes are also less vulnerable to pressures to become the perfect boy or girl or to find attention in notoriety. Helping students appreciate themselves and others, and become engaged in the world, is an essential antidote to the vulnerabilities developed when raw insecurities are instead exploited by larger consumer forces pressuring everyone to purchase excessive products in order to become "super" boys and girls.

Aronowitz's late wife, the prolific feminist writer Ellen Willis, said poignantly in her book *No More Nice Girls*: "People deprived of pleasure don't get kinder and gentler but meaner and nastier."[11]

I believe that change is possible in our schools. If schools are transformed, students who come from these new, more supportive, peaceful, and affirming communities can have a powerful effect on the larger society as they become the future leaders of our country. Together we can move from a destructive one-size-fits-all bully society to more compassionate communities—where students, families, and community members can, instead, thrive.

Appendix

Methodology

I became interested in studying school shootings when I heard the school shooters explain the motives for their crimes. Their complaints were no different from those of average American students across the nation. They were upset about their peers calling them gay, girls that rejected them, teachers who they felt punished them unjustly, and related issues prevalent in most school cultures. So I set out to make more visible the comments the perpetrators made alongside the stories of ordinary youth who raised almost identical concerns. In doing so, I conducted a content analysis of the shootings; I drew on existing statistical research, and I shared my own observations working in high schools and universities over the last twenty years. I also interviewed students, parents, and faculty from schools in disparate demographics—and brought all this information to bear under the scrutinizing light of some of the most powerful and insightful sociological theories available. My methodologies are elaborated below.

Content Analysis

In an effort to systematically analyze factors identified as causing extreme school violence, I have carried out a content analysis of press and scholarly reports of 166 school shootings that took place in the three decades between 1979 and 2009. In a chart, accessible on *The Bully Society* website, I have categorized the motives and contexts of each school shooting—where information is available: http://www.nyu-press.org/bullysociety/dataonschoolshootings.pdf.

At this time, at least 73 of the cases have inadequate information on motives. Of the 166, 7 relate to drugs, money, or political protests unrelated to this study. The remaining shootings are discussed in *The Bully Society* and/or highlighted on the website chart.

In choosing relevant cases to analyze, I combined rampages, targeted attacks, and gang wars. Glenn Muschert categorizes school shootings as follows: rampages, mass murders, terrorist attacks, targeted shootings, and government shootings. In this study, I look most closely at rampages as well as targeted shootings, as they are the types that occur in schools. According to Muschert, rampages are "expressive, non-targeted attacks on a school institution . . . and involve(s) multiple victims, some chosen for their symbolic significance or at random." Targeted shootings, on the other hand, are more directly focused at an individual or group of people—and are less symbolic in nature.[1] Past studies on school shootings tended to focus on rampages and excluded targeted shootings where the shooter specifically attacked and killed individual(s); they also avoided examining gang wars.[2]

In my research I found less distinction between rampages and targeted shootings, or even gang warfare. Most of these crimes are incited by similar masculinity challenges. Therefore, I included high-profile cases of different kinds in my study sample. I gathered public discourse and research (television, radio, newspapers, online news sources, scholarly journals, and books) on school shooting cases, which included indiscriminate murder as well as cases where people were specifically targeted.

I have been studying school shootings since 1997 and I have examined over forty lists of shootings accessible through news, police, and online reports. I conflated this information to compile as complete a list as possible for this part of the study. Nonetheless, some school shootings are not widely reported—either because schools were reticent about attracting publicity or because lack of injuries failed to make these less tragic incidents register as strongly on the national radar. My study sample therefore is not exhaustive—but the cases that I may have missed are few and are unlikely to affect the validity of the conclusions based on these most highly profiled cases.

To identify common themes, I focused on comments by perpetrators, victims, and community members related to "trigger" factors and motivations in the shootings. I also analyzed the importance and depth of treatment that media sources accorded various motivating factors. According to Zipf's law, the most frequent words and phrases mentioned reflect important concerns in every communication. Therefore, quantitative content analysis starts with word frequencies and extends to synonyms and homonyms. In many of these cases, the perpetrators left manifestos—on the web, in diaries, in videos, and in school notebooks—that directly conveyed why they committed their acts. In other cases, others who knew the perpetrators well (students, parents, teachers) or police investigators tried to fill in the missing pieces on the basis of their knowledge of the perpetrator's grievances. The perpetrators' notes or others' perceptions of the crime were then repeated in the media as well as in scholarly sources. Comments that were repeatedly made either verbatim or with similar intent I considered evidence of "trigger" factors. As much as possible I let the perpetrators speak for themselves when they tried to explain why they committed their crimes.

Analysis of hundreds of reports related to these cases reveals twelve themes that have not been sufficiently identified or adequately addressed in previous studies of school shootings and related violence:

1. Perpetrators lashed out against those they perceived to be at the top of their schools' status hierarchies; they targeted those who tried to increase their status by assaulting, harassing, and threatening the perpetrators.
2. Gender issues, including gay and perceived-gay bashing against the perpetrators (almost all of whom identified as heterosexual), played a role in catalyzing the violence.
3. A pattern of sexual harassment and and/or dating violence and perceived rejections characterized many of the perpetrators' relationships with the girls they targeted and/or killed.
4. Perpetrators tried to defeat the boys whom they perceived as threatening their relationships with girls.
5. Perpetrators acted because they felt humiliated after "being dumped" by girls.
6. Perpetrators saught revenge against their school when they believed that no one was willing and/or able to stop the bullying they experienced.
7. White supremacy, related to efforts to demonstrate masculinity, motivated some of the perpetrators to commit their crimes.
8. As a way to retaliate, some perpetrators targeted those who had hurled racist epithets at them.
9. When girls committed violence, they did so for similar reasons to those attributed predominantly to boys.
10. In some cases perpetrators raged against high-stakes tests or low grades which were perceived as creating overwhelming obstacles to future opportunities.

11. Adults too often turned a blind eye to warning signs about imminent violence as a result of deep-seated beliefs that "boys will be boys," "girls will be girls," "school bullying is part of typical adolescence," or "school bullying is a normal way of being in a competitive culture"; adults were sometimes targeted as a result of their perceived "complicity" in related shootings.

12. Community-oriented programs related to preventing bullying, which have been widely practiced in European schools, have been more successful in reducing school violence than the more common zero-tolerance policies practiced in the United States.

The chart on *The Bully Society* website provides a map of the school shootings and predominant motivations. Elsewhere in the book, the perpetrators speak more elaborately about their motivations, and other students, school faculty, and families make corroborating comments. This analysis exposes the link between the school shootings and the shooters' efforts to accrue social prestige by demonstrating typical indicators of masculinity. Further, this work reveals that the perpetrators made direct threats that were repeatedly missed and/or ignored by faculty, parents, peers, or other members of the school community. The lack of response parallels the media's failure to identify the significance of the role of gender-based violence. This shortcoming, rooted in society and reinforced by the media, lies in the effective invisibility of dating violence, sexual harassment, gay bashing, and other prejudiced behaviors, which are often perceived to be normal.

The lack of media attention to gender can be partly blamed on the approach to crime reporting that Neil Websdale and Alexander Alvarez term "forensic journalism" and Chancer refers to as "individualistic journalism."[3] This occurs, for instance, when reporters highlight crime anomalies perceived as being sensational and newsworthy rather than the more common but perhaps less shocking crime that more often takes place. When the perpetrators said they were tired of being called "gay" or "faggot" or that they were enraged that a girl had rejected them, such comments were, until quite recently, seen as commonplace and therefore not attributable factors in understanding the crime. The media repeatedly missed the "mundane" violence that took place in schools every day to such an extent that when there was a significant retaliatory response to such violence they continued to react with surprise.

To find policy and practice responses to school shootings, I conducted an analysis of hundreds of media accounts of a handful of international school shootings that took place between 1996 and 2002; I examined the most popular responses to high-profile school shootings in the United States and elsewhere. I studied predominantly European and U.S. newspapers and wire services, academic journals, law reviews, magazines, and documentaries. Through online searches in Lexis Nexis, Academic Premier, ProQuest, and other electronic resources, I culled information from every European bureau, including Agence France-Presse, Deutsche Presse-Agentur, and Scottish, Irish, and British news sources.

I have categorized these results in a sample of international school shootings and related policy responses in tables 1 and 2 in chapter 9. For the most part, this research exposes different types of policy responses to school shootings in the United States and Europe. The results are striking, as two clear patterns emerge: U.S. responses tends toward increasing security and punishment, while European responses tend toward adding more school social workers, building community, and creating other forms of social support. The differences in responses fall clearly along the lines of the linguist George Lakoff's famous typology articulated in his book *Moral Politics*: the conservative strict-father (U.S.) model and the liberal nurturant-parent (European) model, respectively.[4] As detailed in chapter 9, these distinctions have implications for school faculty and other community members, and they draw attention to the need for fresh and more nuanced approaches.

Statistical Research

The Bully Society uncovers the antecedents to school shooting massacres in the violence that students experience every day, including the aforementioned: status wars, sexual harassment, dating violence, gay bashing (of both students who identify as gay and students who identify as straight), girl bashing, racism, and rage related to high-stakes tests that are perceived as foreclosing future success. Not surprisingly, prior research indicates that social problems are significant issues in our nation's schools. The daily violence in schools reveals that children respond to the same problems to which the school shooters retaliated, with a host of other destructive, though perhaps less visible, reactions.

Research addressed in *The Bully Society* includes the following topics:

1. *Bullying.* Over the last decade, studies demonstrate that a bully culture dominates our schools. In one 2005 national survey, 65 percent of teens reported having been verbally or physically harassed or assaulted during the past year. Students bullied other students' physical appearance (39 percent), actual or perceived sexual orientation (33 percent), and gender expression (28 percent).[5]
2. *Sexual Harassment.* According to *Hostile Hallways: Bullying, Teasing, and Sexual Harassment in School* (2001), based on a study conducted by the American Association of University Women Educational Foundation, 83 percent of girls said they had been subject to sexual harassment at some point in their school lives, while 30 percent said they experienced it often.[6]
3. *Dating Violence.* In a 2001 study, 20 percent of girls from fourteen to eighteen years old experienced physical or sexual abuse by a boyfriend, partner, or date; in a 2006 survey by the Liz Claiborne Foundation, almost a third of girls said they worried about being hurt by a partner, and nearly one in four said they had gone further sexually than they wanted to because of pressure from their partner.[7]
4. *Gay Bashing.* The Gay, Lesbian and Straight Education Network (GLSEN) released its most recent National School Climate Survey in 2003. Four out of five lesbian, gay, bisexual, and transgender (LGBT) students reported being verbally, sexually, or physically harassed at school because of their sexual orientation. Heterosexual students are similarly gay-bashed if they are perceived as deviating from gender expectations.[8]

Arguably, school shootings are the most extreme symptom of these persistent problems, but high rates of suicide, truancy, dropping out, self-cutting and other forms of self-mutilation, eating disorders, and severe depression and anxiety are among the devastating reactions students consistently display because of the social problems listed above and are also empirically noted in the text of this book.

Participant-Observation Ethnography

Following the tradition of Clifford Geertz and Paul Rabinov known for "reflexive" ethnography, which emphasizes the effect a particular culture has on the ethnographer, I include in my comprehensive descriptions of

U.S. school cultures my own experiences as a student in private and public elementary, middle, and high schools as well as my twenty years working in U.S. schools and higher education.

I have six file boxes documenting time I experienced with students whom I worked with in high schools for eleven years as a conflict resolution coordinator, substance abuse prevention and intervention counselor, social studies teacher, school social worker, guidance counselor, college advisor, and school administrator; these include mediation agreements, college personal statements, social work process recordings, and my own notes documenting my experiences as a faculty member immersed in school cultures. As with my more recent interviews with students, parents, school faculty, and other school professionals, I have received written permission according to human subject research regulations to include the specific file excerpts regarding each student's story included in the book.

Over the last decade, I've worked in public and private universities as a sociology, social work, and criminal justice professor. I've had the opportunity to talk with students from all over the country about their experiences in public, private, and religious schools. My work experiences in these schools and universities help inform and bring to life the U.S. school culture analyzed further in *The Bully Society.* I also share in the preceding pages many of the stories students raised in the criminal justice, sociology, and social work courses I've taught. Issues related to bullying come up organically in many of these courses. Social work students who intern in schools find themselves comforting bullied targets and working to resolve conflicts related to complex and entrenched bully cultures. Students share these challenges in the many social work practice classes they take as they pursue their degrees. In sociology and criminal justice classes violence is a common topic, and many students have experienced or witnessed violence in their prior secondary, middle, and elementary schools. Various topics lend themselves to students sharing their own experiences, since sociology covers many of the social problems that take root in schools, including rape, dating violence, sexual harassment, homophobia, and prejudice related to sexuality, gender, ability, race, and class. Students also tend to share their own experiences when discussing violence in schools, the workplace, and in the family—including their own responses to various education policies. When I included stories my students shared in classes, the students often elaborated on their comments in follow-up official interviews after the course concluded.

I included many of my students' stories since they helped make more visible the school settings from which so many of them had recently graduated. In the early part of the twenty-first century I taught social work in a public, largely working-class, urban university and more recently in a suburban, mostly middle-class university. Student experiences from suburban high schools in the last part of this decade were often similar to the experiences inner-city students had raised in the earlier part of the decade. In both cases students discussed their experiences both before and after they knew that I was involved in school bullying research. There were always some students who said they had not experienced or witnessed bullying; yet in these cases, interestingly enough, there were often other students in the class from the same school who insisted that bullying did indeed persist there. When students told their stories, their specificity was at times even corroborated by other students from the same schools. This precluded concerns that students might be exaggerating their stories or telling me what they thought I might want to hear—though of course it is possible that this was at least sometimes the case.

I've seen a lot of bullying. I've worked intimately with students in conflicts with other students from boyfriend-girlfriend difficulties to gang wars. I've seen students bully other students, boys bully boys, boys bully girls, girls bully boys, girls bully girls, teachers bully students, students bully teachers, parents bully children and adolescents, and children and adolescents bully parents, as well as parents bully teachers and school administrators and the reverse. Where relevant, and where confidentiality and human subject research regulations permit, I share some of these experiences to further illustrate the bully cultures described by the statistics above.

Snowball Sample Interviews

From March 2006 to March 2008 I conducted more than sixty interviews with children and adults in the United States. Since I had worked in schools for over twenty years, I had access to students and other members of school communities that I might not have had otherwise. I shared their stories in *The Bully Society* to bring to life the common landscape our children experience and to show the similarities between the school shooters' complaints and those of average American children and adults from our schools. My interviews were conducted according to the International Review Board's human subjects' research standards and expectations.

In the current climate of high-profile negative press coverage for schools and the understandable fear that surrounds school bullying and related shootings, principals were reluctant to let me enter schools to conduct "official interviews." Nonetheless, I had many contacts to begin my interviewing process. Principals, teachers, students, and parents that I knew from working in schools for two decades helped me contact others from schools in disparate parts of the country. Each person with whom I spoke connected me to other people who were interested in telling me their stories. Such a snowball sample was ideal for recruiting a snapshot of school cultures across the nation. In sociology and other statistical research, snowball sampling is a technique for developing a research sample where interviewees recruit others among their acquaintances until the sample group grows like a rolling snowball. As the sample builds up, enough data are gathered to be useful for research. This kind of sampling technique is often used to reveal hidden populations that are difficult for researchers to access. Given the current school climate, I found the snowball sample offered a helpful framework for illustrating the texture of schools from where the perpetrators came. Indeed, many students I interviewed discussed school shooting plots that had been revealed and averted in their schools. The school shooting perpetrators came from average schools across America just like the schools many of the students I interviewed attended.

My interviews included approximately fifteen from working-class environments, fifteen from wealthy environments, and thirty from middle-class environments; there were also approximately fifteen from rural areas, fifteen from inner cities, and thirty from suburban communities. Most of the people I interviewed were white, about thirty; fifteen were at least partly Latino; and fifteen were at least partly African American. I conducted slightly more interviews with white middle-class students from suburbs, since most of the school shootings took place within this demographic. I also interviewed more people from the Northeast. Fewer school shootings took place in this demographic, yet the same bully cultures that led to so many shootings in midwestern and southern states persisted there. Students ranged in age from approximately eleven to twenty-six years. They either were currently in middle school or high school or had recently graduated secondary school and thus discussed their experiences in high school, middle school, and elementary school, as well as their more immediate college experiences where relevant. I also interviewed some teachers and related professionals in their thirties and forties who reflected on the bully cultures in their schools when they had been younger. Sixty percent of my respondents were female; 40 percent were male. Most of my respondents identified as straight, and about 5 percent identified as gay; as explained in *The Bully Society*, straight and gay respondents had equally disturbing stories related to their experiences of being gay-bashed or otherwise bullied. My respondents came from the inner city of Manhattan and the Bronx, working-class rural Maine, wealthy areas in Connecticut, poor parts of North Carolina, and middle-class and wealthy areas in Texas and New York State, especially Long Island and Westchester.

When first names only are used in the text, this indicates an original interview, with a parent or student, conducted for this book (one last name is used for teachers and other school faculty). These names have been changed, and the interviewees are described merely by their most general demographics. Actual first and last names are used only for those individuals whose stories have been reported in the media and for individuals who wanted to be named directly.

Theoretical Analysis

Using the insights of classic and contemporary sociologists and other scholars—including Hannah Arendt, Stanley Aronowitz, Jean Baudrillard, Lynn Chancer, R. W. Connell, Michel Foucault, Paulo Friere, Jurgen Habermas, Michael Kimmel, Karl Marx, J. W. Messerschmidt, and George Ritzer—I examine the cultures in contemporary schools and reveal a "hidden curriculum" informed by our larger society, including dominant values and principles that school young and old alike away from prioritizing relationships in favor of winning and obtaining status and power; these tenets often manifest in school social hierarchies that reify different forms of prejudices related to status characteristics, including gender, sexuality, race, class, and ability. The insights gleaned from these thinkers further corroborate the concerns revealed by the above data and point to the possibility for real change.

In sum: The school shooting perpetrators' statements regarding why they committed school shootings parallel the research, which indicates that their concerns are shared by millions of American children. The interviews I conducted further corroborate related despair statistics as well as the high level of violence students experience daily; my own work experiences further illustrate this crisis in American schools. Finally, the theoretical analysis reveals the hidden mechanisms by which so many of these social problems persist and suggests paths for building more compassionate communities.

Notes

INTRODUCTION

1. Gina Holland, "'I Am Not Insane, I Am Angry': Suspect in Pearl Handed Class-mate a Chilling Note," *Sun Herald*, October 3, 1997, www.newslibrary.com/deliver.com/deliverccdoc.asp?SMH=133002.

1. SOCIAL STATUS WARS

1. "Va. Tech Killer Picked On, Classmates Say," CBS News, April 19, 2007, www.cbsnews.com/stories/2007/04/19/virginiatechshooting/main2703671.shtml.

2. Bill Hutchinson and Paul Schwartzman, "The Anatomy of a Rampage," *New York Daily News*, April 23, 1999, 36.

3. Pierre Bourdieu, *Distinction: A Social Critique of the Judgment of Taste* (London: Routledge, 1979).

4. Brooks Brown and Rob Merritt, *No Easy Answers: The Truth behind Death at Columbine* (Herdon, VA: Lantern Books, 2002).

5. Ibid., 51.

6. Ibid., 50.

7. Ibid., 108.

8. Ibid., 108.

9. Mark Ames, *Going Postal: Rage, Murder, and Rebellion: From Reagan's Workplace to Clinton's Columbine and Beyond* (New York: Soft Skull Press, 2005), 185.

10. Elliot Aronson, *Nobody Left to Hate: Teaching Compassion after Columbine* (New York: Henry Holt, 2001), 71.

11. Ibid., 71-72.

12. Patrice O'Shaughnessy, "Time of Teen Joy Ends in Sorrow," *New York Daily News*, April 23, 1999, www.nydailynews.com/archives/news/1999/04/23/1999-04-23_time_of_teen_joy_ends_in_sor.html.

13. Dave Cullen, "Outsiders, Even among the Outsiders," *Salon*, April, 22, 1999, http://archive.salon.com/news/feature/2000/11/22/columbine/index.html.

14. Ralph W. Larkin, *Comprehending Columbine* (Philadelphia: Temple University Press, 2007), 124.

15. James W. Messerschmidt, "Schooling, Masculinities, and Youth Crime by White Boys," in *Just Boys Doing Business? Men, Masculinities, and Crime,* ed. Tim Newburn and Elizabeth A. Stanko (New York: Routledge, 1994), 89.

16. Jonah Blank, "The Kid No One Noticed," *U.S. News and World Report*, October 12, 1998, 27-29.

17. Katherine S. Newman, *Rampage: The Social Roots of School Shootings* (New York: Basic Books, 2004), 33.

18. Lisa Popyk, "I Knew It Wouldn't Be Right," *Cincinnati Post*, November 9, 1998, ProQuest.

19. Tamar Lewin, "Terror in Littleton: The Teen-Age Culture; Arizona High School Provides Glimpse inside Cliques' Divisive Webs," *New York Times*, May 2, 1999, www.nytimes.com/1999/05/02/us/terror-littleton-teen-age-culture-arizona-high-school-provides-glimpse-inside.html.

20. Adrian Nicole LeBlanc, "The Troubled Life of Boys: The Outsiders," *New York Times Magazine*, August 22, 1999, www.nytimes.com/1999/08/22/magazine/the-troubled-life-of-boys-the-outsiders.html.

21. James Messerschmidt, *Nine Lives: Adolescent Masculinities, the Body, and Violence* (Boulder, CO: Westview Press, 2000), 66.

22. Louis Alvarez and Andrew Kolker, *People Like Us: Social Class in America*, DVD (New York: Center for New American Media, 2001), transcript, www.cnam.com/downloads/plu_ts.pdf.

23. Lucinda Platt, "Making Education Count: The Effects of Ethnicity and Qualifications on Intergenerational *Social Class* Mobility," *Sociological Review* 55 (August 2007): 485–508.

24. Ira Berkow, "Sports of the Times; The Murders over the Sneakers," *New York Times*, May 14, 1990.

25. "Survey: Teens' Cell Phones Indispensable Social Status Linked to Having Coolest New Model, Too," *CNET Tech News*, September 15, 2008, www.cbsnews.com/stories/2008/09/15/tech/cnettechnews/main4449232.shtml.

26. Harvey F. Stein, "Disposable Youth: The 1999 Columbine High School Massacre as American Metaphor," *Journal for the Psychoanalysis of Culture and Society* 5 (Fall 2000): 217–36.

27. Sara Rimer, "Terror in Littleton: The School: Good Grades, Good Teams, and Some Bad Feelings," *New York Times*, April 22, 1999, www.nytimes.com/1999/04/22/us/terror-in-littleton-the-school-good-grades-good-teams-and-some-bad-feelings.html.

28. Brown and Merritt, *No Easy Answers*, 47.

29. Lorraine Adams and Dale Russakoff, "Dissecting Columbine's Cult of the Athlete," *Washington Post*, December 9, 1998, A1.

30. Newman, *Rampage*, 93; J. C. Adams, "In Search of Why: Warning Signs," *Louisville Courier-Journal*, December 9, 1998, ProQuest.

31. "News Summary," *New York Times*, March 29, 1998, A2.

32. Michael Kirk, dir., "The Killer at Thurston High," *Frontline* (Boston: WGBH Educational Foundation, Public Broadcasting Service, 2000).

33. Timothy Egan, "Oregon Student Held in 3 Killings; One Dead, 23 Hurt," *New York Times*, May 22, 1998, A21; Timothy Egan, "Oregon Freshman Goes to Court as Number of Deaths Rises to 4," *New York Times*, May 23, 1998, A21.

34. Allen Barra, "By the Numbers: Bigger and Better?" *Wall Street Journal*, February 15, 2007, W4.

35. Jessie Klein, "Teen Killers Feel Trapped by Masculine Stereotypes," *USA Today*, November 12, 2003, 13A.

36. Alissa Quart, *Branded: The Buying and Selling of Teenagers* (New York: DaCapo Press, 2004), 117.

37. Seth Livingstone, "Fight against Steroids Gaining Muscle in High School Athletics," *USA Today*, June 8, 2005, www.usatoday.com/sports/preps/2005-06-08-sports-weekly-steroids-report_x.htm.

38. Bernard Lefkowitz, *Our Guys: The Glen Ridge Rape and the Secret Life of the Perfect Suburb* (New York: Vintage Books, 1997), 121.

39. Murray Milner, *Freaks, Geeks, and Cool Kids: American Teenagers, Schools, and the Culture of Consumption* (New York: Routledge, 2004), 40–41.

40. J. S. Peterson and K. E. Ray, "Bullying among the Gifted: The Subjective Experience," *Gifted Child Quarterly* 50 (July 2006): 252–69.

41. D. A. Kinney, "From Nerds to Normals: The Recovery of Identity among Adolescents From Middle School to High School," *Sociology of Education* 66, no. 1 (1993): 21–40.

42. P. A. Adler, S. J. Kless, and P. Adler, "Socialization to Gender Roles: Popularity among Elementary School Boys and Girls," *Sociology of Education* 65 (1992): 169-87.

43. Christina Hoff Sommers, "The War against Boys," *Atlantic Monthly*, May 2000, www.theatlantic.com/do/200005/war-against-boys; Michael S. Kimmel, *Guyland: The Perilous World Where Boys Become Men* (New York: HarperCollins, 2008).

44. David Kohn, "The Gender Gap: Boys Lagging, Girls Move Ahead," *60 Minutes*, May 25, 2003, www.cbsnews.com/stories/2002/10/31/60minutes/main527678.sthml.

45. Kimmel, *Guyland*.

46. David Firestone, "Guns and Schools; An Affinity for Weapons, but No Signs of Anger," *New York Times*, May 21, 1999, www.nytimes.com/1999/05/21/us/guns-and-schools-an-affinity-for-weapons-but-no-signs-of-anger.html.

47. LeBlanc, "Troubled Life of Boys."

48. Lawrie Mifflin, "Media: Why Was Network Television So Attracted to the Littleton Shootings? In Part, It Was Bafflement," *New York Times*, May 3, 1999, C13.

49. Todd Calder, "The Apparent Banality of Evil: The Relationship between Evil Acts and Evil Character," *Journal of Social Philosophy* 34, no. 3 (2003): 368.

50. Sigmund Freud, *Civilization and Its Discontents* (New York: Norton, 1989), 121.

51. Anne Fausto-Sterling, *Sexing the Body: Gender Politics and the Construction of Sexuality* (New York: Basic Books, 2000); L. Bowes et al., "School, Neighborhood, and Family Factors Are Associated with Children's Bullying Involvement: A Nationally Representative Longitudinal Study," *Journal of the American Academy of Child Adolescent Psychiatry* 48 (May 2009): 545–53.

52. Calder, "Apparent Banality of Evil," 64.

53. Johanna Meehan, "Arendt and the Shadow of the Other," *International Journal of Philosophical Studies* 10, no. 2 (2002): 183–93.

54. Stanley Milgram, *Obedience to Authority* (New York: Harper-Perennial, 1983).

55. Lee Ross and Richard E. Nisbett, *The Person and the Situation: Perspectives of Social Psychology* (New York: McGraw-Hill, 1991).

56. Bethany McLean and Peter Elkind, *The Smartest Guys in the Room: The Amazing Rise and Scandalous Fall of Enron* (New York: Penguin Books, 2003); Alex Gibney, dir.,

The Smartest Guys in the Room (Jigsaw Productions, 2005), transcript at www.pbs.org/now/transcript/transcriptNOW132_full.html.

57. Hannah Arendt, *Eichmann in Jerusalem: A Report on the Banality of Evil* (London: Faber and Faber, 1963).

58. Peggy Tyre, *The Trouble with Boys: A Surprising Report Card on Our Sons, Their Problems at School, and What Parents and Educators Must Do* (New York: Three Rivers Press, 2008), 104; Christina Hoff Sommers, *The War against Boys: How Misguided Feminism Is Harming Our Young Men* (New York: Simon and Schuster, 2000).

59. Christina Hoff Sommers, interview by Jon Stewart, *The Daily Show*, April 27, 2005, www.thedailyshow.com/watch/wed-april-27-2005/christina-hoff-sommers; Tyre, *Trouble with Boys*, 104.

60. Freud, *Civilization and Its Discontents*, 154.

61. Ibid., 81.

62. Rosalind Wiseman, *Queen Bees and Wannabes: Helping Your Daughter Survive Cliques, Gossip, Boyfriends, and Other Realities of Adolescence* (New York: Crown, 2009), 19.

63. Ibid., 40.

64. Barbara Meltz, "Boys and a Culture of Cruelty: Can We Stop the Cycle?" *Boston Globe*, October 19, 2000, H3.

65. S. P. Limber, "Featured Speaker Address," in *Proceedings of the Educational Forum on Adolescent Health: Youth Bullying*, ed. M. Fleming and K. Towey (Chicago: American Medical Association, 2002), www.ama-assn.org/ama1/pub/upload/mm/39/youthbullying.pdf, 4–17.

66. Michel Foucault, *Discipline and Punish: The Birth of the Prison* (New York: Pantheon, 1975), 77–78.

67. Ibid., 154.

68. A. N. Oppenheim, "Social Status and Clique Formation among Grammar School Boys," *British Journal of Sociology* 6 (September 1955): 228–45.

2. MASCULINITY AND WHITE SUPREMACY

1. Daniel Pederson, "Tragedy in a Small Place," October 11, 2011 from http://www.thedailybeast.com/newsweek/1997/12/14/tragedy-in-a-small-place.html; Jonah Blank, "The Kid No One Noticed: Guns, he concluded, would get his classmates' attention," October 6, 2011, from http://www.usnews.com/usnews/news/articles/981012/archive_004919_3.htm.

2. Katherine S. Newman, *Rampage: The Social Roots of School Shootings*, (New York: Basic Books, 2002), 27.

3. Jonah Blank, "The Kid No One Noticed."

4. Pederson, "Tragedy."

5. Blank, "The Kid No One Noticed."

6. Blank, "The Kid No One Noticed."

7. Blank, "The Kid No One Noticed"; Newman, Rampage, p. 32

8. Newman, *Rampage*.

9. Anne Campbell, *Men, Women, and Aggression* (New York: Basic Books, 1993), 59.

10. William Pollack, *Real Boys: Rescuing Our Sons from the Myths of Boyhood* (New York: Random House, 1998); Joe Pleck, *The Myth of Masculinity* (Cambridge, MA: MIT Press, 1981).

11. Lynn S. Chancer, *Sadomasochism in Everyday Life: The Dynamics of Power and Powerlessness* (New Brunswick: Rutgers University Press, 1992), 132–33.

12. Ibid., 133.

13. Ibid.

14. Ibid., 135.

15. Quoted in Peg Tyre, "The Trouble with Boys," *Newsweek*, January 30, 2006.

16. James W. Messerschmidt, "Schooling, Masculinities, and Youth Crime by White Boys," in *Just Boys Doing Business? Men, Masculinities, and Crime*, ed. Tim Newburn and Elizabeth A. Stanko (New York: Routledge, 1994), 81.

17. R. W. Connell, *Masculinities* (Berkeley: University of California Press, 1995).

18. Ibid., 79.

19. Ibid.

20. Lynne Segal, *Slow Motion: Changing Masculinities, Changing Men* (New Brunswick: Rutgers University Press, 1990), 159.

21. James Messerschmidt, *Nine Lives: Adolescent Masculinities, the Body, and Violence* (Boulder, CO: Westview Press, 2000), 10.

22. Ibid., 13.

23. Sanyika Shakur, *Monster: The Autobiography of an L.A. Gang Member* (New York: Penguin Books, 1993), 381.

24. Jessie Klein and Lynn S. Chancer, "Masculinity Matters: The Role of Gender in High-Profile School Violence Cases," in *Smoke and Mirrors: The Hidden Context of Violence in Schools and Society*, ed. Stephanie Urso Spina (New York: Rowman and Littlefield, 2000), 140.

25. Newman, *Rampage.*

26. Bill Dedman, "Deadly Lessons, Part I: Bullying, Tormenting Often Led to Revenge in Cases Studied," *Chicago Sun-Times*, October 15, 2000.

27. Derald Wing Sue, *Microaggressions in Everyday Life: Race, Gender, and Sexual Orientation* (Hoboken, NJ: John Wiley and Sons, 2010), 42.

28. Jewelle Taylor Gibbs and Joseph R. Merighi, "Young Black Males: Marginality, Masculinity and Criminality," in *Just Doing Business? Men, Masculinities, and Crime*, ed. Tim Newburn and Elizabeth A. Stanko (New York: Routledge, 1994), 64.

29. Ibid., 70.

30. Wayne Martino and Maria Pallotta-Chiarolli, *So What's a Boy? Addressing Issues of Masculinity and Schooling* (New York: McGraw-Hill International, 2003), 123.

31. Gibbs and Merighi, "Young Black Males," 78.

32. Klein and Chancer, "Masculinity Matters"; Connell, *Masculinities*; Michael S. Kimmel, *Manhood in America: A Cultural History* (New York: Free Press, 1996); Messerschmidt, *Nine Lives;* Michael S. Kimmel and Matthew Mahler, "Adolescent Masculinity, Homophobia, and Violence: Random School Shootings," *American Behavioral Scientist* 46, no. 10 (2003): 1439–58.

33. Judith Butler, *Gender Trouble* (New York: Routledge, 1990).

34. Lynn S. Chancer, "New Bedford, Massachusetts, March 6, 1983–March 22, 1984: The 'Before and After' of a Group Rape," *Gender and Society* 1 (September 1987): 239–60; Bernard Lefkowitz, *Our Guys: The Glen Ridge Rape and the Secret Life of the Perfect Suburb* (New York: Vintage Books, 1997); see also the film dramas based on the stories of these crimes, *The Accused* (1988) and *Our Guys: Outrage at Glen Ridge* (1999), respectively.

35. Messerschmidt, *Nine Lives*.

36. Ibid., 130.

37. Ibid., 3.

38. Martin Daly and Margo Wilson, "Discriminative Parental Solicitude: A Biological Perspective." *Journal of Marriage and Family* 42 (1980): 277–88; Robert L. Burgess and James Garbarino, "Doing What Comes Naturally? An Evolutionary Perspective on Child Abuse," in *The Dark Side of Families: Current Family Violence Research*, ed. David Finkelhor et al. (Beverly Hills, CA: Sage Publications, 1983).

39. David P. Barash, "Evolution, Males, and Violence," *Chronicle of Higher Education: The Chronicle Review*, May 24, 2002, B8.

40. Anne Fausto-Sterling, *Sexing the Body: Gender Politics and the Construction of Sexuality* (New York: Basic Books, 2000).

41. Leda Cosmides and John Tooby, *The Adapted Mind: Evolutionary Psychology and the Generation of Culture* (New York: Oxford University Press, 1995).

42. Lucy Bowes et al., "School, Neighborhood, and Family Factors Are Associated with Children's Bullying Involvement: A Nationality Representative Longitudinal Study," *Journal of the American Academy of Child Adolescent Psychiatry* 48 (May 2009): 545–53.

43. Maia Szalavitz, discussion with the author, May 2009.

44. Michael Kimmel, "Manhood and Violence: The Deadliest Equation," *Newsday*, March 8, 2001, www.whiteribbon.ca/newsletter/wrcWinter05.html.

45. Ibid.

3. VIOLENCE AGAINST GIRLS

1. "Teen Guilty in Mississippi School-Shooting Rampage," CNN News, June 12, 1998, www.cnn.com/US/9806/12/school.shooting.verdict/.

2. "*360 Degrees* with Anderson Cooper," CNN News, March 29, 2005, www.edition.cnn.com/TRANSCRIPTS/0503/29/acd.01.html.

3. John Cloud, "Of Arms and the Boy: All Kids Battle Demons. Why Did These Five Lose?" *Time Magazine*, June 24, 2001, www.time.com/time/magazine/article/0,9171,139492,00.html?iid=chix-sphere.

4. Lisa Popyk, "Violence Is Seductive to New Breed of Killers," *Cincinnati Post*, November 9, 1998, ProQuest.

5. J. R. Moehringer, "Tales of Teen Murder Plot Terrify Mississippi Town," *Los Angeles Times*, October 8, 1997, A1.

6. James Messerschmidt, *Nine Lives: Adolescent Masculinities, the Body, and Violence* (Boulder, CO: Westview Press, 2000), 4.

7. American Association of University Women [AAUW] Education Foundation, *Hostile Hallways: Bullying, Teasing, and Sexual Harassment in School* (Washington, DC: American Association of University Women, 2001), www.aauw.org/research/upload/hostilehallways.pdf, 19–30.

8. Christine N. Carlson, "Invisible Victims: Holding the Educational System Liable for Teen Dating Violence at School," *Harvard Women's Law Journal* 26 (2003): 351–93; Nan D. Stein, *Classrooms and Courtrooms: Facing Sexual Harassment in K–12 Schools* (New York: Teachers College Press, 1999); AAUW, *Hostile Hallways*.

9. J. Blank, "The Kid No One Noticed," *U.S. News and World Report*, October 12, 1998, 27–29; Lisa Popyk, "I Knew It Wouldn't Be Right," *Cincinnati Post*, November 9, 1998, ProQuest; David Barboza, "A Life of Guns, Drugs, and Now, Killing, All at 6," *New York Times*, March 2, 2000, A1.

10. Blank, "Kid No One Noticed"; Katherine S. Newman, *Rampage: The Social Roots of School Shootings* (New York: Basic Books, 2004).

11. Rick Bragg, "5 Are Killed at School; Boys, 11 and 13, Are Held," *New York Times*, March 25, 1998,www.nytimes.com/1998/03/25/us/5-are-killed-at-school-boys-11-and-13-are-held.html.

12. "News Summary," *New York Times*, March 29, 1998, A2.

13. Marina Angel, "Symposium: Abusive Boys Kill Girls Just Like Abusive Men Kill Women: Explaining the Obvious," *Temple Political and Civil Rights Law Review* 8 (Spring 1999): 283.

14. Bragg, "5 Are Killed"; Rick Bragg, "Jonesboro Dazed by Its Darkest Day," *New York Times*, April 18, 1998, www.nytimes.com/1998/04/18/us/jonesboro-dazed-by-its-darkest-day.html.

15. "News Summary," A2; Angel, "Symposium," 283.

16. Walter S. DeKeseredy and Martin D. Schwartz, *Dangerous Exits: Escaping Abusive Relationships in Rural America* (New Brunswick: Rutgers University Press, 2009).

17. Mark H. Moore et al., eds., *Deadly Lessons: Understanding Lethal School Violence* (Washington, DC: National Academics Press, 2003), 87.

18. S. Handlin, "Honors Student Kills Teacher," *Court TV Online*, April 26, 2001, www.courttv.com/trials/brazill/bakground.html.

19. "Friend Says She Saw Teen-Ager Pull Trigger," CNN News, May 2, 2001, http://archives.cnn.com/2001/LAW/05/02/teacher.shooting.03/index.html.

20. Handlin, "Honors Student Kills Teacher."

21. Ibid.

22. "Schoolgirl, Six, Shot Dead by Classmate," BBC News, April 21, 1999, http://news.bbc.co.uk/2hi/americas/661564.stm; Keith Naughton, "Did Kayla Have to Die?," *Newsweek*, March 13, 2000, www.newsweek.com/id/83300?tid=relatedcl.

23. Paul W. Efthim, James R. Mahalik, and Maureen E. Kenny, "Gender Role Stress in Relation to Shame, Guilt, and Externalization," *Journal of Counseling and Development* 79, no. 4 (2001): 430–38.

24. "Profile of Georgia School Gunman," Associated Press, May 21, 1999, ProQuest; Steve Fainaru, "Cry for Help Went Unheeded," *Boston Globe*, November 8, 1998, A1.

25. Fainaru, "Cry for Help."

26. Michael Kirk, dir., "The Killer at Thurston High," *Frontline* (Boston: WGBH Educational Foundation, Public Broadcasting Service, 2000).

27. Pam Belluck and J. Wilgoren, "Caring Parents, No Answers in Columbine Killers' Pasts," *New York Times*, June 29, 1999, A1.

28. Blank, "Kid No One Noticed"; Bragg, "5 Are Killed"; John Cloud, 'Just a Routine School Shooting,'" *Time*, May 23, 1999, www.time.com/time/magazine/article/0,9171,991076,00.html; Anemona Hartocollis, "Levy Discloses Flaw in Security in Wake of Shooting in School," *New York Times*, January 24, 2002, B2.

29. Cloud, "Just a Routine"; David Firestone, "Guns and Schools: An Affinity for Weapons, but No Signs of Anger," *New York Times*, May 21, 1999, www.nytimes.com1999/05/21/us/guns-and-schools-an-affinity-for-weapons-but-no-signs-of-anger.html.

30. Al Baker, "Police Arrest School Suspect and Detail Security Breach," *New York Times*, January 19, 2002, B1.

31. "Trial Report: Jacob's Letter to Tonya Bishop," *Court TV Online*, July 27, 1999, www.courttv.com/archive/trials/davis/072799_letter_ctv.html.

32. M. J. Hutt et al., "Further Validation of the Vengeance Scale," *Psychological Reports* 80 (1997): 744–46.

33. R. M. Eisler, J. R. Skidmore, and C. H. Ward, "Masculine Gender Role Stress: Predictor of Anger, Anxiety, and Health Risk Behaviors," *Journal of Personality Assessment* 52 (1988): 133–41.

34. J. Smith and R. J. Epstein, "2 L.I. Students Slain in Arizona," *Newsday*, February 18, 2007, www.newsday.com/news/local/longisland/ny-lishoto219,0,661305.story?coll=ny-main-bigpix.

35. John Ridgeway, "Mass Murderers and Women: What We're Still Not Getting about Virginia Tech Evidence Shows That Many Mass Murderers Begin and End Their Rampages with Violence against Women: With Over 30 Dead in Virginia, Can We Finally Begin to Take the Issue Seriously?," Foundation for National Progress, April 20, 2007, www.ncdsv.org/images/Mass%20Murderers%20and%20Women.pdf.

36. Newman, *Rampage*, 375.

37. Amnesty International, *Maze of Injustice: The Failure to Protect Indigenous Women from Sexual Violence in the USA* (New York: Amnesty International, 2007).

38. Susan Brownmiller, *Against Our Will: Men, Women, and Rape* (New York: Simon and Schuster, 1975); Diana E. H. Russell, *The Politics of Rape* (New York: Stein and Day, 1975); Suzanne R. Sunday and Ethel Toback, eds., *Violence against Women: A Critique of the Sociobiology of Rape* (New York: Gordian Press, 1985); Catharine A. MacKinnon, *Feminism Unmodified: Discourse on Life and Law* (Cambridge, MA: Harvard University Press, 1987); Caroline Sweetman, ed., *Violence against Women* (Oxford: Oxfam Press, 1998); Suzanne E. Hatty, *Masculinities, Violence, and Culture* (Thousand Oaks, CA: Sage Publications, 2000); Lynn S. Chancer, "Revisiting Domestic Violence in Theory and Practice," *Deviant Behavior* 25, no. 3 (2004): 255–75.

39. D. E. Howard and M. Wang, "Risk Profiles of Adolescent Girls Who Were Victims of Dating Violence," *Adolescence* 38 (Spring 2003): 1–14.

40. Stephen S. Hall, "The Troubled Life of Boys: The Bully in the Mirror," *New York Times Magazine*, August 22, 1999; Mark Townsend and Gaby Hinsliff, "Victims of Bullying Strike Back," *Observer*, June 22, 2003, www.guardian.co.uk/politics/2003/jun/22/classroomviolence.childprotection; Nathan Greenfield, "Killings Spark Discipline Drive," *Times Educational Supplement*, May 28, 1999, 22; K. L. Tonso, "Reflecting on Columbine High: Ideologies of Privilege in 'Standardized' School," *Educational Studies* 33, no. 4 (2002): 389–403; H. J. Willert, "Do Sweat the Small Stuff: Stemming School Violence," *American Secondary Education* 30 (Spring 2002): 2–13.

41. Carlson, "Invisible Victims," 351; R. Emerson Dobash and Russell Dobash, eds., *Rethinking Violence against Women* (Thousand Oaks, CA: Sage Publications, 1998); Stein, *Classrooms and Courtrooms*; Messerschmidt, *Nine Lives*; Mark D. Totten, *Guys, Gangs, and Girlfriend Abuse* (Peterborough, Ontario: Broadview Press, 2001).

42. DeKeseredy and Schwartz, *Dangerous Exits*, 4.

43. C. J. Callahan, "Schools That Have Not Protected and Worked with Gay and Lesbian Students Have Been Sanctioned by the Courts," *Education* 121, no. 2 (2000): 313–26.

44. AAUW, *Hostile Hallways*, 19–30.

45. Ibid., 40.

46. Ibid., 14.

47. Catherine Orenstein, *Little Red Riding Hood Uncloaked* (New York: Basic Books, 2002); Frances J. Ranney, "Beyond Foucault: Toward a User-Centered Approach to Sexual Harassment Policy," *Technical Communication Quarterly* 9, no. 1 (2000): 9–28; Emmalena K. Quesada, "Note: Innocent Kiss or Potential Legal Nightmare: Peer Sexual Harassment and the Standard for School Liability Under Title IX," *Cornell Law Review* 83 (May 1998): 1014.

48. Stein, *Classrooms and Courtrooms*, 11.

49. Ibid., 12.

50. U.S. Department of Education, Office for Civil Rights, "Sexual Harassment Guidance," see "Supplementary Information: Purpose of the Guidance," March 13, 1997, www.ed.gov/about/offices/list/ocr/docs/sexharoo.html.

51. Stein, *Classrooms and Courtrooms*, 1.

52. Quesada, "Note."

53. Ibid.

54. AAUW, *Hostile Hallways*, 14.

55. Kristy Castora, "The Butt Remark Dilemma," *Teen Wire*, March 8, 2002, www.teenwire.com/infocus/2002/if-20020308p151.php.

56. Shelly Reese, "The Law and Gay-Bashing in Schools," *Educational Digest* 62 (May 1997): 46–49; Quesada, "Note"; Carlson, "Invisible Victims."

57. AAUW, *Hostile Hallways*, 33.

58. Ibid., viii, 37.

59. Jay G. Silverman, "Dating Violence against Adolescent Girls and Associated Substance Use, Unhealthy Weight Control, Sexual Risk Behavior, Pregnancy, and Suicidality," *JAMA* 576 (2001): 286.

60. Leora Tanenbaum, *Slut: Growing Up Female with a Bad Reputation* (New York: Seven Stories Press, 2003), 141.

61. DeKeseredy and Schwartz, *Dangerous Exits*, 2.

62. Ibid., 2–3.

63. Liz Claiborne Inc., "Teen Relationship Abuse Survey," March 2006, www.loveisrespect.org/wp-content/uploads/2009/03/liz-claiborne-2006-relationship-abuse-hotsheet.pdf, 2–14.

64. Liz Claiborne Inc., "Tech Abuse in Teen Relationships Study," www.loveisrespect.org/wp-content/uploads/2009/03/liz-claiborne-2007-tech-relationship-abuse.pdf, 5–10.

65. Katie Roiphe, *The Morning After: Sex, Fear, and Feminism* (New York: Little, Brown, 1994).

66. DeKeseredy and Schwartz, *Dangerous Exits*, 2.

67. Legal Momentum: The Women's Legal Defense and Education Fund, "Teen Dating Abuse Program," 2009, www.legalmomentum.org/our-work/teen-dating-abuse/.

68. Rosalind Wiseman, *Queen Bees and Wannabes: Helping Your Daughter Survive Cliques, Gossip, Boyfriends, and Other Realities of Adolescence* (New York: Crown, 2009), 12.

69. Liz Claiborne Inc., "Tweens and Teen Dating Abuse Survey," 2008, http://loveisnotabuse.com/c/document_library/get_file?p_l_id=45693&folderId=122160&name=DLFE-729.doc.

70. Carlson, "Invisible Victims," 260.

71. Liz Claiborne, Inc., "Tweens and Teen Dating Abuse Survey, 2008."

72. Carlson, "Invisible Victims," 259.

73. Ibid., 352.

74. Ibid., 361.

75. Kerry Lobel, ed., *Naming the Violence: Speaking Out about Lesbian Battering* (Seattle: Seal Press, 1986); M. T. Huss and J. Langhinrichsen-Rohling, "Identification of the Psychopathic Batterer: The Clinical, Legal, and Policy Implications," *Aggression and Violent Behavior* 5 (2000): 403–22.

76. Martin D. Schwartz and Walter S. DeKeseredy, *Sexual Assault on the College Campus: The Role of Male Peer Support* (Thousand Oaks, CA: Sage Publications, 1997).

77. Hatty, *Masculinities, Violence*, 70.

78. Ridgeway, "Mass Murderers and Women."

79. L. M. Peterman and C. G. Dixon, "Domestic Violence between Same-Sex Partners: Implications for Counseling," *Journal of Counseling and Development* 81 (Winter 2003): 40–47.

80. Kyle Velte, "The Whys? of the Jonesboro Shootings: Gender Bias, the Overlooked Answer," *American Jurist* 1 (May 1998).

81. Bureau of Justice Statistics, "Violence Rates among Intimate Partners Differ Greatly According to Age," press release, October 28, 2001, http://bjs.ojp.usdoj.gov/content/pub/press/ipva99pr.cfm.

82. Donna E. Howard and Min Qi Wang, "Risk Profiles of Adolescent Girls Who Were Victims of Dating Violence," *Adolescence* 38 (2003): 1-14.

83. Stein, *Classrooms and Courtrooms*; Schwartz and DeKeseredy, *Sexual Assault*; S. L. Hills, "Crime and Deviance on a College Campus: The Privilege of Class," in *Humanistic Perspectives on Crime and Justice*, ed. Martin D. Schwartz and D. O. Friedrichs (Hebron, CT: Practitioner Press, 1984), 60–69.

84. Richard J. Gelles, "Family Violence," in *The Handbook of Crime and Punishment*, ed. Michael Tonry (Oxford: Oxford University Press, 1998), 178–206; Bureau of Justice Statistics, "Violence Rates."

85. Luoluo Hong, "Toward a Transformed Approach to Prevention: Breaking the Link between Masculinity and Violence," *Journal of America College Health* 48 (May 2000): 269–79; Elinor Scully, "Boys, Sex, and the Social Landscape: Normality of Harassment" *Independent School Magazine* 60 (Winter 2001), www.nais.org/publications/ismagazinearticle.cfm?ItemNumber=144342; T. L. Davis, "Programming for Men to Reduce Sexual Violence," *New Directions for Student Services* 90 (2000): 79–89.

86. Stein, *Classrooms and Courtrooms*.

87. Hills, "Crime and Deviance."

88. Nina Bernstein, "Behind Some Fraternity Walls, Brothers in Crime," *New York Times*, May 6, 1996, A1.

89. Stein, *Classrooms and Courtrooms*, 33.

90. Bernard Lefkowitz, *Our Guys: The Glen Ridge Rape and the Secret Life of the Perfect Suburb* (New York: Vintage Books, 1997); Stein, *Classrooms and Courtrooms*; Jeff Benedict, *Public Heroes, Private Felons: Athletes and Crimes against Women* (Boston: Northeastern University Press, 1997); Hills, "Crime and Deviance."

91. Lefkowitz, *Our Guys*, 127.

92. Ibid., 138.

93. Peggy Reeves Sanday, *Fraternity Gang Rape: Sex, Brotherhood, and Privilege on Campus* (New York: NYU Press, 2007).

94. Michael Kimmel, *Guyland: The Perilous World Where Boys Become Men* (New York: HarperCollins, 2008), 235.

95. S. B. Boeringer, "Influences of Fraternity Membership, Athletics, and Male Living Arrangements on Sexual Aggression," *Violence against Women* 2 (1996): 134–47; M. P. Frinter and L. Rubinson, "Acquaintance Rape: The Influence of Alcohol, Fraternity Membership, and Sports Team Membership," *Journal of Sex Education and Therapy* 19 (1993): 272–84.

96. T. W. Crosset et al., "Male Student Athletes and Violence against Women," *Violence against Women* 2 (1996): 163–79.

97. Newman, *Rampage*, 146.

98. Hatty, *Masculinities, Violence*, 68.

99. Carlson, "Invisible Victims"; Lobel, *Naming the Violence*; Huss and Langhinrichsen-Rohling, "Identification."

100. Sandra Walklate, *Gender and Crime: An Introduction* (Hemel Hempstead, UK: Harvester Wheatsheaf, 1995); Messerschmidt, *Nine Lives*; R. W. Connell, *Masculinities* (Berkeley: University of California Press, 1995); Michael S. Kimmel, *Manhood in America: A Cultural History* (New York: Free Press, 1996); Michael S. Kimmel and Matthew Mahler, "Adolescent Masculinity, Homophobia, and Violence: Random School Shootings," *American Behavioral Scientist* 46, no. 10 (2003): 1439–58; Jessie Klein and Lynn S. Chancer, "Masculinity Matters: The Role of Gender in High-Profile School Violence Cases, in *Smoke and Mirrors: The Hidden Context of Violence in Schools and Society*, ed. Stephanie Urso Spina (New York: Rowman and Littlefield, 2000); Klein and Chancer, "Normalized Masculinity: The Ontology of Violence in Everyday Life," in *Philosophical Foundations of Crime*, ed. B. A. Arrigo and C. R. Williams (Urbana: University of Illinois Press, 2004).

101. Stein, *Classrooms and Courtrooms*, 5.

4. GAY BASHING

1. Alex Tizon, "Scarred by Killings, Moses Lake Asks: 'What Has This Town Become?'" *Seattle Times*, February 23, 1997.

2. Kai Wright, "Gay Teasing at Roots of Violence," *Washington Blade*, December 18, 1998, www.kaiwright.com/new_more.php?id=267_0_30_0_M.

3. Tizon, "Scarred by Killings."

4. "Groundhogs, Bullies, Lawyers, and Children, Part 1," *On the Other Foot,* February 2, 2006, http://ontheotherfoot.blogspot.com/2006/02/groundhogs-bullies-lawyers-and.html.

5. Jonah Blank, "The Kid No One Noticed," *U.S. News and World Report,* October 12, 1998, 27–29.

6. Terry McCarthy, "Warning: Andy Williams Here: Unhappy Kid. Tired of Being Picked On," *Time,* March 11, 2001.

7. Gay, Lesbian and Straight Education Network [GLSEN] and National Center for Lesbian Rights [NCLR], "Fifteen Expensive Reasons Why Safe Schools Legislation Is in Your State's Best Interest," September 1, 2005, www.glsen.org/cgi-bin/iowa/all/library/record/1913.html.

8. Joseph G. Kosciw and Elizabeth M. Diaz, *The 2005 National School Climate Survey Sheds New Light on the Experiences of Lesbian, Gay, Bisexual, and Transgender Youth in Our Nation's Schools* (New York: GLSEN, 2005), www.glsen.org/binary-data/GLSEN_ATTACHMENTS/file/585-1.pdf, 14.

9. Ibid.

10. Christine Alder and Anne Worrall, eds., *Girls' Violence: Myth and Realities* (Albany: SUNY Press, 2004), 119.

11. Bob Moser, "The Crusaders," *Rolling Stone,* April 7, 2005, www.rollingstone.com/politics/story/7235393/the_crusaders/; Bryan Robinson, "Anti-Bullying Program or 'Gay Agenda'?," ABCNews.com, October 9, 2002, www.beliefnet.com/story/115/story_11503_1.html.

12. Jessie Klein, "Sexuality and School Shootings: What Role Does Teasing Play in School Massacres," *Journal of Homosexuality* 51, no. 4 (2006): 42.

13. Human Rights Watch, *Hatred in the Hallways: Violence and Discrimination against Lesbian, Gay, Bisexual and Transgender Students in the U.S.* (New York: Human Rights Watch, 2001), www.hrw.org/reports/2001/uslgbt/toc.htm; Shelly Reese, "The Law and Gay-Bashing in Schools," *Educational Digest* 629 (May 1997): 46–49.

14. Harris Interactive and GLSEN, *From Teasing to Torment: School Climate in America, A Survey of Students and Teachers* (New York: GLSEN, 2005), 4.

15. Ibid., 13.

16. M. Elias, "Gay Teens Coming Out Earlier to Peers and Family," *USA Today,* February 11, 2007, www.usatoday.com/news/nation/2007-02-07-gay-teens-cover_x.htm.

17. Harris and GLSEN, *From Teasing to Torment,* 4.

18. Trevor Project, "Suicidal Signs and Facts," 2009, www.thetrevorproject.org/suicide-resources/suicidal-signs.

19. National Mental Health Association, "National Survey of Teens Shows Anti-Gay Bullying Common in Schools," press release, December 12, 2002, www.scienceblog.com/community/older/archives/K/1/pub1600.html.

20. C. Shawn McGuffey and B. Lindsay Rich, "Playing in the Gender Transgression Zone: Race, Class, and Hegemonic Masculinity in Middle Childhood," *Gender and Society* 13 (October 1999): 619.

21. American Association of University Women Educational Foundation, *Hostile Hallways: Bullying, Teasing, and Sexual Harassment in School* (Washington, DC: AAUW, 2001), 18.

22. R. W. Connell, *Masculinities* (Berkeley: University of California Press, 1995), 79.

23. Robert Kolker, "Out of Bounds," *New York Magazine*, October 20, 2003, http://nymag.com/nymetro/news/features/n_9391/.

24. Mark Benjamin, "The Abu Ghraib Files," *Salon.com*, February 17, 2006, www.salon.com/news/abu_ghraib/2006/03/14/introduction/.

25. Alfred C. Kinsey et al., *Sexual Behavior in the Human Male* (Philadelphia: W. B. Saunders (1948; repr., Bloomington: Indiana University Press, 1988), 638.

26. Lynn S. Chancer, *Sadomasochism in Everyday Life: The Dynamics of Power and Powerlessness* (New Brunswick: Rutgers University Press: 1992), 132–35.

27. A. Cuesta, "Gay Advocates Say Bullying Contributed to a Rash of School Violence," *GayWired.com*, October 5, 2006, www.gaywired.com/article.cfm?section=9&id=10929.

28. "Teen Accused in Weston Shooting Appears in Court: Witness Says She Tried to Warn School Officials," Channel 3000, April 18, 2007, www.channel3000.com/news/12286464/detail.html.

29. David Cullen, "The Rumor That Won't Go Away," *Salon.com*, April 24, 1999, www.salon.com/news/feature/1999/04/24/rumors/.

30. Wright, "Gay Teasing."

31. A. Chase, "Violent Reaction: What Do Teen Killers Have in Common?," *In These Times*, July 9, 2001, http://surge.ods.org/idle_other/violent_reactions.htm.

32. M. D. Simpson, "Gay Student Battles Bashers," *NEA Today*, October 1997, 23-27.

33. Jamie Nabozny, "20 Questions: Interview," *Philadelphia City Paper*, May 1, 1997, www.citypaper.net/articles/050197/article001.shtml.

34. Ibid.

35. Ibid.

36. American Civil Liberties Union of Illinois, High School Civil Liberties Project, "Teacher ACLU Fact Sheet: Protection from Anti-Gay Violence in Schools," 2006, www.aclu-il.org/legal/highschool/teachers/protection.shtml; Shelly Reese, "The Law and Gay-Bashing in Schools," *Educational Digest* 62 (May 1997): 46–49.

37. Reese, "Law and Gay-Bashing."

38. Catherine Saillant and Amanda Covarrubias, "Oxnard School Shooting Called a Hate Crime:14-Year-Old Is Charged in Shooting of Oxnard Classmate," *Los Angeles Times*, February 15, 2008, www.latimes.com/news/local/la-me-oxnard-15feb15,0,7663055.story.

39. Reese, "Law and Gay-Bashing," 65–68.

40. Ibid.

41. GLSEN and NCLR, "Fifteen Expensive Reasons."

5. GIRL BASHING

1. "Sticks and Stones: School Shooter Describes What Drove Her to the Edge: Elizabeth Bush Interviewed by Connie Chung," *20/20*, April 13, 2001, ABC, www.antidepressantsfacts.com/2001-03-07-ABC-BethBush.htm.

2. Ibid.

3. Elizabeth Lloyd-Richardson et al., "Characteristics and Functions of Non-Suicidal Self-Injury in a Community Sample of Adolescents," *Psychological Medicine* 37 (2007): 1183–92.

4. "Sticks and Stones."

5. Ibid.

6. Robert F. Marcus and Bruce Swett, "Violence and Intimacy in Close Relationships," *Journal of Interpersonal Violence* 17, no. 5 (2002): 570–86; Sibylle Artz, *Sex, Power, and the Violent School Girl* (New York: Teachers College Press, 1998).

7. Rachel Simmons, *Odd Girl Out: The Hidden Culture of Aggression in Girls* (New York: Harcourt, 2002), 175.

8. Michele Burman, "Turbulent Talk: Girls' Making Sense of Violence," in *Girls' Violence: Myths and Realities,* ed. Christine Alder and Anne Worrall (Albany: SUNY Press, 2004), 88.

9. Ibid., 95.

10. "Principal Says School Officials Tried to Thwart High School Hazing," CNN News, May 9, 2003, www.cnn.com/2003/US/Midwest/05/08/hs.hazing/.

11. "The Murder of Reena Virk: A Timeline," CBC News, April 12, 2005, www.cbc.ca/news/background/virk/.

12. Sheila Batacharya, "Racism, 'Girl Violence,' and the Murder of Reena Virk," in Alder and Worrall, *Girls' Violence,* 62.

13. Ibid., 69.

14. Helen Kennedy, "Phoebe Prince, South Hadley High School's 'New Girl,' Driven to Suicide by Teenage Cyber Bullies," *New York Daily News,* March 29, 2010, http://articles.nydailynews.com/2010-03-29/news/27060348_1_facebook-town-hall-meetings-school-library.

15. Leora Tanenbaum, *Slut: Growing Up Female with a Bad Reputation* (New York: Seven Stories Press, 2003), 12.

16. Alder and Worrall, editors of *Girls' Violence,* note that crime statistics are the most unreliable of social facts and that crimes perpetuated by girls have been recategorized in ways that appear to show increases in violence where none exist. In fact, categories related to crimes committed by girls have shifted toward greater criminal culpability. Their book includes a series of essays questioning the increase in so-called girls' violence. James Garbarino argues in his book *See Jane Hit: Why Girls Are Growing More Violent and What We Can Do About It* (New York: Penguin, 2006) that violence has indeed increased; he cites statistics from disparate sources, noted in the text of *The Bully Society,* to support these claims.

17. "The Pack Mentality," *Nightline with Ted Koppel,* ABC, May 10, 2002.

18. Garbarino, *See Jane Hit,* 9.

19. Ibid., 4.

20. Marisa Trevino, "Arrests of Female Teens for Violent Crime Grow," Women's eNews, December 14, 2003, www.womensenews.org/article.cfm/dyn/aid/1642/context/cover/.

21. Deborah Prothrow-Stith and Howard R. Spivak, *Sugar and Spice and No Longer Nice: How We Can Stop Girls' Violence* (San Francisco: Jossey-Bass, 2005).

22. Robin Morgan, *An Anthology of Writing from the Women's Liberation Movement* (New York: Vintage, 1970); Susan Griffin, *Women and Nature: The Roaring inside Her* (Washington, DC: Sierra Club Books, 1978).

23. Carol Gilligan, *In a Different Voice: Psychological Theory and Women's Development* (Cambridge, MA: Harvard University Press, 1993).

24. Nancy Chodorow, *The Reproduction of Mothering: Psychoanalysis and the Sociology of Gender* (Berkeley: University of California Press, 1999).

25. Jody Miller, *Getting Played: African American Girls, Urban Inequality, and Gendered Violence* (New York: NYU Press, 2008).

26. Andrea Dworkin & Catharine MacKinnon (1985) *The Reasons Why: Essays on the New Civil Rights Law Recognizing Pornography as Sex Discrimination* (New York: Women Against Pornography), p. 17.

27. Kathleen A. Bogle, *Hooking Up: Sex, Dating, and Relationships on Campus* (New York: NYU Press, 2008).

28. Ariel Levy, *Female Chauvinist Pigs: Women and the Rise of Raunch Culture* (New York: Simon and Schuster, 2006), 125.

29. Ibid., 121.

30. Garbarino, *See Jane Hit*, 4.

31. Levy, *Female Chauvinist Pigs*, 17–30.

32. Ibid., 30.

33. Miller McPherson, Lynn Smith-Lovin, and Matthew E. Brashears, "Social Isolation in America: Changes in Core Discussion Networks over Two Decades," *American Sociological Review* 71 (June 2006): 353–75; Jacqueline Olds and Richard S. Schwartz, *The Lonely American: Drifting Apart in the Twenty-First Century* (Boston: Beacon Press, 2009).

34. Aaron Kupchik, *Homeroom Security: School Discipline in an Age of Fear* (New York: NYU Press, 2010).

6. CYBER-BULLYING

1. "Special Report: Scared at School," WMBF News, March 2, 2011, www.wmbf-news.com/story/12073987/special-report-scared-at-school.

2. Joel Allen, "Atty: Socastee HS Shooting Suspect Was Bullied," WPDE News, September 24, 2010, www.carolinalive.com/news/story.aspx?id=516521.

3. Tammy Blythe Goodman, "Cyberbullying: Freshman Opens Fire at School in South Carolina," SafetyWeb, September 27, 2010, http://blog.safetyweb.com/cyber-bullying-freshman-opens-fire-at-school-in-south-carolina/.

4. Jesse Lee, "President Obama and the First Lady at the White House Conference on Bullying Prevention," White House Blog, March 10, 2011, www.whitehouse.gov/blog/2011/03/10/president-obama-first-lady-white-house-conference-bullying-prevention.

5. "What Parents Need to Know about Cyberbullying: Teens Are Often Far Ahead of Parents When It Comes to Technology," ABC News, September 12, 2006, http://abcnews.go.com/Primetime/story?id=2425023.

6. Amanda Lenhart, "Cyberbullying Report," Pew Internet and America Life Project, Washington, DC, June 27, 2007, www.pewinternet.org/Reports/2007/Cyberbullying.aspx, 1.

7. F. Mishna, A. McLuckie, and M. Saini, "Real World Dangers in an Online Reality: A Qualitative Study Examining Online Relationships and Cyber Abuse," *Social Work Research*, 33, no. 2 (2009): 107–18, p. 111.

8. "'Happy Slapping Gang Members Admit Killing Ekram Haque," BBC News, June 16, 2010, www.bbc.co.uk/news/magazine/.

9. "Online Video Shows Girl Attacked at Area School," WLWT Cincinnati, October 9, 2007, www.wlwt.com/nes/14295313/detail.html.

10. Deborah Siegel, "Girls Fight, We Watch," *Girl with Pen,* October 10, 2007, http://girlwithpen.blogspot.com/2007_10_01_archive.html.

11. Denise Witmer, "Girls Fighting YouTube Videos: Are Mean Girls Getting Meaner?," *Parenting Teens,* April 19, 2008, http://parentingteens.about.com/b/2008/04/19/girls-fighting-youtube-videos-are-mean-girls-getting-meaner.htm.

12. Fran Smith, "Going after Cyberbullies," *Prevention,* September 2006, 143-44.

13. Susan Keith and Michelle E. Martin, "Cyber-Bullying: Creating a Culture of Respect in a Cyber World," *Reclaiming Children and Youth* 13 (2005): 224-28.

14. John P. Halligan, "If We Only Knew, If He Only Told Us," 2010, www.ryanpatrickhalligan.org/index.htm.

15. Ibid.

16. ABC News, "Parents: Cyber Bullying Led to Teen's Suicide," *Good Morning America,* November 19, 2007, http://abcnews.go.com/GMA/story?id=3882520&page=1.

17. Susan Donaldson James, "Immigrant Teen Taunted by Cyberbullies Hangs Herself," ABC News, March 10, 2010, http://abcnews.go.com/Health/cyber-bullying-factor-suicide-massachusetts-teen-irish-immigrant/story?id=9660938.

18. Emily Friedman, "Victim of Secret Dorm Sex Tape Posts Facebook Goodbye, Jumps to His Death: Rutgers University Freshman Jumped from the George Washington Bridge," ABC News, September 29, 2010, http://abcnews.go.com/US/victim-secret-dorm-sex-tape-commits-suicide/story?id=11758716.

19. Phil McKenna, "The Rise of Cyberbullying," *New Scientist,* July 2007, http://newscientist.com/article/mg19526136.300-the-rise-of-cyberbullying.html.

20. Brian Stelter, "Guilty Verdict in Cyberbullying Case Provokes Many Questions over Online Identity," *New York Times,* November 27, 2008, www.nytimes.com/2008/11/28/us/28internet.html?scp=17&sq=cyberbully&st=cse.

21. Erik Eckholm, "Two Students Plead Guilty in Bullying of Teenager," *New York Times,* May 4, 2011, www.nytimes.com/2011/05/05/us/05bully.html?scp=1&sq=phoebe%20prince%20prosecution&st=cse.

22. "Dan Savage and Terry Miller," *Time,* April 4, 2011, www.time.com/time/specials/packages/article/0,28804,2058044_2060338_2060226,00.html.

23. Sameer Hinduja and Justin Patchin, *Bullying beyond the Schoolyard: Preventing and Responding to Cyberbullying* (Thousand Oaks, CA: Sage Publications, 2009), 164.

24. Ibid., 133, 161.

25. Ibid., 106, 142.

26. Sameer Hinduja and Justin W. Patchin, *Bullying beyond the Schoolyard: Preventing and Responding to Cyberbullying* (Thousand Oaks, CA: Corwin Press, 2008), 42.

27. Mishna, McLuckie, and Saini, "Cyber-Bullying."

28. Mike Masnik, "Technology Induced ADD?," *Tech Dirt,* March 28, 2004, www.techdirt.com/articles/20050328/1051222.shtml; "The Social Problems Being Caused by Technology," *Yahoo Associated Content,* January 27, 2011, www.associatedcontent.com/article/6247420/the_social_problems_being_caused_by.html?cat=25.

29. Sadie Stein, "'Fauxting': How Young People Avoid Human Interaction," Jezebel: Secrets and Lies, May 3, 2010, http://jezebel.com/5530034/fauxting-how-young-people-avoid-human-interaction.

30. C. Franzen, "OMG! Teens Now Text More Than Talk Face to Face," April 25, 2010, www.aolnews.com/tech/article/pew-study-texting-is-now-teens-top-way-to-communicate/19447380.

31. B. Hendrik, "Internet Overuse May Cause Depression Study: Teens Who Pathologically Use Internet May Be About 2.5 Times More Likely to Become Depressed," WebMD Health News, August 2, 2010, www.nhs.uk/news/2010/02February/Pages/Excessive-Internet-Use-and-Depression.aspx.

32. Kimberly S. Young and Robert C. Rogers, "The Relationship between Depression and Internet Addiction," *CyberPsychology and Behavior* 1, no. 1 (1998): 25-28, www.liebertonline.com/doi/abs/10.1089/cpb.1998.1.25; J. J. Kandell, "Internet Addiction on Campus: The Vulnerability of College Students," *CyberPsychology and Behavior* 1, no. 1 (1998): 11-17, www.liebertonline.com/doi/abs/10.1089/cpb.1998.1.11.

33. Lauren D. Laporta, "Twitter and YouTube: Unexpected Consequences of the Self-Esteem Movement?" *Psychiatric Times* 26, no. 11 (2009): 1-4.

34. M. McPherson, L. Smith-Lovin, and M. E. Brashears, "Social Isolation in America: Changes in Core Discussion Networks over Two Decades," *American Sociological Review* 71, no. 3 (2006): 353-75.

35. See Jacqueline Olds and Richard S. Schwartz, *The Lonely American: Drifting Apart in the Twenty-First Century* (Boston: Beacon Press, 2009).

7. ADULT BULLIES

1. Dan Savage, "Fear the Geek," *The Stranger*, May 12, 1999, www.thestranger.com/seattle/Content?oid=915. This quote has been referenced in many places, but there is controversy over its authenticity. See "Journals, Notebooks and Diaries," acolumbinesite.com/diary.html.

2. Brooks Brown and Rob Merritt, *No Easy Answers: The Truth behind Death at Columbine* (Herdon, VA: Lantern Books, 2002), 25–27.

3. Ibid., 28–31.

4. "Kimveer Gill: Chronologie d'une folie," *Technaute*, September 15, 2006, http://kimveer-gill-news.newslib.com/story/9375-1.

5. Andrea Cohn and Andrea Canter, "Bullying: Facts for Schools and Parents," National Association of School Psychologists, October 7, 2003, www.nasponline.org/resources/factsheets/bullying_fs.aspx.

6. "The In Crowd and Social Cruelty," *ABC News Special*, June 3, 2002.

7. Alane Fagin, contribution to "Impact of Hazing on Students, Family, and Community" panel, First National Conference on High School Hazing, Adelphi University, Garden City, NY, September 22, 2006.

8. Cohn and Canter, "Bullying."

9. Ibid.

10. Paul Grafer, interview by the author, January 12, 2008.

11. K. L. Tonso, "Reflecting on Columbine High: Ideologies of Privilege in 'Standardized' Schools," *Educational Studies* 33, no. 4 (2002): 389–403; Bernard Lefkowitz, *Our Guys: The Glen Ridge Rape and the Secret Life of the Perfect Suburb* (New York: Vintage Books, 1997).

12. Tonso, "Reflecting on Columbine High."

13. Shelly Reese, "The Law and Gay-Bashing in Schools," *Educational Digest* 62 (May 1997): 46–49.

14. Hank Nuwer, contribution to "Hazing 101: The Basics" panel, First National Conference on High School Hazing, Adelphi University, Garden City, NY, September 22, 2006.

15. Hank Nuwer, "Hank Nuwer's List of Deaths by Hazing," http://www.hanknuwer .com/hazingdeaths.html; University of Connecticut, "Anti-Hazing," http://www. greeklife.uconn.edu/hazing_stats.html.

16. Hank Nuwer, contribution to "Hazing 101: The Basics" panel, First National Conference on High School Hazing, Adelphi University, Garden City, NY, September 22, 2006; Elizabeth J. Allan and Mary Madden, "Hazing in View: College Students at Risk," hazing study presented at the University of Maine, March 11, 2008.

17. Grafer, interview by the author, 2008.

18. Ibid.

19. Regan McMahon, "Parents, Coaches Who Need Time-Outs: Adult Violence at Kids' Sports Sets a Terrible Example," *San Francisco Chronicle*, November 5, 2006, www.sfgate.com/cgi-article.cgi?file=/chronicle/archive/2006/11/05/ING05M4AHP1. DTL.

20. Fox Butterfield, "Father in Killing at Hockey Rink is Given Sentence of 6 to 10 Years," *New York Times*, January 26, 2002,www.nytimes.com/2002/01/26/us/father-in-killing-at-hockey-rink-is-given-sentence-of-6-to-10-years.html.

21. Vicki Louk Balint, "The Hazards of Teen Hazing," *Raising Arizona Kids,* April 2007, http://www.raisingarizonakids.com/index.php?page=1.library.article_view&ar_ id=283.

22. Karen Savoy, contribution to "Impact of Hazing on Students, Family and Community" panel, First National Conference on High School Hazing, Adelphi University, Garden City, NY, September 22, 2006.

23. Tom Downey, "Hazing and Heroism," op-ed, *New York Times*, January 9, 2004, www.nytimes.com/2004/01/09/opinion/hazing-and-heroism.html.

24. Mary Patterson, "Hazed," *Educational Leadership* 62 (May 2005): 20–23, http:// curriculum.d91.k12.id.us/New%20Teacher%20Program/Resources%20for%20Mentors/Articles/Hazed.pdf.

25. Ibid.

26. Gabriel Sherman, "Revolt at Horace Mann," *New York Magazine*, April 7, 2008, 27.

27. Audrey L. Amrein and David C. Berliner, "High-Stakes Testing, Uncertainty, and Student Learning," *Education Policy Analysis Archives* 10 (March 28, 2002), http:// epaa.asu.edu/epaa/v10n18.

28. Sharon L. Nichols and David C. Berliner, "High-Stakes Testing and the Corruption of America's Schools," *Harvard Education Letter,* March/April 2007, www. hepg.org/hel/article/237.

29. Senator Paul D. Wellstone, "Remarks at Teachers College," Columbia University, March 31, 2000.

30. Richard Ryan, interview by the author, February 28, 2008.

31. Amrein and Berliner, "High-Stakes Testing."

32. American Civil Liberties Foundation of Massachusetts, "Public Advisory," ALCU of Massachusetts, April 11, 2000, http://web.archive.org/web/20030419122504/www.aclu-mass.org/youth/studentrights/mcasadvisory.html.

33. Liz Murray, *Breaking Night: A Memoir of Forgiveness, Survival, and My Journey from Homeless to Harvard* (New York: Hyperion, 2010).

34. Maia Szalavitz, *Help at Any Cost: How the Troubled Teen Industry Cons Parents and Hurts Kids* (New York: Riverhead, 2006).

35. Maia Szalavitz, interview by the author, May 15, 2008.

36. Jennifer Gonnerman, "School of Shock," *Mother Jones*, September 2007, http://motherjones.com/politics/2007/08/school-shock.

37. Michel Foucault, *Discipline and Punish: The Birth of the Prison* (New York: Pantheon, 1977), 178.

38. Howard Gardner, *Intelligence Reframed: Multiple Intelligence for the Twenty-First Century* (New York: Basic Books, 1999).

39. Bill Dedman, "Deadly Lessons, Part II: Shooters Usually Tell Friends What They Are Planning," *Chicago Sun-Times*, October 16, 2000.

40. Ibid.

41. Bill Dedman, "Deadly Lessons, Part I: Case Studies: Secret Service Findings," *Chicago Sun-Times*, October 15, 2000.

42. Katherine S. Newman, *Rampage: The Social Roots of School Shootings* (New York: Basic Books, 2004).

43. Bill Dedman, "Deadly Lessons, Part I: Examining the Psyche of an Adolescent Killer," *Chicago Sun-Times*, October 15, 2000, http://education.ucsb.edu/school-psychology/School-Violence/PDF/psycheshooters.pdf.

44. "Parents, Kids Must Unite to Make Our Schools Safe," *Seattle Post-Intelligencer*, February 2, 1999, http://seattlepi.nwsource.com/local/mose02.shtml.

45. Savage, "Fear the Geek."

46. Dedman, "Deadly Lessons, Part I: Case Studies."

47. Joe Milicia, "4 Hurt, Gunman Killed in Ohio School," Associated Press, October 11, 2007, www.washingtonpost.com/wp-dyn/content/article/2007/10/10/AR2007101001486.html.

8. THE BULLY ECONOMY

1. Stephen Beach, *Instructor's Guide to Prentice Hall/ABC News Video Series* (Upper Saddle River, NJ: Pearson Education, 2008).

2. T. R. Reid, "The European Social Model," in *Solutions to Social Problems: Lessons from Other Societies*, ed. D. Stanley Eitzen (Boston: Allyn and Bacon/Pearson Education, 2007), 12.

3. Robert B. Reich, *Supercapitalism: The Transformation of Business, Democracy, and Everyday Life* (New York: Alfred A. Knopf, 2007).

4. Juliet B. Schor, *The Overworked American: The Unexpected Decline of Leisure* (New York: Basic Books, 1993); T*he Overspent American: Upscaling, Downshifting, and the New Consumer* (New York: Basic Books, 1998); David Callahan, *The Cheating Culture: Why More Americans Are Doing Wrong to Get Ahead* (New York: Harcourt, 2004); Jacqueline Olds and Richard S. Schwartz, *The Lonely American: Drifting Apart in the Twenty-First Century* (Boston: Beacon Press, 2009). Alissa Quart, *Branded: The Buying and Selling*

of Teenagers (New York: DeCapo Press, 2004); Elliott Currie, *The Road to Whatever: Middle-Class Culture and the Crisis of Adolescence* (New York: Metropolitan Books, 2004); Madeline Levine, *The Price of Privilege: How Parental Pressure and Material Advantage Are Creating a Generation of Disconnected and Unhappy Kids* (New York: HarperCollins, 2006); Jean M. Twenge, *Generation Me: Why Today's Young Americans Are More Confident, Assertive, Entitled—and More Miserable Than Ever Before* (New York: Free Press, 2007).

5. D. Stanley Eitzen, "U.S. Social Problems in Comparative Perspective," in Eitzen, *Solutions to Social Problems*, 3.

6. Mark Ames, *Going Postal: Rage, Murder, and Rebellion: From Reagan's Workplaces to Clinton's Columbine and Beyond* (New York: Soft Skull Press, 2005), 219.

7. John P. Walsh and Anne Zacharias-Walsh, "Working Longer, Living Less," in *Illuminating Social Life: Classical and Contemporary Theory Revisited*, 4th ed., ed. Peter J. Kivisto (Thousand Oaks, CA: Pine Forge Press, 2007), 6.

8. Ibid.,16.

9. Ibid., 29.

10. Anders Hayden, "Europe's Work Time Alternatives," in Eitzen, *Solutions to Social Problems*, 142.

11. Ibid., 143.

12. Walsh and Zacharias-Walsh, "Working Longer," 29.

13. R. D. Putnam, *Bowling Alone: The Collapse and Revival of American Community* (New York: Simon and Schuster, 2001); Miller McPherson, Lynn Smith-Lovin, and Matthew E. Brashears, "Social Isolation in America: Changes in Core Discussion Networks over Two Decades," *American Sociological Review* 71 (June 2006): 353–75; Olds and Schwartz, *Lonely American*.

14. "U.S. Stands Apart from Other Nations on Maternity Leave," Associated Press, July 26, 2005, www.usatoday.com/news/health/2005-07-26maternity-leave_x.htm.

15. Jay C. Thomas & Michel Hersen (2002) *Handbook of Mental Health in the Workplace* (Thousand Oaks: CA), p. 401; Bureau of Labor Statistics, "Fact Sheet Workplace Shootings July 2010," October 26, 2011 from http://www.bls.gov/iif/oshwc/cfoi/osar0014.htm.

16. Handgun-Free America, *Terror Nine to Five: Guns in the American Workplace, 1994–2003* (Arlington, VA: Handgun-Free America, 2004).

17. "Sheriff: Michigan Office Shooting Kills 1, Injures 2," CNN News, April 9, 2007, www.cnn.com/2007/US/04/09/michigan.shooting/index.html.

18. "Workplace Shooting Wounds 4 in Indianapolis," Associated Press, July 1, 2007, www.theglobeandmail.com/servlet/story/RTGAM.20070111.wworkshoot0111/BNStory/International/home.

19. Callahan, *Cheating Culture*, 18.

20. Ibid., 19–20.

21. Ibid., 31.

22. Ibid., 39.

23. Ibid., 7.

24. Sue Kirchhoff, "Greenspan Takes One on the Chin, Admits Flaws in System," *USA Today*, October 23, 2008, www.usatoday.com/money/economy/2008-10-23-greenspan-congress_N.htm.

25. Schor, *Overspent American*, 11.

26. Ibid., 38–39.

27. Ibid., 39.

28. Daniel S. Hamermesh and Jeff E. Biddle, "Beauty, Productivity, and Discrimination: Lawyers' Looks and Lucre," *Journal of Labor Economics* 16 (January 1998): 172–201, quoted in K. M. Engemann and M. T. Owyang, "So Much for That Merit Raise: The Link between Wages and Appearance," *Regional Economist*, April 2005, www.stlouisfed.org/publications/re/2005/b/pages/appearances.html.

29. Lynn S. Chancer, *Reconcilable Differences: Confronting Beauty, Pornography, and the Future of Feminism* (Berkeley: University of California Press, 1998).

30. Susan Saulny, "In Baby Boomlet, Preschool Derby Is the Fiercest Yet," *New York Times*, March 3, 2006, www.nytimes.com/2006/03/03/education/03preschool.html.

31. Richard Morrill, "Denmark: Lessons for American Principals and Teachers?," in Eitzen, *Solutions to Social Problems*, 127.

32. Jane Gordon, "Everybody Needs a Friend," *New York Times*, September 14, 2003, www.nytimes.com/2003/09/14/nyregion/everybody-needs-a-friend.html.

33. Naomi Klein, *No Logo: Taking Aim at the Brand Bullies* (Toronto: Knopf Canada, 2000); Alissa Quart, *Branded: The Buying and Selling of Teenagers* (New York: DaCapo Press, 2004).

34. Jennifer Abbott, Mark Achbar, and Joel Bakan, prod. and dir., *The Corporation*, DVD (Vancouver, BC: Big Picture Media Corporation, 2003).

35. Ibid.

36. Schor, *Overspent American*.

37. George Ritzer, "The 'New' Means of Consumption: A Post-Modern Analysis," in Kivisto, *Illuminating Social Life*, 280-98.

38. Ibid.

39. Ibid., 282.

40. Jurgen Habermas, *The Theory of Communicative Action: Reason and the Rationalization of Society*, trans. Thomas McCarthy (Boston: Beacon Press, 1984).

41. Twenge, *Generation Me*, 105-7.

42. Neil Postman, *Amusing Ourselves to Death: Public Discourse in the Age of Show Business* (New York: Penguin, 1985); Aldous Huxley, *Brave New World* (New York: Harper Collins, 1932).

43. Shankar Vedantam, "Antidepressant Use by U.S. Adults Soars, Cost and Risk Questions Mount in Face of Overall Surge in Prescription Drugs," *Washington Post*, December 3, 2004, A15.

44. Victoria Sherrow, *For Appearance' Sake: The Historical Encyclopedia of Good Looks, Beauty, and Grooming* (Westport, CT: Greenwood Press, 2001), 42.

45. Quart, *Branded*, 16.

46. Allison J. Pugh, *Longing and Belonging: Parents, Children, and Consumer Culture* (Berkeley: University of California Press, 2009).

47. M. P. Dunlevy, "How Teens Get Sucked into Credit Card Debt," *MSN Money*, May 31, 2006, http://articles.moneycentral.msn.com/SavingandDebt/ManageDebt/HowTeensGetSuckedIntoCreditCardDebt.aspx.

48. Quart, *Branded*, 27.

49. Richard Ryan, interview by the author, February 28, 2008.

50. McPherson, Smith-Lovin, and Brashears, "Social Isolation in America."

51. Olds and Schwartz, *Lonely American*, 10.

52. Ibid., 10–11.

53. Ibid., 11.

54. Quoted in ibid., 50.

55. Adrian Stone, *Intertwined* (Baltimore: Publish America, 2005), 210–11.

56. Mark Ames (2005) *Going postal: Rage, murder, and rebellion: From Reagan's workplaces to Clinton's Columbine and beyond.* (New York: Soft Skull Press), p. 149.

57. Bruce D. Perry and Maia Szalavitz, *Born for Love: Why Empathy Is Essential— and Endangered* (New York: William Morrow, 2010).

58. Ritzer, "'New' Means," 293.

59. Ibid.

60. John Gray, *Men Are from Mars, Women Are from Venus: The Classic Guide to Understanding the Opposite Sex* (New York: HarperCollins, 1992).

9. AMERICA IS FROM MARS, EUROPE IS FROM VENUS

1. P. Dejong, "Finnish School Shooter Was Bullied," Associated Press, November 8, 2007, http://abcnews.go.com/International/wireStory?id=3837063; "Man Kills Eight at Finnish School," BBC News, November 7, 2007, http://news.bbc.co.uk/2/hi/europe/7082795.stm.

2. Dejong, "Finnish School Shooter."

3. Ibid.

4. John Gray, *Men Are from Mars, Women Are from Venus: The Classic Guide to Understanding the Opposite Sex* (New York: HarperCollins, 1992).

5. Darcia Harris Bowman, "Across the Atlantic, Europeans Take Different Approach to School Safety," *Education Week*, 21, no. 37 (May 22, 2002): p. 17.

6. Ibid, 1.

7. D. P. Barash, "Evolution, Males, and Violence," *Chronicle of Higher Education: The Chronicle Review*, May 2002, sec. 2, B7–B9.

8. D. Stanley Eitzen, "U.S. Social Problems in Comparative Perspective," in *Solutions to Social Problems: Lessons from Other Societies*, 4th ed., ed. D. S. Eitzen (Upper Saddle River, NJ: Pearson Education, 2007), 3.

9. George Lakoff, *Moral Politics: What Conservatives Know That Liberals Don't* (Chicago: University of Chicago Press, 1996).

10. Ibid., 65.

11. Ibid., 65–66.

12. Ibid., 72.

13. Ibid., 108–9.

14. D. Stanley Eitzen, "Schools," in Eitzen, *Solutions to Social Problems*, 117.

15. D. Stanley Eitzen, introduction to Eitzen, *Solutions to Social Problems*, 4.

16. K. Swoger, "Teachers, Students Fear a Coming Culture of Violence," *Prague Post S.R.O.*, May 1, 2002; "German Students March against Education Law in Wake of Massacre," Agence France Presse, May 7, 2002, ProQuest; "U.S. Arms Lobby Says German Killings Prove Gun Controls Don't Work," Deutsche Presse-Agentur, April 27, 2002, Academic Premier; "Roundup: Germany Grieves as Groping for Explanations Continues," Deutsche Presse-Agentur, April 28, 2002, Academic Premier; "Roundup: Germany Set to Raise Age for Buying Guns to 21 after School Massacre," Deutsche Presse-Agentur, April 30, 2002, Academic Premier.

17. Anthony Browne, "Headmaster Shot Dead by Pupil in Lunch Hour," *Times*, January 16, 2004, 19; "Roundup: Student Turns Himself in Following Teacher Shooting," Deutsche Presse-Agentur, June 14, 2011 ProQuest.

18. "German School Siege Ends Peacefully," BBC News, October 18, 2002, http://news.bbc.co.uk/2/hi/europe/2340747.stm.

19. Joe Perry, "Slaughter of the Innocents," *Time Europe*, May 6, 2002, http://aolsvc.timeforkids.kol.aol.com/time/europe/magazine/2002/0506/cover/timeline.html.

20. C. P. Wallace, "Massacre in Erfurt," *Time Europe*, May 6, 2002, 24–29.

21. A. Hall, "'Robert Asked to Lie In That Day, Said He Had Something to Do Later. Now We Know What. We Should Have Seen It Coming . . . We Failed': Mother of Pupil who Slaughtered 16 Speaks Out," *Mirror*, May 6, 2002, 18.

22. "School Shooting in the Netherlands," BBC News, radio broadcast, London, December 7, 1999.

23. "Former Student Shoots Himself after Storming High School," *Deutsche Welle*, November 20, 2006, www.dw-world.de/dw/article/0,2144,2243631,00.html.

24. Andrew Purvis, "Tragedy in Taber," *Time*, May 19, 1999, www.time.com/magazine/article/0,9171,25025-2,00.html.

25. "Argentine Boy Shoots Classmates," BBC News, September 29, 2004, http://news.bbc.co.uk/2/hi/americas/3697678.stm.

26. Tu Than Ha, Ingrid Peritz, and Andre Picard, "Shooter Had Brief Military Service," *Globe and Mail*, September 16, 2006, www.google.com/search?client=safari&rls=en&q=%22shooter+had+brief+military+service%22+peritz+picard&ie=UTF-8&oe=UTF-8.

27. "Groundhogs, Bullies, Lawyers, and Children, Part 1," *On the Other Foot*, February 2, 2006, http://ontheotherfoot.blogspot.com/2006/02/groundhogs-bullies-lawyers-and.html.

28. Martin Kasindorf, "Survivors Attack Violence: Some Parents of Slain Student Shun Lawsuits and Instead Campaign for Political Remedies," *USA Today*, 30 May, 1999, A8.

29. Katherine S. Newman, *Rampage: The Social Roots of School Shootings* (New York: Basic Books, 2004), p. 277.

30. Susan Greene, "Goth-Fashion Crackdown Seen by Some as Fascism," *Denverpost.com*, April 23, 1999, http://extras.denverpost.com/news/shot0423cc.htm; "School Shootings on the Decline," radio broadcast, *Democracy Now: The War and Peace Report*, July 29, 1998, www.democracynow.org/1998/7/29/school_shootings_on_the_decline.

31. "Another School Districts Nixes DARE Drug Program," *OpenEducation.net*, December 5, 2007, www.openeducation.net/2007/12/15/another-school-nixes-dare-drug-program/.

32. John Devine and Hal A. Lawson, "The Complexity of School Violence: Commentary from the US," in *Violence in Schools: The Response in Europe*, ed. Peter K. Smith (London: RoutledgeFalmer, 2003), 332–50.

33. U.S. Department of Justice, Bureau of Justice Statistics, "Indicators of School Crime and Safety," 2007, www.ojp.usdoj.gov/bjs.abstract/iscs07.htm.

34. U.S. Department of Justice, Bureau of Justice Statistics and National Center for Education Statistics, "Student Victimization in U.S. Public Schools: School Crime Supplement (SCS) to the National Crime Victimization Survey," 2005, http://nces.ed.gov/pubsearch/pubsinfo.asp?pubid=2009306.

35. "Study: Schools' Zero-Tolerance Policies Flawed," Associated Press, May 16, 2001 from http://www.foxnews.com/story/0,2933,24954,00.html; Russell J. Skiba, (August 2000). "Zero Tolerance, Zero Evidence: An Analysis of School Disciplinary Practice," Indiana Education Policy Center, Policy Research Report #SRS2, August 2000, www.indiana.edu/~safeschl/ztze.pdf.

36. Skiba, "Zero Tolerance, Zero Evidence," Abstract.

37. American Bar Association, Juvenile Justice Committee, Criminal Justice Section, "Zero Tolerance Policy Report," February 2001, www.abanet.org/crimjust/juvjus/zerotolreport.html.

38. Kim Brooks, Vincent Schiraldi, and Jason Zeidenberg, *School House Hype: Two Years Later* (Washington, DC: Justice Policy Institute/Children's Law Center, 2000).

39. National Research Council, *Deadly Lessons: Understanding Lethal School Violence,* (Washington D.C: National Academies Press, 2003), p. 95; Katherine S. Newman, *Rampage: The Social Roots of School Shootings,* (New York: Basic Books, 2002), 277.

40. Ibid., 95.

41. New York Civil Liberties Union, "Criminalizing the Classroom: The Over-Policing of New York City School, March 2007, www.nyclu.org/files/criminalizing_the_classroom_report.pdf.

42. Bill Dedman, "Deadly Lessons: School Shooters Tell Why," Sun-Times Exclusive (Oct 15-16, 2000). *Chicago Sun-Times*, November 1, 2011 from http://www.icarusplays.com/wp-content/uploads/2010/02/3-Secret-Service-Findings.pdf (pp. 1-19), p. 10.

43. Ibid.

44. Newman, *Rampage,* p. 226.

45. Quoted in Bowman, "Across the Atlantic."

46. Angus Roxburgh and Neil Mackay, "Last Moments of the Quiet Teenager who Launched a Killing Spree that Left 17 Dead," *Sunday Herald*, April 2002, 3.

47. Bowman, "Across the Atlantic."

48. Jacques Pain, "Classroom Initiatives to Reduce Violence in School: 'Pedagogie Institutionnelle' Institutional Teaching Methods," European Conference on Initiatives to Combat School Bullying, May 15-16, 1998, www.jacques-pain.fr/jacques-pain/Article_classroom_initiatives.html.

49. R. Limper, "The Only Way to Combat Bullying Is a Cooperation between All Those Involved in School: Good Practice in the Netherlands Initiated by Parents," paper presented at the European Conference on Initiatives to Combat School Bullying, May 15, 1998.

50. Devine and Lawson, "Complexity of School Violence."

51. Joseph A. Dake et al., "Teachers' Perceptions and Practices Regarding School Bullying Prevention Activities," *Journal of School Health* 73, no. 9 (2003): 347-55.

52. U. V. Midthassel and S. K. Ertesvag, "Schools Implementing Zero: The Process of Implementing an Anti-Bullying Program in Six Norwegian Compulsory Schools," *Journal of Education Change* 9 (June 2008): 153-72.

53. "Norwegian Anti-Bullying Program Recommended by the European Union to Countries in Latin America," *Innovations Report,* July 11, 2006, www.innovations-report.com/html/reports/social_sciences/report-73524.html; Erling Roland et al., "The Zero Programme against Bullying: Effects of the Programme in the Context of the Norwegian Manifesto against Bullying," *Social Psychology of Education* 13 (1): 41–55.

54. Mechthild Schafer and Stefan Korn, "Germany: Numerous Programmes—No Scientific Proof," in Smith, *Violence in Schools*, 100–116.

55. Rosario Ortega, Rosario Del Rey, and Isabel Fernandez, "Working Together to Prevent Violence: The Spanish Response," in Smith, *Violence in Schools*, 137.

56. Pain, "Classroom Initiatives."

57. Ersilia Menesini and Rossella Mondiano, "A Multifaceted Reality: A Report from Italy," in Smith, *Violence in Schools*, 165.

58. Kaj Björkqvist and Viktoria Jansson, "Tackling Violence in Schools: A Report from Finland," in Smith, *Violence in Schools*, 189.

59. Geoff Johnston, "Teenage Gunman Lets Pupils Go Free," *Journal*, Newcastle, UK, October 19, 2002.

60. Ibid.; Erling Roland, Gaute Bjrnsen, and Gunnar Mandt, "Taking Back Adult Control: A Report from Norway," in Smith, *Violence in School*, 211.

61. Georges Steffgen and Claire Russon, "Luxembourg: First Official Steps to Deal with Violence in School," in Smith, *Violence in Schools*; Anastasia Houndoumadi, Lena Pateraki, and Maria Doanidou, "Tackling Violence in Schools: A Report from Greece," in Smith, *Violence in Schools*.

62. Schafer and Korn, "Germany"; Ortega, Del Rey, and Fernandez, "Working Together"; Roland, Bjornsen, and Mandt, "Taking Back Adult Control"; Robert Svensson, "Tackling Violence in Schools: A Report from Sweden," in Smith, *Violence in Schools*; Bjorkqvist and Jansson, "Tackling Violence in Schools."

63. Peter K. Smith, "Violence in Schools: An Overview," in Smith, *Violence in Schools*, 8-9; Bjorkqvist and Jansson, "Tackling Violence in Schools."

64. Smith, "Violence in Schools"; Devine and Lawson, "Complexity of School Violence."

65. Smith, "Violence in Schools," 9.

66. "Gun Law—European Style," *Time Europe*, May 13, 2002, 50.

67. D. G. McNeil Jr., "Not Only in America: Gun Killings Shake the Europeans," *New York Times*, May 1, 2002, A3; "Expelled Students Kills 16, Self at School in Germany," *USA Today*, April 27, 2002; "German Parliament Passes New Gun, Media Laws after Massacre," Agence France Presse; Brian Brady and Stephen Fraser, "Six Years on from Dunblame, Blair Orders Crackdown on Airguns That Can Be Converted to Five Live Rounds," *Scotland on Sunday*, April 28, 2002.

68. James Dob, "D'Amato Cites Storm Aid and Schumer Gun Control," *New York Times*, October 16, 1998, B5; White House Press Secretary Michael McCurry, "School Shooting Address," April 9, 1999; Devine and Lawson, "Complexity of School Violence."

69. Scott Melzer, *Gun Crusaders: The NRA's Culture War* (New York: NYU Press, 2009).

70. "Teen Depression on the Increase," BBC News, August 3, 2004, http://news.bbc.co.uk/go/pr/fr/-/2/hi/health/3532572.stm; David G. Blanchflower and Andrew J. Oswald, "Well-Being over Time in Britain and the USA," *Journal of Public Economics* 88, nos. 7–8 (2004): 1359-86; Jean M. Twenge, *Generation Me: Why Today's Young Americans Are More Confident, Assertive, Entitled—and More Miserable Than Ever Before* (New York: Free Press, 2007).

71. Twenge, *Generation Me*, 69; Bruce D. Perry and Maia Szalavitz, *Born for Love: Why Empathy Is Essential—and Endangered* (New York: William Morrow, 2010).

72. Cindi Seddon, "Stopping the Bully," *Scientific American Mind* 16, no. 2 (2005): 80.

73. Tom McLoughlin, dir., *Odd Girl Out*, based on the book by Rachel Simmons, Lifetime Television, April 4, 2005.

74. Ann Weick, "Hidden Voices," *Social Work* 45, no. 5 (2000): 401.

75. Ibid., 396.

76. Smith, "Violence in Schools"; Weick, "Hidden Voices."

77. Newman, *Rampage;* Jessie Klein, "Teen Killers Feel Trapped by Masculine Stereotypes," *USA Today*, November 12, 2003, 13A; Jessie Klein, interview by Michael Medved, November 14, 2003, *Michael Medved Show,* Salem Radio Network.

78. Amy Sullivan, "Why Does Michigan's Anti-Bullying Bill Protect Religious Tormenters?" November 8, 2011, http://swampland.time.com/2011/11/04/why-does-michigans-anti-bullying-bill-protect-religious-tormenters/; Russell Goldman, "Some School Anti-Bullying Programs Push Gay Agenda, Christian Group Says," ABC News, September 1, 2010, http://abcnews.go.com/US/school-anti-bullying-programs-push-gay-agenda-christian/story?id=11527833; Michael A. Jones, "Long Island Principal Blocks Gay-Straight Alliance, Says Gay Slurs Aren't Really that Offensive," *Gay Rights*, January 20, 2011, http://gayrights.change.org/blog/view/long_island_principal_blocks_gay-straight_alliance_says_gay_slurs_arent_really_that_offensive.

79. M. S. Spencer, "Reducing Racism in Schools: Moving beyond Rhetoric," *Social Work in Education* 20, no. 1 (1998): 25–27.

80. R. A. Astor and W. J. Behre, "Perceptions of School Violence as a Problem and Reports of Violent Events: A National Survey of School Social Workers," *Social Work* 42, no. 1 (1997).

81. Ibid.

82. Smith, "Violence in Schools," 4.

83. Ortega, Del Rey, and Fernandez, "Working Together."

84. Eric Debarbieux, Catherine Blaya, and Daniel Vidal, "Tackling Violence in Schools: A Report from France," in Smith, *Violence in Schools;* Inge Huybregts, Nicole Vettenburg, and Monique D'Aes, "Tackling Violence in Schools: A Report from Belgium," in Smith, *Violence in Schools.*

85. Astor and Behre, "Perceptions of School Violence."

86. Tara Parker-Pope, "When the Bully Sits in the Next Cubicle," *New York Times*, March 25, 2008www.nytimes.com/2008/03/25/health/25well/html.

87. Gary Namie and Ruth Namie, *The Bully at Work: What You Can Do to Stop the Hurt and Reclaim Your Dignity on the Job* (Naperville, IL: Sourcebooks, 2000), 92.

88. Ibid., 101.

89. Workplace Bullying Institute, "Workplace Bullying Still Rampant in U.S.," August 30, 2010, www.workplacebullying.org/2010/08/30/2010-wbi-zogby/; Workplace Bullying Institute, "Stability of Workplace Bullying Prevalence since 2007: 2010 WBI Survey," September 17, 2010b, www.workplacebullying.org/2010/09/17/comparison_2010_wbi/.

90. Namie and Namie, *Bully at Work*, 94.

91. Ibid., 108.

92. Ibid.

93. Ibid.

10. CREATING KINDER SCHOOLS AND CYBERSPACES

1. Vincent Brevetti, interview by the author, February 7, 2008.
2. Richard Ryan, interview by the author, February 28, 2008.
3. Paul Grafer, interview by the author, January 1, 2008.
4. Don McPherson, "Adelphi's Sports Leadership Institute: Returning Altruism to Sports," *Faculty Center for Professional Excellence Newsletter,* Summer 2004, http://fcpe.adelphi.edu/News/Issue6/n6_don.htm.
5. Rosalind Wiseman, "Owning Up Program: What Is Owning Up?" 2008, www.rosalindwiseman.com/html/profdev_about_owningup.htm.
6. Ophelia Project, "CASS: Creating a Safe School Program: What Makes Us Unique?" 2008, www.rosalindwiseman.com/html/profdev_about_owningup.htm.
7. Ibid.
8. Ibid.
9. See this program's website at www.smart-girl.org and its page "Take A.C.T.I.O.N. against Bullying," 2011, www.smart-girl.org/kids-area/take-a-c-t-i-o-n-against-bullying/.
10. Laurie Mandel, interview by the author, May 9, 2007.
11. See Challenge Day's website (www.challengeday.org).
12. Center for Nonviolent Communication, "What Is NVC?" 2008, http://cnvc.org/en/what-nvc/nonviolent-communication.
13. Marshall B. Rosenberg, *Life-Enriching Education: Nonviolent Communication Helps Schools Improve Performance, Reduce Conflict, and Enhance Relationships* (Encinitas, CA: Puddle Dancer Press, 2003).
14. Amanda Lenhart, "Teens, Cell Phones and Texting: Text Messaging Becomes Centerpiece Communication. Pew Internet and American Life Project," April 20, 2010, www.pewinternet.org/Reports/2010/Teens-and-Mobile-Phones.aspx; Carl Franzen, "OMG! Teens Now Text More Than Talk Face to Face," April 25, 2010, www.aolnews.com/tech/article/pew-study-texting-is-now-teens-top-way-to-communicate/19447380.
15. Adele Faber and Elaine Mazlish, *How to Talk So Kids Will Listen and Listen So Kids Will Talk* (New York: Harper Paperbacks, 1999), *Siblings without Rivalry: How to Help Your Children Live Together So You Can Live Too* (New York: Harper Paperbacks, 2004), and *Liberated Parents, Liberated Children: Your Guide to a Happier Family* (New York: Harper Paperbacks, 1990).
16. Bill Dedman, "Deadly Lessons, Part II: Shooters Usually Tell Friends What They Are Planning," *Chicago Sun-Times,* October 16, 2000.
17. Michèle Solá, interview by the author, June 24, 2010.
18. Michelle K. Demaray and Christine K. Malecki, "Perceptions of the Frequency and Importance of Social Support by Students Classified as Victims, Bullies, and Bully/Victims in an Urban Middle School," *School Psychology Review* 32 (2003): 471–89.
19. P. C. Rodkin et al., "Heterogeneity of Popular Boys: Antisocial and Prosocial Configurations," *Developmental Psychology* 36 (2000): 14–24; Rosalind Wiseman, *Queen Bees and Wannabes: Helping Your Daughter Survive Cliques, Gossip, Boyfriends, and Other Realities of Adolescence* (New York: Crown, 2009); Rachel Simmons, *Odd Girl Out: The Hidden Culture of Aggression in Girls* (New York: Harcourt, 2002).

20. Richard Morrill, "Denmark: Lessons for American Principals and Teachers?" in *Solutions to Social Problems: Lessons from Other Societies*, 4th ed., ed. D. Stanley Eitzen (Boston: Allyn and Bacon/Pearson Education, 2007), 124–30.

21. Ibid., 127–28.

22. Ibid., 128.

23. Ibid., 128–29.

24. Ibid., 129.

25. Appreciative Inquiry Commons, "What Is Appreciative Inquiry," n.d., http://appreciativeinquiry.case.edu/intro/whatisai.cfm (accessed February 8, 2011).

26. David Faulkner and Mark de Rond, eds., *Cooperative Strategy: Economic, Business, and Organizational Issues* (New York: Oxford University Press, 2005).

27. "Teen Depression on the Increase," August 3, 2004, BBC News, http://news.bbc.co.uk/go/pr/fr/-/2/hi/health/3532572.stm; David G. Blanchflower and Andrew J. Oswald, "Well-Being over Time in Britain and the USA," *Journal of Public Economics* 88, nos. 7–8 (2004): 1359–86.

28. Alisdair A. Gillespie, "Cyber-Bullying and Harassment of Teenagers: The Legal Response," *Journal of Social Welfare and Family Law* 28 (June 2006): 123–36.

29. Quoted in Phil McKenna, "The Rise of Cyber-Bullying: In the Internet's Always-On Playground, Schoolyard Harassment Can Turn Deadly," *Readers' Digest*, July 19, 2007, www.readersdigest.com.au/article/15893%26pageno=3.

30. Julia Saldino, "Hold the Phone: The Incongruity of Prosecuting Sexting Teenagers under the Prosecutorial Remedies and Other Tools to End Exploitation of Children Act of 2003," *Journal of Gender, Social Policy, and the Law* (2009), http://works.bepress.com/cgi/viewcontent.cgi?article=1000&context=julia_saladino25.

31. Guttmacher Institute, State Polices in Brief As of November 1, 2011; Sex and HIV Education, November 2, 2011 www.guttmacher.org/statecenter/spib_SE.pdf.

32. "Bill Text: NY Senate Bill 4921-2011 General Assembly," April 29, 2011 http://e-lobbyist.com/gaits/text/299291.

33. Winnie Hu, "Bullying Law Puts New Jersey on Spot," November 2, 2011, http://www.nytimes.com/2011/08/31/nyregion/bullying-law-puts-new-jersey-schools-on-spot.html?pagewanted=all.

34. Faber and Mazlish, *Siblings without Rivalry*, 101.

CONCLUSION

1. Robert N. Bellah et al., *Habits of the Heart: Individualism and Commitment in American Life* (Berkeley: University of California Press, 1985), 101-2.

2. Joseph Servan, *Discours sur l'administration de la justice criminelle* (1767), quoted in Michel Foucault, *Discipline and Punish: The Birth of the Prison* (New York: Pantheon, 1977), p. 103.

3. Stanley Aronowitz, "Against Schooling: Education and Social Class," *Workplace* 6 (February 2004), http://louisville.edu/journal/workplace/issue6p1/aronowitz04.html.

4. Ibid.

5. Stanley Aronowitz, interview by the author, May 17, 2008.

6. Richard Ryan, interview by the Author.

7. Seth Kreisberg, "Transforming Power: Toward an Understanding of the Nature of Power in the Experience of Education" (PhD diss., Harvard University, 1986), 203.

8. Ibid., 223.

9. James W. Messerschmidt, *Nine Lives: Adolescent Masculinities, the Body, and Violence* (New York: Westview Press, 2000).

10. Aronowitz, "Against Schooling."

11. Ellen Willis, *No More Nice Girls: Countercultural Essays* (Hanover, NH: Wesleyan University Press, 1992), back cover.

APPENDIX

1. Glenn Muschert, "Research in School Shootings," *Sociology Compass* 1 (September 2007): 60-80, 62.

2. Katherine S. Newman, *Rampage: The Social Roots of School Shootings* (New York: Basic Books, 2004); Mark H. Moore et al., *Deadly Lessons: Understanding Lethal School Violence* (Washington, DC: National Academies Press, 2003).

3. Neil Websdale and Alexander Alvarez, "Forensic Journalism as Patriarchal Ideology: The Newspaper Construction of Homicide-Suicide," in *Popular Culture, Crime and Justice,* ed. Frankie Y. Bailley and Donna C. Hale (Belmont, CA: Wadsworth, 1998), 123-41; Lynn S. Chancer, *High-Profile Crimes: When Legal Cases Become Social Causes* (Chicago: University of Chicago Press, 2005).

4. George Lakoff, *Moral Politics: What Conservatives Know That Liberals Don't* (Chicago: University of Chicago Press, 1996).

5. Anthony Cuesta, "Gay Advocates Say Bullying Contributed to a Rash of School Violence," *GayWired.com,* October 5, 2006, www.gaywired.com/article.cfm?section=9&id=10929.

6. American Association of University Women Educational Foundation, *Hostile Hallways: Bullying, Teasing, and Sexual Harassment in School* (Washington, DC: AAUW, 2001).

7. Jay G. Silverman, "Dating Violence against Adolescent Girls and Associated Substance Use, Unhealthy Weight Control, Sexual Risk Behavior, Pregnancy, and Suicidality," *JAMA* 576 (2001): 286; Liz Claiborne Inc., "Teen Relationship Abuse Survey," March 2006, www.loveisrespect.org/wp-content/uploads/2009/03/liz-claiborne-2006-relationship-abuse-hotsheet.pdf.

8. Joseph G. Kosciw and Elizabeth M. Diaz, *The 2005 National School Climate Survey Sheds New Light on the Experiences of Lesbian, Gay, Bisexual and Transgender Youth in Our Nation's Schools* (New York: Gay, Lesbian and Straight Education Network, 2005), www.glsen.org/binary-data/GLSEN_ATTACHMENTS/file/585-1.pdf; R. W. Connell, Masculinities (Berkeley: University of California Press, 1995).

Index

About the Author

JESSIE KLEIN is Assistant Professor of Sociology and Criminal Justice at Adelphi University. She holds a PhD in sociology, an MSW, and an M.Ed. Over the past two decades Klein also led and administered high school guidance programs: she served as a supervisor, school social worker, college adviser, social studies teacher, substance abuse prevention counselor, and conflict resolution coordinator. She also worked as a social work professor.